LLYFRGELL CARTREFLE LIBRARY, NEWI. CARTREFLE, WREXHAM, CLWYD, LL13 9NL.
tel:- (0978) 290390

Please return this book ON OR BEFORE THE LAST DATE STAMPED BELOW.

Dychweler y llyfr hwn AR NEU CYN Y DYDDIAD OLAF ISOD.

16 FEB 1991

22. March 1991

13 JUN 1994

27 APR 2001

2 1 NOV 2005

15 OCT 2002

20 SEP 2000

1 2 MAR 2010

2 9 SEP 2000

2 2 OCT 2001

4 MAY 2011

LIBRARY   NEWI
CARTREFLE COLLEGE WREXHAM

Accessions No. 115,732
Class No. 271.1625 SMI

D0307880

Industry in the Primary School Curriculum

Industry in the Primary School Curriculum

Principles and Practice

edited by

Duncan Smith

Coordinator for National Research
School Curriculum Industry Partnership

 The Falmer Press

(A Member of the Taylor & Francis Group)
London, New York and Philadelphia

for the School Curriculum Development Committee

UK   The Falmer Press, Falmer House, Barcombe, Lewes, East Sussex, BN8 5DL

USA   The Falmer Press, Taylor & Francis Inc., 242 Cherry Street, Philadelphia, PA 19106–1906

Copyright © SCDC Publications 1988

All rights reserved. No part of this publication may be reproduced, stored in a retrieval system, or transmitted in any form or by any means, electronic, mechanical, photocopying, recording or otherwise, without permission in writing from the Publisher.

First published 1988

British Library Cataloguing in Publication Data

Industry in the primary school curriculum:
    principles and practice.
    1. Industry — Study and teaching
    (Primary) — Great Britain   2. Industry
    — Study and teaching (Secondary) —
    Great Britain   3. Industry and education
    — Great Britain
    I. Smith, Duncan *1944–*
    388'.007'1041   LC1081

    ISBN 0–85000–335–1
    ISBN 0–85000–336–X Pbk

Library of Congress Cataloguing in Publication Date

Jacket design by Caroline Archer

Typeset by Katerprint Typesetting Services, Oxford
Printed in Great Britain
by Taylor & Francis (Printers) Ltd, Basingstoke

Contents

Contents

Acknowledgements

I would like to acknowledge the advice and encouragement which I have received from a number of colleagues and friends throughout the period of this book's preparation. The members of the Schools and Industry (5–13) Research Group offered a number of ideas and suggestions in the early stages; Alan Blyth, John Garwell, Alistair Ross and Patrick Waite, in particular, provided valuable advice throughout the entire period of its preparation. I am also indebted to the five other members of the School Curriculum Industry Partnership's Central Team, Margaret Matthews, Andrew Miller, Jack Peffers, John Storey and Alan Wilkins, for their help and encouragement.

Without the tremendous amount of hard work and commitment of the heads, teachers, industrialists, trade unionists and children who developed the work reported in the case studies, this book would not have been written; my grateful thanks to them, to the Local Education Authorities and the companies for giving their permission to publish.

Finally, special thanks are due to Jean Nightingale who typed and helped prepare the final draft of the manuscript.

Duncan Smith
Coordinator for National Research
School Curriculum Industry Partnership
Centre for Education and Industry
University of Warwick, 1987

Foreword

The link between education and industry — manufacturing, extractive, distributive and service — has had an up-and-down history in this country. Heights of involvement inspired by a variety of motives, some worthier than others, have interspersed with troughs of indifference, even hostility.

The general tendency over the centuries has been towards separation. The typical curriculum, originally designed to fit pupils for the priesthood, was adapted to suit the needs of the Empire — and not of that other great British phenomenon, the Industrial Revolution. The later debate between the science school of Ruskin and Huxley and the 'pure' educationalists led by Matthew Arnold reached no final conclusion — except perhaps to leave the arts side uneasily in control. The most sought-after education was obtainable chiefly in green and wealthy counties far removed from the smoky towns where the wealth was created.

Today we are entering a period of closer cooperation between industry and education, thrust upon us, to an extent, by the economic and educational facts of life — industry needs trainable recruits, education needs money and other resources.

But the cooperation is based on more than a narrow view of what constitutes self-interest. An increasing number of teachers are now less inclined to look upon 'industry' as an inevitable threat to the values of the classroom, and have come to see the potential for good that industry-related teaching has for other parts of the school timetable. They also realise that industry is how the country earns its living, and whatever the level of employment, how their pupils will eventually feed, clothe and house themselves. Business people, for their part, no longer assume that a strictly vocational education is the best or only preparation for a successful career in industry.

Enlightened self-interest is the order of the day. Industry is part of society, and can only flourish when society flourishes — and vice versa. Conservation of resources, preservation of the environment, safety at work, quality of product and service, are all areas in which industry's own interests coincide with those of the rest of society. Education is another — which is why cooperation is so important.

However, the benefits of the cooperation so far have been felt mainly in the universities and in secondary schools. There are innumerable examples of joint projects, ranging from specific research and development contracts with universities and the funding of academic posts, to school visits in both directions, teacher/executive exchanges, vacation employment, and collaboration in the production and supply of a very wide range of educational aids.

Industry Year 1986 gave a boost to all this activity, and to a newer form of it — cooperation between industry and primary and middle schools. Children in these schools, in the 5 to 14 age range, are no strangers to industry. They see its products all around them, they enjoy some of the activities linked with industry, such as shopping or TV advertising. And, perhaps rather more romantically, they see industry, the 'world of work', as part of that magic grown-up world that they will one day inherit (their attitudes tend to change as they enter adolescence!). So, in a sense, industry is more real to them than their older brothers and sisters, and as a result they often show a livelier interest.

Certainly industry as a 'subject' has a great deal to offer children in this group — whatever their precise age. It can be used as the basis for many different kinds of 'projects' — all of them capable of stimulating manual and social skills and of providing real-life opportunities for testing and developing academic disciplines such as mathematics, science, history and geography. It also helps the schools themselves to cultivate links with local firms — of long-term interest to both sides.

One of the benefits of the cooperation is the realisation that industry does not consist of a series of hanger-type buildings with large dirty chimneys, most of them defunct. It can be the fifteen-strong firm making china teapots down the road, or the farm on the hill, or the coach service started by two brothers who left school a couple of years ago, or the High street post-office, or the software company set up in that big house just behind the playing fields.

Another important benefit is that children gain an insight into how business is run, that even 'big' business is run by people, and that it can work, and produce the products that are needed, only because people *enjoy* making it work.

The most significant benefit for children is their own early appreciation that work offers endless opportunities for the development and expression of every kind and size of talent, that a narrow specialisation is no substitute for a broad outlook, that personality skills can be as valuable as academic attainment, and that a sense of responsibility towards society as a whole is a prerequisite for long-term success.

The gain for industry and commerce is part and parcel of its identification with society. Children introduced to the workings of factories, farms, laboratories, offices, shops and drilling rigs while they are still comparatively young, are less likely to be either over- or underawed by them when they enter the adult world, and as a result, more able to adopt or adapt them to their own and society's advantage.

Industry is infinitely adaptable — if the people who run it are sufficiently enterprising. Our late Georgian and Victorian forebears had enterprise in abundance. Men like Josiah Wedgwood, George Stephenson, Michael Faraday — most of them with little more than a rudimentary formal education behind them — accelerated the transformation of a largely agricultural and occasionally starving country into a society capable of providing high living standards and economic freedom for the vast majority of its members.

The opportunities for improvement today are as numerous as ever, and will remain so. The continuing North Sea development — already this country's biggest and most sophisticated technological achievement since the railway building boom of 150 years ago — the new horizons opened by microchip, laser and satellite, new advances in biotechnology, and much else, all promise that enterprise and initiative at every level will continue to have the scope needed for fulfilment.

The best reason for introducing young children to industry and commerce is that it gives them early experience of enterprise and initiatives in action, and encourages them to think how their talents and qualities might be developed in the future — to the advantage not only of themselves and of industry and commerce, but of society as a whole.

At Shell, we have been deeply involved for many years in cooperation at the secondary level, and we are delighted to be helping in this newer form of cooperation. We are supporting the School Curriculum Industry Partnership's 'Under Fourteen Research Project', and look to it, and to other initiatives, to help clarify the ways in which the cooperation can be even more beneficial all round.

This book itself will be of major value to any primary or middle school intending to develop collaborative links with industry. We wish all such efforts every successs.

Henry Durowse
Marilyn Elliot
Shell Education Service
Shell UK Limited
January 1987

Section A
Industry Education: The Principles

Chapter 1

Industry and the Primary School Curriculum

Duncan Smith

Background to a Debate

The growth in the number of primary and middle schools eager to develop links with local industrial and commercial organizations has been considerable over the last two to three years. In 1984, Jamieson, in his introductory chapter to *We Make Kettles: Studying Industry in the Primary School*,[63] remarked on the small amount of schools-industry work taking place in primary schools. In spite of extensive enquiries throughout England and Wales, he was forced to conclude that there were 'hardly a dozen examples of primary schools engaged in clear-cut work on industry'.

In 1987, the School Curriculum Industry Partnership (SCIP) is working with 62 Local Education Authorities, and the coordinators in more than a third of those report that they are supporting the work of primary schools in their efforts to develop links with industry. While it is difficult to be precise about the exact number of schools with well-established links with industry, the SCIP network alone represents something in the region of 200 schools. This is one measure of the development in this area of the primary curriculum over the last three years. The stimulus and motivation for establishing those contacts has come from a variety of quarters.

Schools-Industry Organizations

Over the last decade the schools-industry movement has witnessed a rapid expansion in the number of agencies involved in helping teachers, industrialists and trade unionists work together to improve children's understanding of the 'working world'. For the most part, their efforts have been concentrated on secondary schools and in particular the 14–16 age range. In the last three to four years, however, agencies such as the School Curriculum Industry Partnership and the Science and Technology Regional

Organization (SATRO) have become increasingly involved in working with primary schools.

The School Curriculum Industry Partnership, for instance, has since 1982, through its research programme, brought together a group of people involved in schools-industry practice with the 5–13 age range. Some of the most successful initiatives reported by that group were published in *We Make Kettles*. In 1985, SCIP organized the first national primary schools and industry conference at Edge Hill College of Higher Education. For SCIP, the process of creating links with industry has been facilitated by the presence in the Local Education Authority of a schools-industry coordinator whose responsibility is to help schools develop their curriculum with the assistance of local industry. It was only a question of time before some of these coordinators, appointed initially to work with secondary schools, saw the potential of industrial links for primary schools. Some coordinators chose to approach their local primary schools with offers of help, others were invited by the head and staff to become involved in a project which they had devised.

Although few had experience of working in primary schools, what they brought with them were insights into the ways of using industry and trade unions in the classroom on such things as mini-enterprise, work shadowing, work experience and industrial visits. Their aim was to support the schools in developing links which matched the needs and interests of teachers and children within the framework of the primary curriculum. In a few cases, Local Education Authorities have gone one step further and seconded a primary teacher to act as a coordinator for this work rather than add it to the already busy workload of the secondary schools coordinator.

Government

The designation of 1986 as Industry Year also acted as a stimulus for teachers and industrialists to give greater consideration to the primary curriculum. Throughout the year regional workshops were organized which introduced teachers to both the philosophy and practice of industrial links. A national primary schools industry competition was also a feature of Industry Year activities.

It was during the course of 1986 that the Department of Education and Science and the then Secretary of State for Education, Sir Keith Joseph, reiterated the view expressed in the White Paper 'Better Schools', 'that some awareness by school pupils of economic matters is a prerequisite for citizenship and employment'. Among the objectives for the primary curriculum, reference was made to helping children understand how people earn their living. In one sense this was the culmination of a series of reports, including, *A Framework for the School Curriculum*,[25] *The Practical Curriculum*,[98] and *Primary Practice*,[99] which had made reference to the need for children to have some understanding and appreciation of the economic and industrial world. In *The Practical Curriculum*, for instance, it was suggested that children be helped, 'to acquire understanding of the social, economic and political order . . . to prepare for their adult lives at home, at work, at leisure . . .'

In the sequel to that report entitled *Primary Practice*, reference is made in a suggested approach to the curriculum through the study of problems, to the possibility of consumer education and issues such as energy and conservation featuring in young children's learning.

Responses to the Government's initiative came from thirty-eight organizations representing industry and education, some of whom reminded the Secretary of State that economic awareness could usefully form part of the primary curriculum, provided that the concepts were dealt with in a manner which was appropriate to the children's age range and the tendency to oversimplify the subject was avoided. As a first step in the development of this initiative, the School Curriculum Development Committee, the organization set up by Sir Keith Joseph in 1983 to replace the Schools Council, was invited to investigate what was required to encourage further development of this area of the curriculum.

Alongside these various initiatives and recommendations, there was pressure also on primary schools to introduce a technological dimension into the curriculum. Such pressure was not simply a response to the growth of new technology in all aspects of modern day life, but stemmed from a belief that the education of society to cope with changes brought about by technology had to begin with young children. The opportunities which this created for linking with industry were quickly seized by some schools, particularly those which had companies in the high-technology industry close at hand. Support for the idea of introducing technology into the primary curriculum also came from Government, in particular the Department of Trade and Industry's Micro's in Primary Schools initiative. Between 1982 and 1984 over 27,000 schools took up the Department's offer to provide a computer for use with children of the primary age range. Subsequently, this was supported by an education software scheme.

Industry

The pressure from industry for greater collaboration with education has been directed very largely at the secondary sector. The amount of cooperation which some primary schools have received from industry has, however, been extensive as the case studies in this book illustrate. In general, however, primary school teachers have to work twice as hard as their counterparts in secondary schools to get an initial contact established. On the positive side, the commitment of companies to maintain those links, once established, and their very positive feed-back on teachers' and children's enthusiasm, is a very encouraging dimension to this work.

Why Industry Education in the Primary Curriculum?

Education about Industry

One immediate answer to such a question might be that industry is a part, albeit in some cases a declining part, of the environment in which young children are growing up and that schools should be helping them make sense of an aspect of society of which they already have a partial understanding. 'Education about industry' therefore, a phrase used by Blyth in *We Make Kettles*[63] in an attempt to identify objectives for such work, is concerned with the central question of what it is that children of the primary age range need to know about the 'world of work'.

This key question facing teachers, industrialists and trade unionists is one on which, as yet, there is no real measure of agreement, though Ross'[83] analysis of ninety-three teachers' responses to the question provides some interesting answers. The following statements are in rank order of priority as perceived by a group of teachers who attended that first national schools-industry conference:

> understand structure of industry
> relate school learning to world of work
> know industry creates wealth
> know industry pays for services
> understand rate of change of work today
> understand people at work
> understand technology changes work
> decision-makers/carriers-out relation
> appreciate team-work requirements
> understand why trade unions developed
> know problems solved by teamwork
> experience problem-solving exercises
> experience meeting new people
> understand union-management relations

trade union benefits

assess, test, discuss own abilities

Among the responses, there appeared to be a strong preference for helping children understand how a company works, the roles and functions people perform, and how wealth is created by industry. Of somewhat less significance was the human or social dimension, namely working as a team or understanding union-management relations.

Ross and Smith[91] also identified some of the concepts which children might explore as part of a project on local industry:

Concept	
Structure	How a workplace is organized, physically to allow for the flow of items or ideas, and managerially to allow for clear decision-making and responsibility.
Location	The factors influencing the position of a workplace in a particular area. The impact of that workplace on the area.
Capital	Money needed to start an industrial enterprise, coming from a variety of sources, including in a cooperative, the workers themselves.
Price	The amount paid for a product or task.
Value	The negotiated agreement between the buyer and the seller of a commodity or service.
Division of Labour	Work shared, with different people performing different tasks.
Inter-dependence	Different groups of people depend on others to be able to work well themselves.
Authority	Some people influence others through personal characteristics, others through their position.
Cooperation	People working together at every level to achieve a common goal.

The case studies reported in this book provide evidence that children between the ages of 7 and 11 can be helped to understand some of the concepts identified in the table above.

In the Forsbrook case study, Fitzpatrick reports on how the children discussed the price of the mugs in terms of what they thought people would be prepared to pay. A slump in demand after the early sales also had to be discussed and new advertising and marketing strategies identified. Decisions about the dividend to be paid were also part of the learning.

In the Catbrook case study, Richard's work with a mixed-age class involved the study of an hotel's organization and structure. Later, those same ideas were explored within a different context, namely a local vineyard.

Burleton in her work at Freshfield, refers to the way in which the children, during a factory visit, discovered the concept of piece-work and how this affected the working environment. Questions were also asked about profits for the year and why they sometimes varied. Some understanding of the use of technology, in particular the storage of information, the linking of head office to the stores and the concept of electronic mail, was also gained by the pupils.

Other concepts which emerge from project work in the schools, included marketing, competition, supply and demand, equal opportunities and division of labour. For many of the children it was their first encounter with these ideas; an important question for all those involved in developing links with industry, is what strategies exist for helping the children develop those ideas in greater complexity as they progress through the educational system. Progression and continuity are key issues for this, as for other areas of the curriculum, if schools are to avoid the criticism of this being an isolated experience.

Education through Industry

Blyth's[63] second form of categorizing school–industry work was contained in the phrase 'education through industry'. In essence this views industry education as a process which helps young children develop some of the intellectual and social skills appropriate to their age and ability. *Primary Practice*[99] in its various definitions of the curriculum, describes the 'curriculum as process', 'in terms of the opportunities it gives to practise and acquire these skills and qualities'. Included in that list are communication, study skills, ability to define problems, find solutions and make decisions, practical and technical skills. Among the personal and social qualities it includes coping skills and adaptability, ability to work cooperatively with others, sensitivity and creativity.

One attempt to develop this classification of skills a stage further was featured in the work of the *History, Geography and Social Science 8–13 Project, Man in Place, Time and Society*.[100] Skills were categorized as intellectual: the ability to locate information, communicate findings, interpret data, evaluate information and formulate and test hypotheses; social skills: including participation, individual and group relationships, empathy; and physical skills: the ability to manipulate equipment, use expressive powers to communicate ideas and plan and carry out expressive activities.

From the research by Ross[83] on a group of teachers' perceptions, came the following priorities in terms of developing children's intellectual and social skills through industry education:

experience meeting new people
appreciate team–work requirements
experience problem–solving exercises
understand people at work
know problems solved by team–work
relate school learning to world of work
assess, test, discuss own abilities.

Evidence from the teachers' case studies suggests that the children were employing a number of these skills during the course of their projects with local industry.

In the Higham School case study, Hales refers to the skills involved in the interviews with industrialists, the design of the questionnaire, the interview itself, and finally in the analysis of the data. A number of problem-solving exercises were carried out testing the wear and tear of leather and polyurethane, the strength of plastics, metals and solvents. In their enterprise, the children worked together to devise a series of television and magazine advertisements.

Holdsworth and Murphy, in the St Mary's School case study, report on the extensive amount of data collection and analysis which the children carried out in their local community and how this was fed into a computer in order that the children could undertake a more complex analysis.

At Arael School, Garwell and Anderson record the way in which the 'story of the ammonite' was translated into a drama and at Forsbrook School a role play and simulation were used to reinforce the visit to a local company.

All of the projects have involved the children in collaborative group work, in negotiation and consultation with 'adults other than teachers' and in elements of compromise and conflict. Many, through these projects, seem to have developed an empathy towards other people and their responsibilities in the workplace.

One of the frequently quoted reasons why schools and industry need to work more closely is in order to combat some of the negative attitudes which both teachers and children have of industry and commerce. Most of the research in this area has been directed at the secondary age range.[65;7;76] Critics of schools-industry links, particularly as far as the primary school is concerned, view some of the projects with suspicion on the grounds that industry is often presented in very positive terms particularly by industrialists and that the children are encouraged to adopt similar attitudes in their responses.

Schools and industry links, like any other area of the curriculum, will suffer from time to time from bad practice, but teachers are aware of the need to help children make critical judgements and to question stereotypical attitudes to a whole range of industrial practice. While it may be true of some children and maybe some teachers, that they adopt an unquestioning, non-critical stance towards industry, many more do challenge attitudes and practice on a whole range of issues. However, there is no room for complacency in this matter of challenging attitudes and values.

Relating School-Based Learning to the 'World of Work'

A further justification for the 'world of work' having a place in the education of primary school children is that it helps to relate aspects of what they learn in school to the world outside the classroom. The definition of the curriculum as the exploration of key areas of human knowledge and experience is one adopted by a number of primary reports.[98;99] The latter invites teachers, for instance, 'to consider whether their pupils are having and should have, opportunities to enter each of these areas of knowledge and experience'.

In a number of areas of human knowledge and experience, such as humanities and social studies,[69] social abilities or experimental and observational science,[26] the 'world of work' as a context through which a study can be carried out, has been seen as increasingly appropriate. Equally, the areas of aesthetic education, language and drama, can play a part in educating children to understand the economic and industrial world.[91]

In the case studies which appear in this book, there are clear attempts to relate much of the industrial topic work to particular areas of human experience and knowledge. Almost all refer, for instance, to the way in which the work helped to improve the language and communication skills of the children. Discussion on the initial idea for a project, negotiations within the group and with the teacher, meetings with 'adults other than teachers', the design of a questionnaire or the presentation of the findings through drama, were just a few of the processes whereby the children's language skills were enhanced. One interesting aspect of the language work was the way in which the children began to use certain technical terms; Benfield makes this point in her report on the link with Agecroft Colliery. Blyth[9] points to the need for communication skills to include what he calls 'the new symbolic systems based on modern technology', including computer language and graphicacy. Elsewhere, children were using such terms as cost, the market, supply, the consumer, profit and job satisfaction. Written work, in the opinion of many teachers, also improved, and the phrase 'writing for a purpose' is often mentioned, particularly when the children were writing for an audience outside the school.

Science is an area referred to in a number of the case studies, for instance, experiments involving textiles at Freshfield and the work on electricity at Forsbrook, as a result of the link with Creda and Staffordshire Potteries. At Ascension, the class used the science laboratories of the nearby High School to carry out tests on the burning of coal. Links such as this are one important way of helping children through the process of transition and may also help teachers plan for greater progression in learning.

A number of children, particularly those who became involved in enterprise, experienced something of the aesthetic dimension of human experience, in such areas as art, craft and design, music and drama. The areas of social, moral and political awareness were not overlooked. Many of the projects encouraged the children to consider social and environmental factors in the workplace, while others explored the impact of the industry on the physical and human environment. At Arael, the project involving links with the mining industry took place during the miners' dispute and explored conflict as an issue. Health and safety was a subject to which children frequently referred during their visits, in particular those who were studying the textile industry in Lancashire. The children at Manor School were particularly interested in the special provision for the blind workers in the workshops at Newham.

The impact of the industry on both the physical and human environment was certainly brought home to the children who worked on the textile projects in Lancashire and the mining industry in South Wales. At another level, the children at Manor were able to see the contribution which the workshops made to one particular disadvantaged group within the community.

Experiential Learning

Learning through experience has been one of the central tenets of schools-industry work; the School Curriculum Industry Partnership, for instance, made this one of its key principles from the very beginning.[65] Blyth[9] identifies four ways in which the term experience can be used: a particular occurrence, the sum of a number of events, an acquired competence and finally, as a technical term in either philosophy or psychology, the concept of experience. It is with the first two of these that education and, in particular, industry education has been associated. Work experience, enterprise, work shadowing, role play, and games and simulations are just a few of the processes whereby children can experience aspects of the working world.

Blyth also points to a fact which is often forgotten among educationalists, that children build on experiences which they have before they start school, acquire experiences alongside those which the school provides, and go on gaining experiences beyond school. One of the justifications for schools working with people from the local economic and industrial community is that it is a means of providing additional experiences of the working world complementary to those provided by the school. In an adaptation of Dewey,[31] Blyth expresses the problem in these terms: 'the central problem of an education based on experience is to select the kind of present curricular experiences that live fruitfully and creatively in subsequent curricular and general experiences'.

What do we Mean by Industry?

Teachers' Perceptions of Industry

The term 'industry' is variously interpreted by teachers depending on such factors as where the school is located, the proximity of industrial locations and even perhaps the teachers' own upbringing and education. No substantial piece of research has been carried out into primary school teachers' perceptions of industry; such work has almost exclusively been undertaken with secondary school teachers. Jamieson and Lightfoot[65] surveyed the attitudes and perceptions of secondary school teachers to industry and trade unions in twenty-five schools in five Local Education Authorities as part of the research and evaluation of the Schools Council Industry Project (SCIP). The teachers were given twenty-two statements about industry and twenty-six about trade unions with which they were asked to agree or disagree. Overall, the conclusion reached by the authors was that teachers generally hold a favourable view of industry, a fact which might surprise those who are apt to claim teachers have anti-industry attitudes. As to trade unions, while there was support among teachers for their role in bargaining for such things as wages and conditions, there were doubts about certain trade union principles and practices.

Images of Industry: Continuity and Change

Primary school teachers have for some considerable time involved members of the local community in their work with young children. The 'world of work' at the infant school has frequently been represented in topics, such as, 'people who help us' or 'our town' and the support of such agencies as the police and social and welfare services has generally been appreciated by the schools. The development of such work with infants to include more advanced concepts is clearly evident in some of the case studies. At Forsbrook, for instance, not only were the infants involved in visits to a company to see a manufacturing process which they later simulated back in the classroom, but they were eventually given the opportunity to design, market and sell their own product in a small scale mini-enterprise. The children at St Phillips and Freshfield made a detailed study of the textile industry both past and present, and at Higham the shoe trade was the focus of the first part of the project. Children involved in the Shell Oil project in Staffordshire were able to follow the process of oil exploration and extraction through to supplying the customer at the garage.

With the junior age range, environmental studies has often been the context for exploring aspects of the 'world of work' and, as Lawton[70] pointed out, many of the early examples of these schemes concentrated on the physical environment, and industry or work was explored through concepts such as structure or location. Social studies, humanities and integrated studies were also curricula contexts in which children explored the 'world of work' as illustrated by projects such as *History, Geography and Social Science 8–13; Man in Place, Time and Society*. In some cases, such schemes chose to emphasize the social or human dimension rather than the physical.

Ross and Smith[91] emphasize the fact that manufacturing is, however, only one aspect of British industrial society and in some areas is currently a very small part of the local economy. This decline has often been accompanied by a reluctance on the part of some of those companies still operating, many with a substantially reduced workforce, to devote time to schools-industry links. Nevertheless, time and expertise have still been made available to schools, though often it has depended on individuals being prepared to give up their non-work time to help. In addition to the contacts being made in this sector of industry, many schools are now beginning to turn to the service and retail industries, and distributive trades and agriculture as contexts for their work. Links have been established with local stores, banks, travel agencies, garages, hospitals, farms and hotels.

Links with small businesses are sometimes difficult for both secondary and primary schools to arrange. It is not always possible for those smaller organizations, perhaps with less than ten employees, to find time to work with teachers and pupils. Those who have succeeded in making a link see benefits in terms of helping the children understand the business operation and, in particular, the concept of scale. Pupils from a school in Worcestershire[106] studied the ceramics industry from three perspectives. They investigated a one-person operation working from home, a small twelve-person company making exclusive products, many of which were for export, and finally the larger Royal Worcester Spode Ltd, part of the London International Group, with a total workforce of 2,400 in Worcester and Stoke-on-Trent and with selling outlets in the USA and Canada.

Primary schools have developed successful links therefore, with organizations in both the public and private sectors of industry, in which the management and worker roles are very clearly differentiated. Equally, some schools have also introduced children to cooperative business ventures, thus allowing them to make some comparisons between the style and structure of different organizations. Children who have had the opportunity to work with self-employed people have been able to gain some understanding of the problems, risks and benefits which those who run their own business experience.

Perhaps one of the more contentious areas of schools–industry links in the primary school has been the suggestion to involve trade unionists. Ross[83] in his analysis of teachers' responses to schools–industry practice noted that both what he termed the 'instrumentalist' and 'process' groups rated understanding of trade unions as a priority for primary schools very low. There appears to be a variety of reasons for such a position, uncertainty as to what they can contribute, uncertainty about whether young children can understand their role in industry, worry about bias and the lack of balance and perhaps concern over some parental reaction.

Nevertheless, as some of the case studies in this book and others reported elsewhere[106] illustrate, trade unionists can make a valuable contribution to children's understanding of industrial issues. They have provided insights and experience from their work to help children simulate situations in industry, as Fitzpatrick illustrates in the Forsbrook case study. In one instance they helped the children involved in a mini-enterprise set up their own trade union.[106] As with any visitors to a classroom, careful briefing of the trade unionist with details about such things as the children's ability, ways of working and level of response is vitally important, together with information on how the trade unionist's contribution fits into the overall project.

The most successful use of trade unionists would appear to be in those instances where they have used their everyday experience of working as a trade union representative, looking after members' interests and negotiating with management. From time to time the differences of opinion between these two groups will be raised; some of the older juniors will undoubtedly have heard through the media or from parents about the behaviour of some trade unionists with which some might disapprove. These opinions in themselves may well contain elements of bias and prejudice and therefore an opportunity for discussion of these differences to take place should be accepted by schools. The overwhelming evidence from those primary school teachers who have used trade unionists, however, is that their experience and knowledge have been welcomed by the children and any worries about extremist viewpoints being introduced have been totally without foundation.

At the same time, teachers' worries about industrialists using the opportunity solely to promote the benefits of capitalism are also largely unfounded and the overwhelming evidence is of both groups exercising considerable care and consideration in their handling of the topics with young children.

Developing Wider Concepts of Work

While it is important that young children have some understanding and appreciation of what might be described as the traditional images and settings of industry and work, people from both education and industry believe that alternative perceptions of work can be introduced to children in the latter stages of their primary education.

There is within the present-day economy a considerable group of people who might be described as working outside the mainstream of industry and commerce as defined in popular terms. Some of these people do in fact contribute successfully to both the mainstream and 'alternative' structures. (Such groups should not, however, be confused with those associated with what has come to be termed the 'black economy'). Many of these people work within community groups, some on a paid, others on a voluntary basis. Housing cooperatives, local support groups, welfare agencies such as meals on wheels or hospital taxi services and community newspapers are just a few of the organizations for which people work mainly from a sense of community responsibility. Many primary schools, of course, do invite organizations such as Help the Aged or the NSPCC to talk to the children, but often it is not perceived by them as 'someone coming to talk about what I think of as my work'. The point which is being stressed here is that although in some people's opinion these groups would not be classified as wealth creators, as a part of the economy their individual or group needs, their resources and organizational structures are capable of being examined. At another level most are contributing directly to the well-being of their community and the social cost implications of their work is something to which children can be introduced.

This widening of the concept of 'work' has, by some people, been taken further. Many, for instance, have turned leisure pursuits into a form of work, organized along quite formal lines; the person who paints from home and sells in local shops, the author who writes for pleasure, but has work published through local sources, the person who breeds birds as a hobby but finds there is a local demand, or the person who entertains a theatre queue. Extending the concept to include work in the home, the role of a mother or father, the skills of organizing and managing the household would also be considered as a dimension of the concept by some people.

The purposes behind working with such people is firstly, to discover whether the children perceive of these activities as work and secondly, for them to discover such things as people's motives, level of satisfaction, skills and attitudes in relation to the activity.

The Issue of Unemployment

For children in some parts of the country, the picture of industry is one of decline, closure and unemployment. The physical environment is characterized by old, dilapidated and unattractive buildings, many of which have long-since closed, others with only a fraction of the workforce they once employed. In human terms, the experience for some children is of family unemployment; some will not remember, for instance, the last occasion when father or mother worked, others will associate work with part-time casual employment.

In these circumstances, industry-related project work can appear as irrelevant to some children as a study of the Vikings or the Netsilik Eskimos. The key question is, should children be helped to understand the problems associated with unemployment and the decline of certain sectors of industry? For most teachers faced with such a situation, the solution has been to tackle the issues as and when the children choose to raise them, rather than to deliberately impose the topic on the project. In some cases the natural curiosity of the children has raised the issue, 'how many people do you employ; how many did you employ five years ago; why are there fewer people here now; are you still producing the same number of items as you did five years ago'? It is the top junior classes who most frequently pose such questions to industrialists and to trade unionists. Blyth and

Derricott[100] in the *History, Geography and Social Science 8–13 Project* suggest that a theme for 10-year-olds on workers and local industry might focus on such key concepts as power, similarity and difference, or continuity and change. The development of such concepts might well involve issues related to unemployment and industrial decline.

The topic has arisen on occasions in conversations with trade unionists when terms such as redundancy were used in reply to questions about how a company might deal with falling demand for its product or what a trade union does for members made redundant.

Simple business games and simulations can often help children to understand the problems faced by a company when, for instance, new technology is able to perform the function of large numbers of employees or when a similar, but cheaper product to theirs arrives in this country from abroad. While it is not appropriate to deal with the more complex issues related to industrial decline or unemployment, some underlying principles can be communicated to children during the latter stages of the junior school.

Issues

Progression in Learning

One of the most important issues related to the planning of children's learning is that of progression. The need for concepts and skills to be developed in a sequentially structured framework is as crucial in industry education as in any other area of learning. The issue is, of course, related to the wider curricular debate on the overall aims and structure of primary education. A key question for all those involved in this particular area of education, therefore, concerns how schools can build progression into industry-related work in the same way as they do in the areas of language or numeracy. The question is not an easy one to answer, partly because the 'subject matter' is less familiar to teachers than some others.

In one sense, the case studies illustrate the way in which progression, at least in the area of intellectual and social skill development, has been achieved. Frequent reference is made, for instance, to how the children's handling and presentation of information improved or how interpersonal skills were enhanced. Clearly, these were skills which the children had already begun to develop and the industry topic served to assist progression. Future topics using, for instance, group work, role play and simulations would build on these skills.

The answer as far as the 'subject matter' is, however, less precise.

How does a teacher, for instance, build on the experience which some children have of the way in which a product is designed, manufactured or marketed, or the way in which a company is structured? How can the children's knowledge and experience of running their own business be developed at some future time? The danger is obvious, namely, that both the knowledge and experience acquired remain isolated and unrelated to subsequent work in which the children are engaged. The question is, why use industry, in particular, as a resource for learning, if this is the case.

There is, of course, the important point, continually stressed in recent reports on primary education, that it is the process whereby the children learn which is important. This is a central principle of much of the work described in this book. Nevertheless, the question must be asked: if a child's only experience of the 'world of work' is as part of an enterprise at 8 years of age, visiting a factory in the first year of secondary school and doing a week's work experience in the final year, does this constitute progression in this area of learning? Clearly, it is an issue which those concerned with this aspect of the curriculum will continue to debate.

The Focus of the Learning

A further fact which emerges from an examination of much of the industry education work with the primary age range is the variety of ideas and concepts which are introduced. In what are often quite small scale projects, there appears to be a tendency to introduce the children to a considerable number of concepts. Often, the reason for this lies in a visit or series of visits which the children have made which produce a whole range of possible areas for investigation. Occasionally, the explanation lies in the attempt by the teacher to integrate as many areas of the primary curriculum into the project as possible.

While it is important for children to understand the interrelationship of different sectors and operations within a company, there also appears to be a need, in some cases, to focus the study more precisely on just one or two key ideas. Some of the case studies in this book refer to the fact that a prior visit to a company by the teachers was of great value in helping them focus specifically on a particular aspect of the operation. It might also be argued that this process also helps the company to provide a more coherent learning experience for the children. Both teachers and industrialists agree that concentrating on one or two key elements of a company's operation still provides considerable scope for the development of the children's intellectual and social skills.

Integrating the Industrial Experience into the Curriculum

The scepticism shown by some teachers and by many industrialists to bringing industry into the primary curriculum is undoubtedly challenged by the case studies contained in this book. A variety of objections are encountered by those trying to develop links with industry; the children are too young to appreciate the way industry works, it's not a safe environment to bring young children to, learning about industry should be left until they are older when choice becomes more crucial, there's a danger of giving these children too rosy a picture of industry. All these criticisms have at one time or another been levelled at those involved in such work.

As to the age of the children being a problem, the key to their understanding lies in the teachers and industrialists working together to develop appropriate strategies and processes by which the knowledge and skills can be acquired. A number of the teachers in the case studies refer to how they and the industrialists were surprised by the level of sophisticated questioning displayed by the children when, for instance, they had the opportunity to investigate a particular aspect of a company. The same conclusion was reached by those teachers who witnessed the children operating their own small businesses.

As far as the safety issue is concerned, there will always be environments which are deemed unsafe for young children. Often the problem, however, lies in the attitude of some industrialists who use this as an excuse for not getting involved. Teachers and industrialists have usually been able to find ways around the problem without in any way endangering the safety of the children. The experience of the children at Arael school, who were taken down the museum pit with retired miners, was probably just as meaningful as that which they would have had down a 'working' pit.

For some people learning about industry should be left until the children reach the secondary school where it becomes more relevant. The question of relevancy is always a difficult one to confront; which is more relevant, learning about how a large department store is run or learning about how Stonehenge was built? The need is for a balance between the different types of experiences which the children receive, between the direct experiences of the world in which they are growing up and between those from other times and other cultures which will also contribute to their development. Within such a framework, the 'world of work' as a context for their learning can play a part.

The question of bias and imbalance in the attitudes and values which the children encounter is a very important one. Undoubtedly, there will be times when the children will experience prejudice and questionable value-judgements. Teachers have encountered this, not only with industry, but with other sections of society with whom they have worked. Two observations are relevant here. Firstly, some of this practice is remarked upon by the children themselves, examples of apparent discrimination, for instance, have been picked up by children visiting companies. Their questioning of the employer or employees has allowed for some discussion of the issue. Secondly, the teachers are able to use the experience in subsequent discussions with the children, in some cases, with the industrialists also present. Helping the children to come to terms with some of these ideas, rather than trying to avoid them, would seem to be a more appropriate approach to education and industry work.

The way in which this work has contributed to the professional development of the teachers is referred to in a number of case studies; working with industralists to plan and implement a project, seeing how industry approaches a particular problem, using someone from outside the school to assess the children's learning. These and a number of other benefits have convinced teachers that their own professional horizons have been substantially widened by the experience of this particular piece of collaborative learning.

Chapter 2

Children's Understanding of the Social and Economic World

Alistair Ross

Education does not prepare children for society: they are already members of society and have been for five years before they start school. They have many experiences of the social groups and activities around them and are beginning to classify and generalize from these before they reach school. At school, these experiences may be extended, useful concepts developed that help them understand these experiences in a broader context, and useful skills developed that allow them to seek out and use information about societies. But school does not begin work on a blank sheet.

This is true also of the economic understanding of the child. Children are aware of industry and commerce around them. Very young children visit shops with parents and see transactions going on, they are aware of parents either going to work, or desiring to have work. Exactly what 'work' is may be a bit of a mystery if it involves a parent going away from the home each day, but it is clearly an activity that adults rate highly, that they often do in special places, with other people, and for which they are given money. Some children have a much greater appreciation of the nature of work while they are still infants, especially those whose parents work or trade from home. Children whose parents are, for example, home workers in the clothing industry know a great deal about the pressures of piecework, relationships between employees and managers, and the economics of employment. More children are getting substantial amounts of information about the employment and the economy from the media; take this 10-year-old boy discussing the effects of automation:

> There's so many factories (closing) — like all last week I heard on the news that there was three factories closing down in one week alone and there's about three million people out of work now. They're just going to close down factories and keep it like that.[84]

More than Mere Close Observation

Children, then, have a great wealth of experience of the world of work. But they need to do more than simply make observations. There is a school of thought that primary education is concerned to facilitate children to 'closely observe and respond'. This belief seems to ignore several points. Firstly, observations are rarely neutral: what is perceived is the result of a series of social and personal expectations of the meaning, significance and context of that particular experience of perception. Of the whole variety of sensory data we perceive at a given moment, we only choose to give significance to a fraction; and that fraction is often culturally determined. For example, while a townsperson would see a handful of soil in very simple terms, an agricultural worker would notice its friability, moisture content, humus content, potential agricultural use — a wealth of observations conditioned by an economic experience not shared by the townsperson.

Secondly, observation in itself is not enough. In primary education we also intend that children analyse and criticize their observations. Many teachers also hope that they acquire the confidence to challenge and change their social and natural environment. Powers of analysis and of criticism are developed in several ways.

Children, even very young children, build up sets of abstract concepts that they modify and extend as they encounter fresh experiences. To begin to develop a concept, a child needs to classify an object or experience as similar to an object or experience encountered before. To take a concrete example, children of 18 months have little difficulty distinguishing dogs from other animals, despite the great varieties of dog that exist — differentiated by colour, size, even shape. They are able to hold an abstract conception of a dog and this enables them, on encountering a new animal, to look for a sufficient combination of doggy features to classify it as dog or not. Some concepts are more abstract, the notion of the division of labour, for example. A 6-year-old might first come across the idea that work is shared out among different members of a family; the concept develops when the child meets another example of work being shared, perhaps in the organization of the school, and relates the two experiences as having elements in common. As more examples are encountered and classified, so the concept is refined and redefined.

Children develop the autonomy to control and manage their own learning as well as the associated skills. They use concepts as a basis for questioning and organizing their experiences. The child developing the concept of the division of labour encountered, at the age of 9, a theatre group who had come to school to enact and explain family life among the

Netsilik Eskimo peoples. When the opportunity came to question the actors in role, he sidled up to one and asked 'Who's in charge in your family? Who tells them which jobs they've got to do?' Here, he was using two different concepts together, the concept of power or authority and that of the division of labour; moreover he was using them as a basis for questioning and for further organizing his perceptions of the social group he was studying.[60]

Observations are not in themselves value-free. They are conditioned by a variety of previous experiences. With older children and adults, many of these will be the shared preconceptions and prejudices of our society; with younger children, this is less apparent. Younger children are often prepared to be more critical and blunt. This comes partly from their inexperience of adult work, so, for example, they ask questions that may seem naive, such as 'Why do you need managers? Couldn't you all just get on with your work and decide for yourselves what to do?' This is a fundamental observation about the organization of economic groups that is rarely asked by adults because their perceptions have been differently conditioned. The experience of many primary aged children (and particularly so in the case of the child just quoted) is of a classroom in which children are encouraged to be autonomous and responsible for organizing their own work. Many inhibitions about asking particular questions about economic life have not yet been acquired. 'How much pay do you get each week?', a 9-year-old asks the managing director of a medium sized company in the presence of several other workers from the firm![64] Older children visiting a workplace may often be constrained by their own ambitions or fears of finding work.

Children's Social Understanding

It might be appropriate at this point to look at developments in educationalists' attitudes towards the teaching of social understanding in the primary age child. The *Plowden Report*[19] made no specific mention of social studies. There was a brief discussion of work in history and geography, which, though critical of the level of generalizations found in the available textbooks, and advocating detailed case-studies, was fairly superficial. Vincent Rogers, a visiting American educationalist, castigated Plowden's lack of rigour in its consideration of the social areas of the curriculum: he searched the index for references to any of the social sciences,

> and despite the concern expressed in the section on the Aims of
> Primary Education for an education that would, among other

things, help children cope with social and economic change, critically analysing their own society, understanding the nature of a democratic society, etc., I find no reference to any of these disciplines. This straightforwardly states the Committee's views far more eloquently, I think, than would an explanatory paragraph or two. Obviously, in Plowden's view, the insights of the social sciences are not perceived of as necessary, useful or an appropriate segment of the primary school curriculum.[82]

At least one reason for this state of affairs was the influence of Jean Piaget on British primary education. Piaget had suggested that political units such as the nation, and concepts such as nationality, could not be grasped before children were at the formal operations stage.[77] Not till the age of 11 did most children grasp the idea of the country with its related and included parts.[78] Primary children cannot, Piaget concluded, consider different possible explanations or make generalizations and hypotheses.[79]

Piaget's conclusions on children's understanding of the social environment were summarized by McNaughton: primary children 'will not, without considerable prompting, stand back from what they have read about other people to compare with others and themselves.'[74]

Vincent Rogers laid the blame for the lack of coherent work in primary school social studies directly at the door of Piaget, whose findings, Rogers claimed,

> have had an undue influence . . . often leading to overtly simplistic, intellectually undemanding studies emphasising the 'concrete', and (therefore) the nearby, while consistently putting off the more challenging approaches that might begin to develop more complex thinking strategies at much earlier age levels.[82]

English critics of Plowden were also concerned by the dominance of local studies: W.A.L. Blyth, for example, referred to this work as the 'arcadian and bucolic . . .opiate of the peasantry'.[10] Work followed that challenged many of Piaget's findings on the levels of sophisticated thinking possible by children on social issues. David Russell summarized criticisms from the United States[94] and this was followed by work in Britain by Margaret Donaldson[34] and Barbara Tizzard and Martin Hughes[114] which suggested that considerably more sophisticated thinking was possible, even by pre-school children, in many common social contexts.

Curriculum Development in Social Studies

A series of practical curriculum developments followed Plowden's neglect
of social subjects. The Schools Council responded to Plowden's suggestion
for middle schools for 8 to 13-year-olds, by holding a conference in 1967
on what the curriculum might be for such schools: three papers were
presented on the social studies curriculum.[101] The paper by Dennis Lawton
was the most significant: his argument provided cogent reasons for
development in the area, not in order to produce any kind of social
conformity, but to develop a critical awareness of society. He suggested a
sequential syllabus based on Bruner's spiral curriculum model, with a core
of social concepts that were yet to be developed.

The Schools Council commissioned Lawton and his colleagues to
report on good practice and to make recommendations. Some interesting
examples of economic education were reported: particularly notable were
Margerison's island simulation, where for a day a week through a whole
school year a third-year junior class created their own society — including
manufacturing, trading and other economic activities,[75] and Downton's
simulations of productions with third year juniors.[35] Lawton suggested
that social studies 'was a very important area of learning which often
overlaps with other areas'; in the middle years of education, however,
children should focus more on the materials and methods of the social
sciences. A project should be established to suggest how teachers could
plan successfully in this area, because there was so much superficial work
going on in schools that good foundations were not being established.[71]

The curriculum development project eventually known as *Place, Time
and Society 8–13*, directed by W.A.L. Blyth and his team at Liverpool
University, was the result.[11] The published materials were of two kinds: a
book and associated series of booklets for teachers on curriculum planning
and a set of exemplar classroom materials. The planning book identified a
set of key concepts, continuity/change, similarity/difference, and made
suggestions as to how teachers could select from these in planning the
curriculum. It also listed skills that might be fostered through the social
sciences, history and geography. The teaching materials, apparently produced at the request of some of the trial schools against the better judgment
of some of the members of the planning team, were less successful.

One of the most relevant of these classroom packs to this study was
the unit called *Money*. This attempted to explore a range of economic
concepts, through children making a case study of the trading system of
the Tikopia in Polynesia, playing a trading game based on the informal
exchange economics of Prisoner of War camps, and through considering
their own experiences of money as a token of exchange, store of value.

A number of developments sprang from the *Place, Time and Society 8–13* project. In Merton, for example, a team of teachers from first, middle and high schools, led by Eileen Harries, worked in 1977–79 to consider continuity and development in social science learning.[102] 'Whatever happens in schools', they concluded,

> pupils develop an economics perspective on their world. If teachers wish to ensure that this is a rational perspective, they must help their pupils to build a conceptual framework and to develop thinking skills which enable them to make sense of economic experience. (Teachers of) first school pupils . . . should not ignore the development of thinking processes.

Another local authority to build on the *Place, Time and Society 8–13* project was the ILEA. They developed a series of primary classroom curriculum development materials, *People Around Us*, and an explanatory teachers' guide, *Social Studies in the Primary School*.[117] These suggested eight core concepts: the division of labour, power and authority, cooperation, interdependence, social control, social change, tradition and conflict, that were drawn partly from Blyth's project and partly from the work of Hilda Taba in the United States.[112] The *People Around Us* project's use of concepts went beyond that suggested by the Blyth project: they were no longer listed to help teachers select content, but to help teachers and children organize content matter. The dissemination of the project has been reviewed elsewhere by the writer.[85]

The final unit, *Work*, is the most significant in this review. It presents a series of photographs to children of a variety of people at work: housewives, professional footballers and the unemployed as well as factory workers, and related activity sheets ask children to compare various everyday economic and social experiences to these photographs. Two books explore further dimensions of work: *Changes* looks at how patterns of work have changed through the eyes of four individuals; and *Toy Factory* is a case study of the manufacture of a toy tractor, presented through the words of the production line workers and those in the managerial hierarchy of the firm. The teacher's guide suggests that children might interview workers and visit workplaces to follow up work on the books.

Developing Language Skills

One of the common threads running through all these projects has been an emphasis on the development of language skills and the crucial role that these play in the formation of social and economic concepts. Young teenagers were found to be able to discuss social stratification, but many of them were limited by their lack of knowledge of the vocabulary of social class.[55] Jahoda's study of 6 to 10-year-olds' perceptions of class found that while children of 7 could identify class and social stratification from non-verbal clues, few were able to explain this.[62] Campbell and Lawton's interviews with primary school children, designed to elicit their grasp of social relationships, concluded:

> . . . children's social thinking at about nine or ten seems to be outstripping their vocabulary. We may be underestimating the quality of their thinking, not overestimating it, by using interviews that rely on the children's abilities to put their thoughts into words. Alternatively, of course, their thinking may be limited because they have not developed the necessary skills with words.[18]

The language skills that appear most useful to develop in this context are oral skills: of discussion, listening and interview. As Barnes observes,

> pupils' talk . . . is a major means by which learners explore the relationship between what they already know, and new observations and interpretations which they meet.[6]

Discussion skills are frequently marginalized by teachers. It takes some time, ingenuity and planning in order to establish patterns of inter-child communication in a class. What often passes for class discussion is a series of dialogues between the teacher and an individual child. Typically, the children are seated at their desks and the teacher asks a question, one child responds and is then subjected to further related questions. The rest of the class are passive, until the teacher launches a new series of questions. The child that is selected to respond to the first of these (not, incidentally, the child in the first dialogue) will then be the participant in this series of questions. Eventually, one child will say something that has already been said before and may be admonished for not listening.

The point here seems to be that children have been misinterpreting the nature of discussion (or perhaps interpreting the teacher's needs too well). They regard such sessions as being a series of individual oral tests. The questions are asked not because the teacher wishes to elicit real information, but to test the powers of recall or argument of the particular child. They do not therefore concern the other children in the group; they feel that they may legitimately opt out of this part of the proceedings. A more fundamental attitude to the nature of knowledge underlies this: children in this situation perceive knowledge as something that the teacher alone possesses. Other children in the class cannot have useful experiences, information or opinions, so they need not be listened to.

Discussions in small groups without the class teacher are equally likely to go wrong. Giving a stimulus photograph or picture to a group and asking them to discuss it, presents problems. The most frequent occasion on which most children are asked to comment on pictures is in 'comprehension' exercises in the more common (and poorest) English language textbooks. They will be shown, for instance, a picture of workers in a production line and be asked a series of questions: 'How many people are in the picture?', 'Describe the person to the right of the one in the blue overall'. These encourage superficial considerations and tend to be used by children as the benchmark for the level of their own 'discussions'. If the same group are asked, of the same picture, 'Who do you think is in charge here?' or, 'Do you think that these people enjoy doing this all day?' they will at first be nonplussed.[72]

Experiences such as these discourage many primary school teachers from going any further with discussion in social studies. There are, however, several techniques that teachers have found that may make discussions more successful.

Many find that it helps in any discussion if all those taking part can clearly see each other's faces. When a conversation becomes relatively unstructured, as inevitably it does in a group discussion, then non–verbal signals between participants become particularly important. They give cues to speakers about how what they are saying is being received: they allow listeners to signal to each other and to the speaker when they want to make a contribution. With a large group or class, the satisfactory solution can be to clear a space of desks and sit in a circle.

The teacher's role will change as discussion skills develop with a class. Initially, the teacher may need to chair the discussion and be fairly directive as to who should speak. But it is important that at the same time they are a participant: this becomes one of the ways that they provide a model of how the children should contribute. Thus teachers as participant/chair find that they can comment on each contribution to show that all comments are valuable and also indicate that they may not necessarily agree with all comments. It is important to create an atmosphere in which all children feel able to take part if they wish.

In order to help children realize that they should listen to all those who speak, not just the teacher, many find that repeating the gist of each contribution as soon as it is made helps in several ways. Repetition emphasizes the contribution, underlining the point that the class should have listened, and offers an opportunity to those who didn't listen a chance to hear it again. It shows that the teacher values the fact that a contribution was made; and it may offer a chance to rephrase the child's words in a more succinct or powerful way, giving a model back to the child; and finally, it allows the teacher to possibly cue in a fresh speaker on the same point ('. . . but do you agree with that, Mukesh?'). This is not to suggest that every contribution in a discussion is slavishly repeated back to the class!

Several children wanting to talk at the same time is a very common problem, although it is a sign of success in choosing a good subject for discussion. In William Golding's *Lord of the Flies* the meetings of the shipwrecked boys decided on a rule to prevent this happening: a conch shell was passed around and only the person holding it could speak. In some classes something like this has formed a useful way of developing self-control: the important thing seems to be that children learn that they must catch the present speaker's eye before they can make their point. Only when he or she has passed the token can they talk. Very often such devices can be dropped after a few discussions.

Not every child may participate in a particular discussion. This is not necessarily a problem. They may have nothing they wish to contribute — and they may be learning just as much by listening as by talking. But it seems important that the teacher tries to ensure that everybody who wishes to speak has a chance to do so somewhere in the discussion. It may also be necessary to monitor the relative contributions of boys and girls: there is evidence that boys tend to dominate at the expense of girls. Teachers often understandably, and unconsciously, use their power as chairperson to cue children to speak who may potentially be more disruptive, and this form of social control often gives boys the lion's share.[109]

As discussion skills develop with a group, many teachers find that their role begins to change. They become less a formal chairperson and more an ordinary participant. This seems particularly true if discussions are centred around the exchange of experiences, opinions and values and not based on the recall of facts. The subject for a discussion is evidently important: much more may materialize from talking about topics such as:

— whether women should be able to work on the factory floor?
— could men be good secretaries?
— are the managers really necessary?
— who should get paid more than someone else?

than, for example, trying to recall a list of products made in a factory.

Interviewing people also calls for the development of particular skills. Asking the right questions is a skill. Sometimes classes prepare for an interview by making lists of questions to be asked. This often leads to stilted interviews. Children regard certain questions as 'theirs' and wait for their 'turn' to ask it. The list becomes something to get through, rather than a framework from which to expand. Interesting points are left hanging and not followed up. Perhaps, above all, the major disadvantage is that children feel if the question is written, the answer should be written too, and not many children can write fast enough. It can be frustrating to see an interview turn into a session where the interviewees spend most of their time waiting for the next question while their answers are recorded — or even being asked to spell out what they have said.

There are techniques to get round this. If the teacher and the children feel happier with a sheet of paper in front of them, it may help to suggest that they look carefully at the way that interviewers in television discussions use their notes — they are lists to which they occasionally refer, not detailed questions that are obsessively worked through.

Keeping a record of an interview as it progresses is a hard task for any interviewer. There are several alternatives. Making a tape-recording of the interview gives a complete record, but it can be hard to find particular answers or points. It is possible to transcribe a tape: Sallie Purkis has had teams of 9-year-olds transcribing interview tapes in the primary class, but this is very time consuming.[81] An alternative is to ask children, after an interview, to quickly list all the headings that they can remember, select the three items that seemed most important to them, and then make more detailed notes on these. Most of the important items will be covered somewhere in the class if this technique is used; and there can be an interesting discussion about why lists differ.[86]

Another problem may be that interviews become disjointed, with successive questions bearing little relation to each other. This may be each child regarding a particular question as 'his/hers', and keeping it until it is his/her 'turn' to speak. Several teachers have overcome this by practising interview skills on parents: the teacher insists that every question must take up a point in the previous answer and build on this. This ensures that every would-be questioner listens very intently to what has been said. Some children may also become skilful at picking up a point that a speaker has made and turning it around to raise a fresh point. After a few interviews like this, the need to insist on 'following on' is less important: the advantages of a more satisfying interview are apparent to the children.

Young children will sometimes ask questions that seem straightforward to them, but are sensitive to many adults — such as 'How much do you earn?' There doesn't seem an easy way around this: they will learn not to do so by the responses that they get. There are other ways by which this information can be acquired; the teacher can ask 'Do people like you get paid more than the people who do X?', for example. The teacher could get the wages structure of a workplace to discuss in class afterwards. Wage differentials seem an entirely legitimate area for children to discuss, and they are bound to do it in the context of individuals with whom they have met and talked.

Surveys may be another important way of gathering information for children. A street survey of a couple of hundred passers-by can be accomplished in a morning with a class of junior-aged children. The skills of designing a questionnaire so that it can be filled in rapidly are well worth exploring; the exercise will generate interest particularly in the consumers' view of an industry or a service. The results may also be easily analysed using an information retrieval program with the school's microcomputer.

Forming Concepts

These skills are, at one level, those of communication. In the context of children discussing other people's experience, and, in particular, of talking with 'adults other than teachers', industry/work projects offer a very wide range of possibilities to develop such skills. It is, however, the growth of such skills in the particular context of industry education that allows the development of specific socio-economic conceptual understandings.

Take, for example, the term 'work' itself, a seemingly straightforward word. But it is already ambiguous to the school child: it may mean something that some adults do, as in 'men at work', or something that only children do at school as in 'get on with your work!'. Taking only the application to adults, if children consider a range of different kinds of people working, they will quickly find that the concept is in fact quite complex. Is a professional footballer 'working' when playing a league game? How is this different from when the school team play a match? Or when the same professional footballer kicks a ball around with his son in the park? What about people who claim that sitting in a chair thinking and talking is work? What about a person who is home-making and looking after children? They are not paid, nor do they have specified hours of work. Can an unemployed person be working when they are looking for a job? Quite quickly a term that probably seemed to the child simple, clear-cut and straightforward becomes complex, murky — and rather interesting.

The processes by which this development of a concept occurs can be seen as a series of stages; the children:

- draw on their own experiences and define a category in these terms;
- exchange experiences with their peers, exploring what others include in the same category;
- redefine their own definition, to include some or all of these other examples;

- seek out (or are directed towards) other groups' uses of the concept, sometimes by direct contact, and sometimes at secondhand, through media such as books, papers, television and film;
- again redefine their concept to encompass the new information.

These last two stages form a never-ending loop: through life they will go on adding to their understanding of a term.

The concept cannot be acquired by learning a definition; it has to be encountered through a series of examples, and the common threads that help define and broaden the category have to be noticed, explored and brought together in some discrete statement. The role of the teacher might be seen as providing opportunities to meet examples, to guide the noticing, exploration and synthesis, and to help the child realize that the knowledge achieved is only provisional.

In terms of education through industry, a number of concepts might be seen as particularly appropriate. Cooperation, interdependence, conflict, power and authority, social change, tradition, social control and division of labour were concepts suggested in the ILEA social studies project.[61] The *Place, Time and Society 8–13* project suggested the following: communication, power, values and beliefs, conflict/consensus, similarity/difference, continuity/change, and causes and consequences;[12] while the School Curriculum Industry Partnership added these particular economic concepts to the earlier suggestions of social concepts: capital, added value, value, price, wage, location, hierarchy and structure.[93]

How do children develop and use such abstract concepts? Take, for example, the concept of hierarchy. This is a useful way of exploring the relationships in many institutions: it does not occur universally, but is common in a wide range of social groupings. The first encounter with the notion of a hierarchy might come when first-year junior children draw their family tree. Strictly speaking, this shows the relationship between generations, but to young children these often correspond to at least their perception of power relationships. Even drawing a tree of the immediate family is not easy, but when children can compare the variety of family structures, they soon detect basic similarities and the range of possibilities.

Their next encounter with a hierarchy might be a year later, in a study of their own school. They interview and draw all the members of the staff. The teacher suggests that they might like to cut out their portraits and arrange them as a collage 'that explains how the school works'. Often the children themselves will suggest that the headteacher's picture goes at the top: 'They're in charge'. Sometimes they may suggest the school caretaker or the school secretary go at the top: they may perhaps be 'in charge' in that school! The ideas of different forms of control between different people within a hierarchy might be explored. Third year junior children might differentiate 'controls', 'advises' and 'informs' in a diagram of the school's relationships that included the Cabinet and themselves. At this stage the word hierarchy has probably not been introduced. The children may refer to 'the school's family tree', for example.

In the third year, perhaps the same group of children look at a local manufacturer. After visiting the works on two or three occasions, and having talked to a wide range of workers, their teacher encourages them to devise a hierarchical chart of the organization of the workplace. This involves several checks with workers about who tells whom what to do. Some children refer to this as the 'factory tree', but the teacher introduces the word hierarchy, and some children pick this up.

In the fourth year juniors, the same class is at work on a project on the middle ages. When the feudal system is described, several children immediately describe it as a hierarchy. Most children are able to construct independently a hierarchical chart showing, sometimes with small inaccuracies, the relationships between different orders of feudal society.

Transferability of Concepts

This example of the accumulation of a concept, based on the experiences of a real class, illustrates how a concept needs to be encountered in a variety of contexts, over a period of time. It is by making the connections between the examples that the concept is formed and refined; and the proof that the concept has been successfully grasped by the child lies in the way that they use it to help them organize new information. The notion of transferability is important here: the concept is only fully understood if the child can independently recognize the concept's application in a different context.

It seems that such concepts can be transferred by junior age children. The writer was involved with a school-based project in industry education in which each class made a detailed case study of a particular industry. Afterwards, a random sample of children were asked to perform a number of tasks associated with entirely unrelated examples of work and industry. A strong correlation between transferability of concepts and age was discovered ($+0.71$): there was no significant correlation with verbal reasoning quotients measured with standard NFER tests ($+0.19$) or sex. Comparisons of results between children of a similar age involved in different industry activities showed a differential ability to transfer particular concepts. The differences between the mean scores reported here all fall within a 97.5 per cent confidence limit (that is, there is only a one-in-forty chance that the difference reported has arisen by chance).

For example, two fourth-year junior classes respectively looked at a local bank and formed a cooperative to publish their own magazine. The bank group interviewed the manager and staff of a high street bank and were particularly interested in how banks decide to lend money, the kinds of collateral needed, the kinds of venture backed. The parallel class each bought an equal number of shares in a company of their own that prepared and sold four issues of a magazine. The capital was needed for purchasing paper and stencils: they used the school's word processor, stencil scanner and duplicator to prepare and print the copies. A board of directors was elected, who in turn appointed editors for each issue and decided how much of the profits should be disbursed to members of the cooperative and how much retained for the business.

When all this work was over, the children were shown a picture of a man deep in thought, with a 'thinks' bubble over his head containing a picture of a factory. They were told that the man wanted to have a factory to make things: where would he get the money to build and run the factory? Both groups mentioned borrowing from a bank; but the 'bank' class commented much more on the need for the would-be entrepreneur to have securities to advance the borrowing (52 per cent against 26 per cent of the other class), while the 'magazine' class put forward more strongly the idea of raising share capital (42 per cent compared to 8 per cent). Younger children, whose projects had not considered the capital needs of industry in any detail, tended to suggest that the man save his money; a few suggested robbing banks or marrying a rich woman.

When the children were shown a tin of beans, and asked how the shop distributed the money it collected when it made a sale, there were again differences. Both groups mentioned items like wages, overheads and restocking; but the 'magazine' group also emphasized that some money represented profits for the owner (74 per cent), while the 'bank' group were less emphatic on this (36 per cent).

Two third-year junior classes had visited respectively a light engineering works where there was a distinct line of production and a noticeable hierarchy, and a local independent supermarket in which the flow of goods was less simple, and the management structure not as explicit as in the factory. The engineering group were all better able to categorize the pictures of the factory workers (84 per cent to 62 per cent) and to generally arrange the pictures into a hierarchical arrangement (86 per cent to 68 per cent). When shown a picture of a production line of workers in a food factory, they were better able to describe the division of labour that was portrayed (61 per cent to 47 per cent).

One second-year class made a series of visits to a local record shop which specialized in exchanges; a parallel class made two visits to a large local hotel. The hotel had a clear departmental structure, and children made more detailed studies of particular departments. When children from both groups were shown a flow diagram of an engineering works and asked to explain the effects of a delay in one department on the flow of production, the 'hotel' group were better able to explain the interdependence between the departments (82 per cent to 68 per cent).

These results suggest two things. Firstly, that children are able to demonstrate transfer of concepts that are acquired in the socio-economic area; and secondly, that such conceptual grasp is clearly related to the nature of the industrial experiences of that group of children. A clear subjective impression was given in the interviews that children whose parents were actively involved in small businesses were more articulate and informed about the issues raised in the evaluation exercise.[87]

Continuity and Progression

It seems clear that if there is to be development in children's acquisition of these skills and in their grasp of conceptual understandings, then a primary school will need to develop a clear policy on the kinds of industrial concerns to which children are exposed over their school years, and on when such work should occur. In both the series of language skills and intellectual skills described above, and in the development and refinement of concepts, it has been shown that long periods of time are needed, and multiple exposure to examples of particular concepts.

Without wishing to be too prescriptive, it would seem desirable if a school sought to develop in its pupils the socio-economic skills and concepts that have been described; it would seek to ensure that over their primary years children had at least three distinct opportunities to study people at work in local workplaces. In addition, all children might at some time examine their own school as a place of work. In these case studies, the emphasis would need to be placed on talking with a wide range of people who had worked there for as long a period as was possible. Children might also at least once in their primary school career be able to participate in some mini-enterprise, where some service or goods were actually provided by the children in a work arrangement that gave the children as much independence as possible. Some other activities such as simulations of work practices might also be built in to such a programme.

The workplace studies might cover a variety of activities. Infants might look at certain limited aspects of the agricultural industry, for example. Junior children might look at a manufacturing industry and some public service, or an office, or supermarket. Many infant classrooms have activities centred on a shop; these might be extended to include problems of restocking and overheads. More realistic enterprises might follow in the junior years, though there is no reason why infants should not run their own businesses.[116]

Careful monitoring and record-keeping is essential in this process. Teachers need to be aware not only of the area of work that a class has covered — for example, 'Visited magazine publisher' — but also the specific skills and concepts that the class teacher thought had been well covered. It does seem helpful if a class record of work can be passed on up through the school, so that work can be monitored and, more importantly, planned to extend and build on what the class has done before. Children's personal records may not need to be so detailed.

The social and economic understandings that have been described in this chapter are an exciting area of education. They relate very clearly to the real world in which children live, and sensitive teaching can allow children to use activities in this area as a basis for the exploration of issues such as sex-roles in work and unemployment. The activities and processes described here are, above all, enabling: they give children a repertoire of tools with which they can describe their world, analyse their world and — most importantly of all — take control of their world.

Chapter 3

Appraising and Assessing Young Children's Understanding of Industry

Alan Blyth

In Industry Year 1986, it seems obvious that industry education justifies itself. We may not always be quite sure whether we are trying to produce operatives or inventors or shareholders or managers or salesmen or even masters of robotics who can get tasks done by proxy, but it does appear self-evident that we are ready to join hands and do real jobs and move together into the twenty-first century, rather than staying in ivory towers or behind desks in the relics, as is sometimes thought, of the nineteenth. So it seems almost indecent to enquire what evidence we have that young children are actually gaining something from industry education.

If we consider the arguments for industry education found elsewhere in this book, along with the impressive examples of industry education in action, its seems scarcely necessary to look further than the gleam in the eyes of the children, and of the teachers, to find proof positive that industry education works. Indeed, if too many questions are asked about its effectiveness, there will be more than a hint that the ugly spectre of evaluation is being brought into this triumphant spectacle.

Yet that is what this chapter is about. Behind all the rhetoric, and through all the variety, of what counts as industry education for young children, it is possible to discern some distinctive common features, some general objectives of a non-behavioural kind, that most proponents of industry education would endorse. If it is important for all children that they should encounter these common features and benefit from them, then there must be some way of deciding whether children have in fact benefited, and whether some have benefited more, or in different ways, when compared with others.

A Framework for Appraising and Assessing Industry Education

To find a way of doing this, it is useful to draw up a tentative chart of curriculum process, based on a set of relevant skills, task procedures, concepts and attitudes in one dimension, and a focusing upon industry education in the other. The assumption behind any chart of this kind is that the skills, task procedures, concepts and attitudes acquired through any work in industry education will not just be capable of reproduction or 'playing back' of material related to that work, but will also be available for transfer to the understanding of other similar examples of industry or commerce or agriculture, and eventually for generalization across examples that are less similar. For this is a general model of how, if we are allowed one neologism, children who are learning to be literate, numerate, orate, graphicate, and all the rest, can also become 'industriate'.

It is important to emphasize that this kind of chart represents a comprehensive, all-embracing model of the relevant curriculum process. No one school could or would possibly attempt to engage in more than a small part of it; but whatever a school, or a class within a school, did decide to do could be represented somewhere within the model and could generate an assessment procedure derived from it. Moreover, the existence of the model could help the school or class to decide more positively the grounds on which that particular part of the whole has been chosen, and at the same time to become more firmly convinced why industry education is not just an additional, temporary fad for Industry Year 1986, but an important addition to the basic curricular repertoire for all young children. Figure 1 (pp. 40-1) represents a chart of this kind.

The classification used in Figure 1 itself requires to be explained and justified. The horizontal rows are generally well established now, and in the case of the *skills* and *concepts* they have been discussed so fully in relation to curriculum development that a case is often made out for arranging each of them in a ladder or hierarchical series, with the 'higher' elements introduced one by one as the learning process continues. No such ladder or hierarchy is embodied in Figure 1, partly because that would make it still more complex, and partly because there is incomplete agreement as to the order in which the elements do in fact arise, and as to whether they arise uniformly in all children and all curricular situations. Meanwhile, in common with the usage developed in *Place, Time and Society 8–13*,[13] a distinction is maintained between substantive and methodological concepts, that is, between those that refer to the ideas central to a subject area and those that are concerned with ways of classifying data. It is important to remember that some of both are virtually common to humanities/social studies and to science/technology, while others in each classification are more characteristic of one of these two curricular areas. For the present purpose a third kind of concept is added, one with Kantian overtones, namely the two categorical concepts of space and time, within which the perspectives of understanding of both broad subject areas are necessarily established.

The chart is further developed through the introduction of a major classification not usually found in such contexts, that of *task procedures*. It is included because any area of the curriculum is characterized by distinctive ways of mobilizing skills and concepts for specific tasks such as data collection and analysis, and also by particular modes of thought. Being a geographer, for example, involves more than using mapwork skills and concepts such as settlement patterns. *Attitudes* are included next, because of their central significance in relation to curriculum aims, though, as will become evident later, their openness to appraisal and assessment is distinctly problematical. As for *content*, the actual material to be learned, it is allocated a relatively subordinate role; but it remains important, partly in its own right (for example in the case of local studies of industry) and partly because some specific content is actually necessary for the development of skills, task procedures, concepts and attitudes.

As for the vertical columns, they represent in very general terms a classification of the curriculum process, on the major assumption that there are two broad areas of the primary curriculum, humanities/social studies and science/technology, that are epistemologically intermediate between the whole curriculum on the one hand and industry education on the other. Such an assumption does presuppose that each child's construction of knowledge will eventually lead to some such framework. At the same time it does not imply that all the real learning must be derived from two academically-recognized sectors of the curriculum and must, as it were, be piped into industry education in order to impart a backbone of respectability. In an adequate model of primary education, the process is just as likely to work the other way round, using the experience of industry education as a means of developing wider understanding in the two curricular areas. Of course, both areas are too complex and wide-ranging to allow industry education to become their only gateway; yet industry education is in itself sufficiently complex and wide-ranging to claim to be an important gateway to both.

If appraisal and assessment of industry education were confined to the science/technology aspect, there would be room enough even so for controversy and difference of opinion about what should be emphasized. For example, teachers might concentrate on the basic processes involved, or alternatively on creative technology and problem-solving. But it is when the social dimension is introduced that the major controversial issues arise. For there are profound disagreements about the nature of industrial, commercial and agricultural society. Economists, politicians, psychologists

Curricular element	General	Relevant elements in humanities/social studies	Relevant elements in science/technology	Specific exemplification in industry education
Skills	Observational Representational classificatory (taxonomic) manipulative Reasoning and problem-solving	Sketches, photos and descriptions mapping: time scale Use of equipment with computers	Sketches, photos and descriptions and graphing Use of classifications Use of computers, apparatus and construction kits	Sketches, photos, graphs and descriptions Typology, etc. Origins and distribution Photography; taping: modelling
	Hypothesising Probabilistic thinking Communicative Interactive	Social reasoning and problem-solving Social hypothesising Best-fit explanation Presentation of data Questioning: interviewing	Scientific reasoning and problem-solving Experimentation and trial Best-fit explanation Presentation of data	Asking pertinent questions Suggesting explanations Industrial simulations, etc. Recording and presentation of data Meetings with personnel
Task procedures	Information retrieval	Library/ Database/search Records Sampling Case studies Systematic observation	Database search	Use of published materials, handouts, etc. Visits to workplaces Simulations of technological innovations and of industrial organization
	Compilation of new data		Use of kits and materials, experimentation and measurement	
	Analysis of data	Analysis of data	Analysis of data	Quantification of data Debriefing
	Interpretation of data	Historical, geographical and social-scientific interpretation	Scientific interpretation	Application of relevant modes of interpretation
Methodological concepts	Similarity/Difference Continuity/Change Causality (and its limitations)	Similarity/Difference Continuity/Change Cause, consequence, prediction and concomitance in social affairs	Similarity/Difference Continuity/Change Cause, consequence, prediction and concomitance in the natural world	Coarse and fine differences Continuity/Change Cautious approach to explanation, estimation, planning, etc.
Categorical concepts	Space	Spatial distribution and relations	Spatial measurement	Location of industry, etc.
	Time	Historical dimension	Temporal measurement	Time-scale in retrospect and in planning ahead

Curricular element	General	Relevant elements in humanities/social studies	Relevant elements in science/technology	Specific exemplification in industry education
Substantive concepts	Communication	Personal and mechanical communication, verbal and non-verbal	Modes and media of communication	Marketing Investment Supply and demand Unions: negotiation
	Conflict	Conflict/consensus		
	Value	Values and beliefs	Materials	Price: value, added value
	Matter		Energy	Tradition Production
	Power	Social power		Management, employment
	Interaction	Interdependence	Interactive systems	Division of labour
	Investigation	Role Social enquiry	Testing and experimentation	Innovation Market research Quality control
Attitudes	Loyalty: Readiness to consider evidence Readiness to plan and to undertake study Toleration of uncertainty	Recognition of positive value of communities and institutions Readiness to explore in place, time and society Readiness to question stereotyped certainties	Commitment to scientific method and accuracy Readiness to invent, to experiment, to engage in technological trial and error and to undertake creative design Readiness to consider the adequacy of explanation	Recognition of ambiguities in attitudes towards aspects of industrial society Readiness to value and to initiate innovation Readiness to accept uncertainties to economic life
Content	(Too extensive and diffuse to specify)	Local studies and samples of human life contrasted in place, time and society with the local environment, built up systematically in relation to skill concept and attitude development	Physical, biological and technological phenomena, especially in immediate or vicarious experience in relation to skill, concept and attitude development	Straightforward examples of local (and some other) industry, agriculture and commerce, chosen in accordance with teachers' professional judgment

Figure 1: Chart of Curriculum Elements as Guide for Appraisal and Assessment of Primary Industry Education

and sociologists, and theologians and men of letters too, are all constrained to offer differing interpretations of what industrial society is, and even more so to offer differing prescriptions for what it should be. Therefore it is impossible to decide fully how to assess or appraise the children's development until a decision has first been made about what counts as desirable development. It is hardly possible to sing the praises of small enterprises and at the same time to convey the impression that society is moving inexorably towards centralized state socialism or co-operative communities in a participatory democracy, or towards a fundamentalist Islamic republic. It is not even possible to applaud both competition and co-operation among children in a class unless a clear decision has been made about how the one can be reconciled with the other. For that reason it may seem easier to retreat into the purely science/technology area. But to do so would itself in fact be to make a social judgment, to the effect that only these matters should figure in the education of young children and that the wider social issues could not, and should not, be open to consideration in primary schools. In the present discussion, it is assumed that these wider issues should be considered, though not in any one way, so that nobody is going to be either entirely satisfied or entirely dissatisfied.

Even if this rather perilous stance is taken, the table still appears uneven. Some of the boxes are heavily weighted with important material; others are more thinly peopled. Indeed, as its implications become apparent, it is evident that a whole chapter could be devoted simply to commenting on this one table. Nevertheless, it serves as a practicable device for the discussion of actual procedures of appraisal and assessment. These, and their applicability at different age-levels and in different school situations, can now be considered. For this purpose it is necessary next to survey in outline the procedures that have been formulated for the purpose of assessment in primary education generally.

The Process of Appraisal

First it is useful to bear in mind the process of observing children as they work, which goes on, day in, day out; estimating what they are capable of doing next, and then challenging them to do it. This I would term *appraisal*, taking the term from the work of Joan Tough on communication skills.[115] It involves procedures that each teacher works out for himself or herself, two of the most notable examples being those recounted by Armstrong[5] and Rowland.[95]

Where the whole process of learning and teaching reaches this level of sophisticated interaction, it indeed becomes difficult to isolate the part of it that constitutes appraisal; but appraisal is implicit throughout. In such studies it is also difficult to locate appraisal of any one curricular area separately, since the whole growth of children is under scrutiny, though each episode of learning can be associated with one particular form of understanding, such as mathematics. Now, what distinguishes the work of people such as Rowland and Armstrong from the generality of primary teachers is the quality, sensitivity and consistency of their observation, and their appreciation of the importance of procedures such as participation in discussions.[88] All primary children are observed; not all are 'closely observed' in this sense. But most teachers consider that their classes are observed closely enough for practical purposes. When pressed about detail, the nature of their observation does not always impress by its plenitude, or by its capacity to diagnose the next steps.

A quiet girl, rather lacking in confidence in her own powers.

Always ready to 'have a go'; a pity that he does not take more trouble about his written work.

Such comments may symbolize and express inadequately a fuller but unformulated intuitive impression in a teacher's mind, and may indeed be sufficient to place a child in a rank order or a typology of the teacher's own choosing, based on inexplicit, internalized criteria, and quite often defended through some terminology such as:

I just *know* how they are doing.

Clearly there may be considerable substance in that claim; yet it is necessary also to note where it falls short.

For this purpose it is worth while to look again at the two fictitious but representative descriptions of children in the previous paragraph. In the second case, it is not difficult to forecast what a teacher will do. She will encourage this boy — how often it is a boy — in class discussions, and then will privately urge improvement in the standard of his topic work or creative writing or whatever he has to do. Yet there is no clue as to whether, for example, there is a difference between creative writing and topic work in the degree of accuracy or of motivation that he shows. If pressed, the teacher might well be able to draw such a distinction, but does not explicitly volunteer to do so when asked to appraise the boy's work. In another case, some specific interest might be singled out, such as being 'mad about football' or having a deep interest in living things, but there is in this no indication of his undistinguished but still relevant performance in, for example, social studies or music.

If however we look at the first example, the quiet girl who keeps her head down, a more difficult situation is indicated. Although her lack of confidence in her powers is noted, there is no suggestion about what those powers are, or of how she might be encouraged to develop more confidence in them. There would seem to be far too many children like this, going warily through primary education and always outbid for the teacher's attention — if indeed they want it — by somebody else who is more bright or more stupid or more ostentatious or more disruptive than they are. These children are readily identifiable in studies such as ORACLE[49;80;126] as well as in everyday experience. The problem is that the very nature of their appraisal precludes diagnosis of their potential. They are afraid of being challenged, and they manage not to be challenged. Others, such as the boy who is ready to have a go, risk earning applause or objection or ridicule according to the outcome and its social evaluation. But the wary ones risk nothing, lose nothing, and gain nothing, except a row of ticks on humdrum work that may fail by a wide margin to match their cognitive potential.

So, however impressive the appraisals made by an intuitive teacher may be, they are not always a sufficient guide for the diagnosis of every child's potential or for the design of individual and group tasks intended to realize the next step towards that potential. What is more, they involve the dangers of typifications and self-fulfilling prophecies, impelling children to be what they expect and are expected to be, rather than to defy and break the mould of prediction.

One of the most useful ways of extending encouragement through appraisal is for the children to learn to appraise their own and each other's work. For not only are they remarkably candid, and not always damning, in their estimation of each other, but they may well learn in this way how to be more accurate and more encouraged about their own potential. And a little encouragement from teachers in this context can sometimes achieve a notable breakthrough.

The Process of Assessment

In addition to appraisal there comes the more explicit process that can be, and usually is, termed *assessment*. It involves some kind of procedure, which can range from a mark or grade given to a piece of artwork or a topic book to a fortnightly test of mental arithmetic or even a full-blown examination. Quite often one of the principal indicators of the movement from infant to junior, or from first to middle, school is the introduction of a regular assessment procedure which is characteristically centred on language and mathematics and sometimes touches upon little else. This may well be symptomatic of the rest of the curriculum, the distinction so clearly brought out in Alexander's analysis of primary teaching.[1] It is true that constructive attempts have been made by Harlen[53] and others in primary science, and more tentatively in the field of social studies,[21] to develop effective assessment procedures that could bear comparison with those in mathematics and language, and indeed to combine these with systematic appraisal procedures too; but in practice teachers usually include among their taken-for-granted assumptions the requirement that assessment in language and mathematics is important, while the rest of the curriculum can be left to intuitive appraisal. Responsibility for that assumption may even be displaced on to other shoulders:

The Head prefers it.

The parents expect it.

or even, perhaps with a virtuous shrug:

That's the sort of society we live in.

Where specific assessment does take place, there is of course plenty of guidance about its procedures. It may be norm-referenced (when candidates are considered primarily in relation to each other's performance), criterion-referenced (when performance on particular tasks is noted irrespective of the other candidates), or self-referenced (when comparison is made with one's own previous performance). In any case it raises the question of yardsticks: a norm of what? a criterion in what? a previous performance in what? All of these issues have been frequently discussed by authors such as Broadfoot[14] and Shipman[105] as well as by others concerned mainly with secondary education. The relevant arguments need not be rehearsed here, though it is worth noting that norm-referenced testing seems to go more readily with traditional teaching styles in which all the children are engaged in the same or similar work, whereas criterion-referencing and self-referencing lend themselves more directly to a curriculum built around skills, procedures, concepts and attitudes and also allow more readily for individualized programmes. But they do also make much heavier demands on whoever does the assessing.

Another important consideration in assessment, not always remembered, is the *range* of understanding that is involved. Some forms of assessment are virtually confined to ensuring that the actual work undertaken has been understood. If an event or a process has been studied, then children may be expected to show that they have grasped that particular process or event. But if the experience has been a truly educative one, then they may be expected not only to have grasped the particular content but also to have understood how the thinking they have done in this instance can be transferred to others. 'Transfer of training' used to have a black reputation, but when properly guided it is important both as an objective of cognitive development and as an index of cognitive attainment.[120] If a child cannot apply what he or she has learned in one situation to a rather different one, then the learning is unproductive. What is more, the higher the level of generalization derived from an instance of learning, the wider the field of transfer to which it can be, cautiously and critically, applied.

In the following discussion, the terms *recall assessment* and *transfer assessment* will be used to denote these two types of procedure. Actually, there is a continuum from recall through cognate transfer (i.e., transfer to quite similar situations) and then to general transfer, which in fact itself represents a sequence of learning and development. It should be noted that this is true irrespective of the form of assessment used. There can be norm-referenced, criterion-referenced, and self-referenced procedures both in recall assessment and also in all kinds of transfer assessment. The importance of this distinction between recall and transfer assessment will become evident when its relationship to age-levels is considered.

The rest of this chapter will be concerned with how those techniques of appraisal and assessment can be related to the skills, procedures, concepts, attitudes and content associated with primary industry education and embodied in Figure 1. Of course, these techniques are not confined to industry education, or even to humanities/social studies and science/technology, though they will be discussed in the industry education context. Figure 2 embodies an attempt to show how this relationship to curriculum can be worked out.

Strategies for Appraisal and Assessment of Industry Education

In Figure 2, a number of procedures are named. Some of them are familiar enough. Recall items are in frequent use and serve a valuable purpose provided that they are crisp and unambiguous:

What tool was the man in the second room using?

Why was that tool important?

Cloze procedure (supplying missing words) and sentence completion are almost as familiar, and both often figure in the ubiquitous worksheets found in primary as well as in secondary schools. They save time, if not paper. Of the two, cloze procedure is more attuned to recall:

To make glass, you need . . . and . . . and . . . and . . .

Curricular element	Appraisal	Recall assessment	Cognate transfer assessment	General transfer assessment
Skills	Systematic observation of individuals and groups noting skill acquisition (from initiation to mastery) and readiness to apply newly acquired skills	Direct application of skills such as map-making, map-interpretation, sequencing, information retrieval and manipulative skills	Applications of these skills to analogous situations in other industries and occupations	General application of these skills to other issues in Industry, Education and beyond*
Task procedures	Observation of response of individuals and groups to set tasks, and of readiness to plan, carry out and express the outcome of projects	Oral and illustrated accounts of the actual procedures used	Individual and group tasks to plan procedures similar to those used in the study programme, for use in similar but not identical situations	Individual and group tasks to plan approaches to quite different issues in industry, agriculture and commerce generally
Concepts	Noting of responses to specific questions and problems and of readiness to mobilize a particular repertoire of concepts in oral and written work	Procedures such as cloze and sentence completion, absurdities tests and picture or toy sorting to test attainment of specific concepts derived from the study programme	Procedures such as cloze and sentence completion, absurdities tests and picture or toy sorting designed to test application of attained concepts in similar situations	Testing of general application of relevant concepts to issues in industry education and beyond*
Attitudes	Estimation of attitudes as revealed in interaction, towards: — industry education — specific tasks — the teacher(s) — each other	Carefully devised creative writing, simulations and work in other media, designed to show patterns of attitude, motivation, etc. Questionnaires; Interviews	Application of expressive and projective methods to similar but imaginary situations	More general use of creative studies to indicate attitudes to industry, agriculture, commerce and other aspects of industrial society and activity
Content	Noting understanding by means of current observation, questioning, and discussion	Oral, visual, verbal and perhaps microcomputer methods of testing the study programme: Who . . . . Where . . . . When . . . . How . . . . Why . . . . What	Possibly, inference of understanding of closely analogous examples	Possibly, inference of understanding of more general examples

* Particularly suitable for summative assessment at the age of transfer to secondary education

Note: All the assessment categories are open to norm-, criterion- and self-referenced procedures.

Figure 2: A Framework for Appraisal and Assessment of Primary Industry Education

while sentence completion can go more clearly into transfer:

Before you can build a new factory, you have to . . . . . .

Absurdities tests were originally designed to probe concepts such as sequence and time (Note A) but need not be confined to temporal absurdity. It is possible to devise items which would embody spatial or economic or societal absurdities too and which could stimulate independent critical thinking:

You could get twice as much bread for the same price if everybody in the factory worked twice as hard.

Children's learning often moves from a stage of genuine puzzlement about absurdities, through one of increasingly amused confidence, to a superior stance which pities a teacher who could ask such silly questions; at which point they can be challenged to ask better ones. Often the real test of understanding is not so much the capacity to answer questions as the capacity to ask them.

As for the use of visual stimuli, they serve to reinforce as well as to assess, and form a useful epitome of a scheme of work. There is value in getting children themselves to take photographs for this purpose, with the incentive that they may be able to catch the teacher out. In fact this is doubly valuable, because it not only provides the teacher with a ready-made test for the class as a whole, but also affords another sensitive medium for appraisal of the children's perception of what is important. Of course there are circumstances in which they would not be permitted to take photographs, but there are others, for example on the public highway, where there is no objection, and a teacher may find it well worth while to be caught out in the process of gaining such insights. Teachers are themselves learners, both about children and about industry education.

In the same vein, there is a place hardly yet recognized for using a microcomputer program with items inserted by the teacher — or, better, by the children, (Note B) — to test recall and, potentially, transfer.

It will be apparent that the suggestions in Figure 2 about assessment of *attitudes* omit any reference to the more sophisticated techniques of attitude measurement familiar to social psychologists. This is because such techniques lie outside the scope of the practicable for most classroom teachers and because anyway they go beyond what is really necessary for the present purpose. The procedures that are recommended, namely simple questionnaires and enquiries, and the judicious use of the creative aspects of the curriculum that are likely to reveal affective responses, go quite far

enough. For attitude change, rightly regarded as among the most important aims of industry education, is by far the most difficult to assess with
any degree of certainty.

There are many other ingenious procedures that could be and have
been employed, and good luck to the teachers who have developed them,
often quite unpretentiously and unawares, with their own pupils. But these
are among the most serviceable. All of them can be used in recall and, as
already indicated, they can also be adapted, some more readily than others,
to different kinds of transfer assessment.

For example, cognate transfer could be probed systematically by
questions involving a measure of hypothesising:

> If we had visited the supermarket in the winter, what differences
> might we have noticed?

> (here perhaps the question could be made more specific by refer-
> ring to goods, demand, management, etc.)

> (and it could be amplified in relation to concept development by
> asking what would not be different in a different season).

Or there could be another kind of reasoning from one industry to another:

> If we had visited a shoe factory, what differences might we have
> noticed?

> (and here again the categories of difference could be specified, and
> perhaps similarities also requested)

General transfer would then involve further questions with a greater
component of *generalization* such as:

> What do managers of supermarkets have to remember about
> differences from one part of the year to another?

or even, reinforcing the concept of division of labour:

> Think about the things we have been making. What do we all have
> to remember about how to make things as quickly as possible?

All of these questions could be put orally to small groups and the answers
recorded; or in a pencil-and-paper form to a whole class, which may be the
only practicable procedure once they are sufficiently literate. If necessary
they can be adapted to allow answers to be drawn, or chosen from
drawings or symbols or even models, in order to avoid verbal blockages.
In any event, it is important to remember that questions of this kind do not
call for straight right/wrong answers, but rather for a capacity to perform

problem-solving operations effectively and to express tentative answers in cautious and linguistically appropriate ways.

It is hoped that the provision of these tentative examples, devised by one person for imaginary though not improbable situations, will be taken at their face value and not used gratefully as a model. Most teachers could think of examples much more suitable for their own classes. For teachers, as for children, it is the process of devising such questions, and not the questions themselves, that I am advocating. If the effort involved in that process seems disproportionate, it is worth remembering (as has already been indicated more than once) that just as all teaching situations are also appraisal situations, so all assessment procedures are also teaching procedures. Children learn through being tested, and teachers cannot help teaching as they assess. Moreover, since the aim of assessment is to monitor the progress of individuals rather than to devise traps for them, it is all to the good if they do learn even as they are being tested. Sometimes, the slightly more subdued atmosphere of the test itself assists learning. In any case, it is appropriate enough, in a consideration of industry education, that procedures should be advocated which effect a real economy of time and effort and do not, as might at first appear, make a further demand on both.

Sequencing Appraisal and Assessment

The next step in considering appraisal and assessment in primary industry education is to translate the techniques embodied in Figure 2 into an age-level distribution. Figure 3 has been devised for this purpose, and is intended to represent a general strategy of appraisal and assessment across the statutory age-span of primary education

It is not easy to represent such processes diagrammatically, and in any case industry education is still in its early stages and it is only now that pioneer schools who have initiated ventures in this field are learning how to follow up their first venture with even one more. The assumption behind Figure 3 is that a further stage has been reached, in which it is normal for schools to plan for an element of industry education, broadly conceived, to figure in the whole curriculum from 5 to 11 or beyond, and thus in the educational experience of young children throughout their primary-school life. It is necessary to establish a framework of this kind, even though it goes beyond what is yet normal, in order to slot in the particular instances of appraisal and assessment that follow.

The relation of Figure 3 to Figure 2 will become clearer as the argument develops. But some general explantory comments are necessary at the

Mean age level	Appraisal	Recall assessment	Cognate transfer assessment	General transfer assessment
5–7	General observation of groups and individuals especially in relation to skills and concepts			
7–9	ADD Direct interrogation about tasks in hand	Occasional simple testing, by written and other means of skills, concepts and content inherent in schemes of work	Oral questioning of a semi-formal kind, to probe capacity for limited transfer	
9–11	ADD Appraisal of capacity to design and to carry out tasks ADD More forming of emergent interests and attitudes	ADD More searching and varied testing related to actual learning episodes	ADD More formal testing of capacity to apply skills and concepts from one situation to another	ADD Summative assessment on more standard basis (at age of transfer) and more generally ADD Further, varied, general testing of skills and concepts
OVER 11 (where applicable)				

Figure 3: Developmental Sequence for Appraisal and Assessment of Primary Industry Education

outset. First, as previously indicated, at the infant/first school level appraisal is allowed a virtual monopoly. Even here, it would be possible to envisage a semi-formal situation in which the children assemble triumphantly in front of their final exhibition or collage or after their oral presentation or simulation and answer carefully-devised questions about what they have done. This is however more in the nature of a collective appraisal than a formal assessment.

In the early junior years a more comprehensive procedure becomes possible, reflecting the general change in assessment at this age. The term 'interrogation' is used in Figure 3 to imply a more searching questioning of individuals and groups, while 'problems' suggests that within the general theme, individuals may be allocated tasks and observed tackling them.[38] Meanwhile the end of a piece of work on a factory or farm or industry can be marked by some piece of lively and carefully-devised assessment, making only slight demands on writing skills, but sufficient to indicate that everyone has retained some of the key information derived from that piece of work. For example, there could be a naming of raw materials; a multiple-choice cloze question on the role of a foreman requiring the insertion of a word on a worksheet; the arrangement of symbolic figures to represent a hierarchy;[89] or an identification of an important part of a manufacturing plant from a slide projected on the screen or on a wall.

Older juniors can and should be expected to undergo more rigorous appraisal and assessment. Their skill and concept development undergoes a sharp enhancement; their interests develop; their attitudes become more established; and their mastery of procedure can be impressive. At this age-level, close observation and regular monitoring can often yield appraisal of their interests, while their capacities are open to a more varied kind of periodic assessment, not just through recall testing but through transfer testing too: the use of maps and time-scale; the identification and understanding of a process and of a hierarchy; the general grasp of economic concepts such as division of labour or added value and their application in other situations; and many more.

All the examples of assessment hitherto discussed are basically *formative*, that is conducted with an eye to planning future work for individuals and groups through appropriate matching of tasks to children. In addition, there is a case for the introduction at the end of the junior or middle school of some more general, *summative*, test of the children's understanding of industry education as a whole, with procedures common to a number of schools in an area as well as those particular to individual schools. For there are some features of such universal significance that they can be claimed as necessary components in any programme of industry education. Examples in addition to those already mentioned are raw materials; assembly lines;

computerization; location; supply and demand; roles in industry; and indeed most of the elements in the final column of Figure 1. It is evident that these elements form part of a wider complex of humanities and science/technology as was also apparent in Figure 1, and so there is a strong case for making this summative assessment at the apex of primary education apply not just to industry education but to the whole of these two broad areas of the primary curriculum. Indeed, it would be valuable if the impetus derived from Industry Year 1986 and from the present surge in primary industry education could result in a greater general emphasis on assessing humanities/social studies and science/technology, rather than on still further concentration on assessing language and mathematics in the belief that these alone provide the 'grounding' required for a lively and inventive industrial society.

Maybe some people will take this suggestion in the wrong way. For it could easily be regarded as equivalent to the re-imposition of the shackles on primary education that are alleged to have been removed when the eleven-plus was abolished (where it was abolished). That is certainly not the intention. No form of *selection* is implied. It is simply a matter of informing a secondary school of the particular bent and manifest capacity of individuals in important fields, which they can and should be encouraged to develop. Nor does it involve a uniform programme of industry education for primary schools in a locality or more widely. Each school would continue to follow its own curriculum, but with the reasonable condition that each school will, in its own way, cater for the development of skills, procedures and concepts that are generally agreed to be important. This is how a 'process curriculum'[8] operates.

Appraisal and Assessment in Practice

The importance of appraisal and assessment is evident in other discussions of primary industry education in this volume and elsewhere. Alistair Ross' treatment of the development of children's social understanding[90] suggests how a sequence of skills and concepts can be developed systematically and progressively and rendered transferable; a policy of appraisal and assessment is needed in order to monitor the effectiveness of such an approach. Particular emphasis is laid on the importance of guided discussion in the diagnosis and assessment of individual development. Meanwhile Patrick Waite's account of research[121] indicates ways in which one-to-one interaction between teacher and pupil can probe more deeply into the processes by which pupils learn skills and concepts in particular, and indeed shows at the same time how difficult it can be to distinguish between testing and teaching; maybe it is a false distinction anyhow. Together, these two chapters point the way towards a framework of shared expectations about young children's growing understanding of industry, as part of a considered strategy of curriculum planning on the lines already suggested in this chapter. This may, in turn, enable teachers to approach the task of appraisal and assessment with greater confidence.

The case studies included in this volume also indicate some awareness of the importance of appraisal and assessment, thus affording a parallel in practice to the more general issues already considered. It is instructive to observe how far these instances relate to the suggestions outlined in this chapter, and how far they diverge from those suggestions.

Some systematic use of *appraisal* is to be found in all of them, and there are some stimulating variations on the basic patterns of observation already discussed. In addition to general monitoring of individual children, Sheila Burleton,[16] Shirley Fitzpatrick[40] and Ciaran Clerkin[20] all make specific reference to the focusing of appraisal on children's contributions to discussions. Ciaran Clerkin also mentions explicitly the appraisal of social skills and of the positive impact of his school's Braille project on the general behaviour of the children. In addition he provides an excellent example of children's appraisal of each other's work. Perhaps the most systematic procedure in this set of case studies is the one devised by Steven Hales[52] who developed three-point scales for the appraisal of individual attainment in respect of various skills, concepts and attitudes across the curriculum, and a parallel set of three-point scales for effort, and introduced this system throughout the infant and junior years. A sophisticated form of profiled appraisal such as this can readily include also some individual instances of specific assessment, especially if, as in this case, members of staff come to regard this kind of appraisal as a continuing and necessary part of their own role-expectation.

Assessment, as defined in the present chapter, appears to be in less frequent use. There are some references to regular classroom tests, presumably mostly in language. More strikingly, references to explicit assessment include some assessment of attitudes, for Sheila Burleton used attitude questionnaires before and after an episode in industry education, and Ciaran Clerkin made systematic use of creative writing in the manner suggested earlier.

Thus the picture emerging from these case studies is one of effective appraisal, depending largely on global, undifferentiated monitoring but occasionally referring to particular skills, concepts and attitudes, combined with more spasmodic assessment procedures designed for specific ends. There is little distinction between what has here been termed recall assessment and transfer assessment, whether cognate or general. This does not imply that the procedures followed in these case studies are to be weighed in the balance of our model and found wanting. Logically, it could be equally justifiable to weigh the model against the practice and to find it over-ambitious and irrelevant. It is very likely that the contributors have all given the whole matter due thought and have come to the conclusion that all the outcomes intended in this chapter, including effective transfer, can for them be attained without more specific assessment procedures or any similar augmentation of classroom planning. In their hands, this is probably true, especially in the light of their own ambitious and successful schemes of industry education, for global affirmations about successful innovations, especially those involving attitude change, are often made by palpably effective practitioners. Yet the possibility remains that by placing their own work in the wider context of appraisal and assessment in humanities/social studies and science/technology, they might gain further insights into the development of their own pupils and hence might be able to plan still more effectively in subsequent years. Indeed, some schools have already made use of a draft version of Figure 1[122] for this purpose, and it seems likely that instances of systematic assessment and appraisal of primary industry education will be introduced more widely.

The value of a broad perspective of this nature is likely to become more apparent where — as Steven Hales has indicated — a scheme for a whole school is developed. The need to monitor children's growth year on year, and to present an adequate and systematic profile record at the age of transfer to secondary education, will become more evident as the importance of continuity and progression in industry education, and its place in relation to humanities/social studies and science/technology, becomes more fully established in the whole-school curriculum.

For without an adequate system for assessment and appraisal, primary industry education will lack its own quality control. Only teachers can really devise a system of this kind. They can look to others, including the contributors to this book, for ideas, and they will reserve the right to reject those ideas if they find them wanting. In the English context, teachers may be convinced, but they cannot — hitherto — be overridden, or obliged to do something in which they do not believe. Moreover, as the GCSE saga has shown, they cannot espouse any substantial innovation, however desirable, without the time and resources that are necessary. So if industry education with younger children is to show clear evidence of positive outcomes, there is a need for each school that responds to its challenge to go further and, by means of a staff development programme perhaps in relation to an IT-INSET initiative (Note C), to work out its own scheme of pupil monitoring and record-keeping for industry education within the framework of humanities/social studies and science/technology and indeed within the whole curriculum. In the process, they can become more confident in their own powers of self-appraisal, and more able to convince others that they are genuine professionals, mindful of standards and striving and excellence, whatever anyone may say, and quite capable of being masters in their own enterprise.

I am grateful to Professor Wynne Harlen of the Department of Education, University of Liverpool, and to my fellow-members of the Schools/Industry (5–13) Research Group for their generous advice on this chapter in its draft stage, and to my fellow-authors in this volume for allowing me to refer to their own procedures of appraisal and assessment which indicate that these matters can be effectively handled in schools for younger children.

Notes

A   Temporal absurdity components were introduced into some of the earlier intelligence tests, and have also been used in a number of investigations into children's historical understanding.

B   An interesting innovation was introduced at Coal Clough Primary School, Burnley, in relation to industry education, by a former member of staff, Mrs Gloria Varley. Upper juniors entered multiple-choice items on a standard program, mostly for recall purposes, but with evident potential for transfer and for higher thinking skills. Further focused research on the potential of microcomputers for such purposes will have considerable significance for assessment in humanities/social studies and science/technology.

C   This could in fact be one of the issues to be taken up collaboratively with an institution of teacher education, for example as part of an IT-INSET programme within the framework developed through the Centre for Evaluation and Development in Teacher Education at the University of Leicester. One useful aspect of the IT-INSET pattern of organization is that more time and opportunity become available for effective appraisal.

Chapter 4

Economic Awareness: Context, Issues and Concepts

Patrick Waite

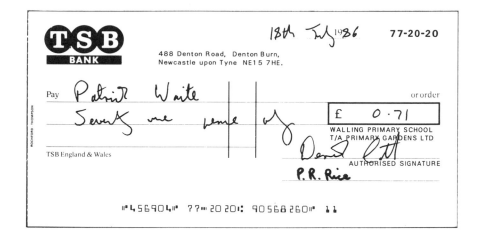

A Place for Industry in the Primary School Curriculum

The thrust throughout the 1980s for industry-related activities to appear within the curriculum for children 5–13 has come from those responsible for the curriculum[27] and from those who seek to influence teachers.[33;57;58] The resulting examples of curriculum case studies from knowledgeable, concerned and enthusiastic teachers offer 'how to' accounts of useful methodology, suggested workable activities and clever ideas.

They appear similar to developments observed in related fields, particularly in the USA in the late 1970s.[67] The case studies are all based on purposeful, concrete first-hand experiences which form the base of the cone of experience on which all children's learning and communication is constructed and the basis for all the visual and verbal symbols that they use in reading, writing, talking and listening.[23]

The teachers' accounts acknowledge that the 'working world' is part of the social and physical environment in which the children are growing up[107] and that the experience must be based on local industry and its employees:[37;118;123]

> Previously my topics related to minibeasts under the hedgerow, and then missing out the cardboard manufacturing and packaging plant, we would continue our topic by obtaining water samples from the Leeds–Liverpool canal. (Deputy Headteacher)

The packaging plant represents the working world of today with its computerized line employing some local parents. Others, however, find themselves unemployed due to the new technology:

> In common with many schools we have, for some time, taken the view that the school curriculum is not solely contained within the school building or its teaching force, nor does it stand in isolation from its environment or culture.[73] . . . The future has to be discussed honestly and if the subject arises it has to be talked about. For some it can be disturbing, because it's a problem close to home.[54]

Learning About and Learning Through Industry

The study of local industry is often the first experience children have of a workplace; their base has previously only been as a large group of consumers buying articles. This very central part of everyday life has tended to be neglected in primary schools. The teachers' accounts, however, show that children's experience of local industry helps develop a range of communication skills through discussion, interviewing and presentation of information and opinion, based on meeting a range of 'adults other than teachers'. The area manager of a British Rail region, the signalperson, announcer, ticket clerk, the train guard, the salesmanager of a brick company, the owner of a nursery centre, the production director of a company manufacturing pulp products, a flight captain, are just a few of the people who have met children aged 5–13 in their own working environment through visits. They have also been willing to work with the children in the school. The school visit in particular has assumed a new role and purpose and a particular venue is no longer chosen simply because it might prove interesting or enjoyable as with the traditional outing to the fire or police station.[50] This is where the links are made between the schools and industry.

Industry as a Classroom Resource

The teachers' accounts also indicate that the use of industry-related activities provide the resource for a wide range of curricula areas. The infant children aged 5–7 visit a pottery and then invite a hand potter, a parent, to demonstrate his own personal practical skills. He discusses the properties of the clay with the children making their own clay insects for sale. Is this experience just in the art and craft area? The pertinent questions flow from the children's natural curiosity:

> Do you always sell everything you make; how do we decide how much we are going to put on the price ticket?

These questions raise other issues; the experience is leading to the need for wider discussions, debriefing and reinforcement of the issues outside the immediate curriculum area.[68] Similarly, the instance of the works manager from the local slipper factory who discusses frankly the need to introduce a computerized sewing machine and his dilemma as to whether to continue to employ machine operators from the local community (the children's parents) where his is the only works still open, raises many moral and ethical issues for the children.

The conclusions from the teachers' case studies appear to indicate that for children who undertake this type of industrial-related topic there is a raising of their consciousness on economic issues. There is a growth in their economic awareness based on their practical, first-hand experiences. It arises from a range of social, political and ethical dimensions which the children experience from local micro case studies. This subject is not new to primary schools; it is, for instance, included within a number of existing curricula areas as suggested by the DES consultative letter 'Economic Awareness in the School Curriculum'.[28] The replies to the letter from 38 bodies[39;96;113] who represented a spectrum of interest and opinion were incorporated into the invitation to the School Curriculum Development Committee to undertake additional development work in order to attain the aim of equipping all pupils by the age of 16 with some economic awareness and understanding. More particularly:

> Many of the replies also recognized that aspects of this can properly find a place within the curriculum for the primary phase, provided that care is taken not to introduce too sophisticated concepts at an early age and to avoid the pitfalls of over-simplification.[29]

Developing a Conceptual Framework

At present, there appears to be no predetermined map of the concept field under consideration for the primary phase, although the economic awareness gained by direct practical experiences might lead a child to an understanding of, for example, the particular social and economic concepts suggested by Ross and Smith.[92]

It is clear that a study of such concepts as interdependence, power, added value, change, conflict, value, price, wage and location has been raised and is now on the agenda for consideration and discussion for the curriculum of children aged 5-13 across the full ability range. The question must be asked as to how these concepts are to be developed. Are they to form part of a linear progression or 'spiralling' within the whole curriculum from 5–16?

Examples abound of children of all ages showing understanding. David, aged 8 years 2 months, reading age 10.6 who visited a circus as part of a topic on 'the circus' and discussed many aspects with the ringmaster in school, suddenly explained to his teacher how he could possibly get the pound coin he paid of his entrance money, back in his own pocket — 'the journey of a coin'. Direct experience such as the setting up of a mini-enterprise in the classroom can stimulate learning in a number of directions. The problem of raising the capital to manufacture the chosen product is immediately evident. Many ways have been tried; the school fund, a bank or, of course, share certificates.

Kerry was a founder member in December 1985 of Primary Gardens Ltd and bought her share for ten pence. In February 1986, I offered one pound for any share in Primary Gardens and Kerry decided to sell me her share. At that time she pointed out that:

> if we sell all our plants, your share will be worth sixty-five pence. But we have planted more seeds so your share will be worth more later in the year.

In July 1986, she wrote the following

> I am sorry to say that your share is only worth seventy-one pence and you paid one pound for it. Your seventy-one pence is in a cheque not cash. By the way I sold it to you because I needed to buy a present for my mam for mother's day. The reason why you only got seventy-one pence is because we grew lots of plants, but could not sell them all.

Examples such as this indicate that there is a continuum from awareness to

Share
Certificate

This is to certify that

KERRY LOWTHER

is the holder of a
One Hundredth Share
of Primary Gardens Ltd
As witness of the above I
sign this day, December
1985

Joanne Wright Company Sec.

Registered address: The Walling Primary School,
NEWCASTLE upon TYNE, NE5 3PL

an understanding of the economic concepts leading ultimately to economic competence and capability.[97] However, it must be noted that Blyth in Chapter 3 widens the agenda involved to include not only concepts, but also skills, task procedures, attitudes and content.

Assessing Children's Understanding of the Concepts

The case studies indicate that learning situations are being set up which will accelerate the children's conceptual understanding by using a number of different strategies, but only rarely are teachers attempting to assess that understanding in the classroom (Ross, Chapter 2). There is, however, no apparent evidence of teachers accounting for the difficulties experienced by individual children in developing particular concepts. The child must be the centre of the activity, the 'centre of gravity'[32] by virtue of the fact that most of his or her economic awareness is acquired through information channels outside the classroom. This is based on three elements a child brings to school in his or her economic awareness 'backpack':[32] economic attitudes, unprocessed direct experiences, and a developing cognitive capacity. The first two are influenced, for example, by parents and the society into which the child was born and is growing up. It is enlarged by breakfast-table conversation, television, visits to the bank, post office and supermarket and trade with friends. A vivid example of this was Solomon, aged 9 years who, according to his teacher, was always tired, yet knew all about buying, price, value and selling for he got up every morning at 04.00 hours and visited the fruit and vegetable market with his father.

Evidence from research

In order to be able to develop the economic awareness 'backpack' for children into one of economic understanding, knowledge of selected research studies appears to be essential. Most investigations involving children's cognitive capacities have shown a marked preference for the study of concepts about the physical world rather than the social world. However, the following are summarized in order to assist a recognition of the probable 'critical periods'[32] for children aged 5–13 in the area of children's understanding of economic concepts.

The studies selected commenced in the 1950s and concentrate on what young children think about economic-related ideas and problems. They all use interview techniques with a varying number of initially structured questions and problems. The researchers base their conclusions on the children's own words which reflect the manner in which children go about making sense of their social world.[42] In almost all the studies the cognitive development theory of Piaget has provided the theoretical guide. They use close replication of Piaget's methods in examining another aspect of cognitive development. Furth[43] maintains that the processes whereby children understand the social world are not fundamentally different from those used to help them make sense of the physical world. It follows, therefore, that the key stages in the development of their social experiences can be charted in a similar manner to that used by Piaget for children's physical thinking.

Developments in Children's Understanding of Certain Economic Concepts

Money

This review specifically concentrates on the literature pertaining to children's understanding of dealing with money and was started by Strauss (1952) who investigated 'the development of monetary meaning' among 66 children in Indiana.[111] His was the first research and he categorized his sample of children aged 4–11 into nine developmental stages, each of which represented a change in the form of children's reasoning.

The complexity of children's thinking, he concluded, was determined largely by age, but qualitatively it was different from that of adults. Children move from one stage of reasoning to another, building sequentially on the learning and ideas acquired in the previous stage.[103]

Six years later, Danzinger (1958), using ten standard questions dealing with various economic processes, interviewed 41 Australian children on their understanding of selected economic concepts which included those of buying and selling, and money. The questions he used which specifically deal with the area under review were:

> Why do we have to give money when we buy things in a shop?
> What does the man at the shop do with the money he gets?
> Where does the money come from?[24]

He concluded that there was, for children aged 5–8, a developmental sequence from simple to complex. Using the concept of money, he found that the children at first thought of money exchange as a ritual with no real purpose, but at a later stage of development they understood that the customer's pay is used to buy goods from the shop with money serving as a medium of exchange.

Exchange and Value

More recent studies by Burris (1976), Fox (1978) and Furth (1979) similarly examine the development of economic understanding in children from a developmental perspective. The 44 interview questions used by Burris (1976), broadly related to children's social understanding and in particular to the area of economic relations. Eighty children aged 4–5, 7–8 and 10–12 were interviewed on six broad topics of which two, those of exchange and value, are here considered. Burris (1976)[17] found three distinct developmental stages in children's thinking about the ideas of economic exchange. The first stage was very much characterized by the child's personal and individual view of monetary change. In the second stage there was evidence of the child's understanding of the reciprocal or one-to-one relationship in the process of exchange. The final stage, however, contained evidence of the child's ability to see it as part of a whole system whereby money was exchanged within a very large network of individuals and groups.

He further argued that this development pattern would appear to satisfy each of Piaget's four criteria for the identification of cognitive developmental stages. The children's responses at each stage were qualitatively different from those which preceded them and a further analysis according to age, supported the hypothesis that the stages were sequential in their development.

The stages are illustrated in the research reported later in this chapter, of answers given by four children, two aged 8 and two aged 12 to the question, why do we give money when we obtain goods in a shop, supermarket, petrol station or at a farm? The two 8-year-olds answered in terms of: paying for what you buy, breaking the law, money for more stock, so that you can't just get things that are worth a lot of money or take them from the shop, you would have to pay for them, it is stealing. The two 12-year-olds replied in the following terms: to pay people we bought them off, so that you can buy it again, so that if we pay them $£x = VAT + \text{whatever}$, pays them for making or buying from the wholesalers, pay for them, pay a 'little bit' more than they've cost to give them profit, a 'little bit' of money for them.

The table opposite from Burris (1976) shows the distribution of responses to the most basic of questions, why we give money when obtaining goods at the shop? Burris drew two conclusions from this data about the stages in children's developmental thinking concerning economic exchange. Firstly, that it pointed to the fact that the stages form a hierarchy, with the ideas not only increasing in their complexity but also becoming more closely interrelated rather than fragmented. Secondly, that the stages do not relate to ideas of economic exchange alone but provide a way of looking at the development of all social concepts.

The three distinct stages and all four of Piaget's criteria are seen in Burris' (1976) investigation of the child's construction of a concept of

Type of Response	Percent Giving Response*		
	4–5	7–8	10–12
Responses which fail to indicate reciprocity of money/goods exchange			
Transaction explained by moral or legal imperative	66.7%	23.8%	0.0%
Transaction viewed as exchange of money for money	33.3	0.0	0.0
Responses which emphasize the reciprocity of the transaction			
Transaction explained as exchange of money for goods	0.0	28.6	23.1
Payment is necessary because goods are valuable	0.0	42.8	3.8
Responses based on the rationality of the total system of circulation			
Payment necessary because store must recover its expenses	0.0	4.8	65.4
Payment serves as a means of rationing	0.0	0.0	7.7
TOTAL	100.0%	100.0%	100.0%
	N=9	N=21	N=26

* Excludes "don't know" responses and responses which were judged to be tautological (i.e., which merely agreed that money must be given, but failed to provide any explanation for this fact).

Significance: Taub for cross-tabulation of three major categories of response with grade level equals 0.788 (p<0.001).

Burris (1976 Table 5.1)

exchange value, summarized in the table below. Again, two 7-year-olds and two 12-year-olds in reply to the question, what are we paying for when we obtain a can of drink?, illustrate this line of reasoning. From the 8-year-olds came, can of drink — the tin — can of drink — drink — can. From the 12-year-olds, drink — VAT — shopkeeper (profit) — people who made it — goods put into it — expenses for travelling — profit/if cheap not much/more is more profit — buying other goods — living; drink — people who made it — people who made can — all machines that make it — lighting (electricity) in factory — some tax.

Fox (1978) particularly concentrated on younger children and observed that they have an awareness of aspects of the economic world prior to school age, but that confusion is sometimes caused by the more abstract exchanges which then take place. An example of this confusion about money transactions in shops arises when children see adults using cheques and credit cards for purchases. This change to more abstract exchange makes the function of money even more abstract for children

Stage	Median age*	Location of exchange value	Quantification of exchange value
I	4.11 years	Physical-technical attributes of object from point of view of *perception.*	Based on physical size of the object.
II	8.1 years	Physical-technical attributes of object from point of view of *consumption.*	a) Based on hierarchic ordering of functions served by different objects. b) Based on the durability of the object.
III	11.2 years	Physical-technical attributes of object from point of view of *production.*	a) Based on value of raw materials. b) Based on labor-time expended in production.

* Median age of those children whose modal response is of the given type.

Burris (1976 Table 6.3)

The basic features of the stages in the child's conception of exchange value

who are only able to deal with concrete, experience-based notions of the world.[41]

An example of this occurred when the winners of the North West regional final of the National Primary School Industry Competition 1986, a lower junior class of children, received a cheque for £200 and the teacher wrote to say:

> This afternoon we all went to the bank to deposit the cheque. By arrangement, the bank manager took them to his office where he filled the silver cup with 200 £1 coins.[22]

Cost

Such concrete, experience-based notions of the world as illustrated in the previous quote were observed in answers to the question:

How does the person at the store decide what things will cost?[41]

Basically, explanations centre on one facet of the question and fail to comprehend the relationship between price and other factors. They were tautological, 'they decide' (age 5.6); literal, 'with his mind and with his brains' (age 4.10) or based on authority, 'because it's stamped on the top' (age 5.7). A few of the 8-year-olds began to show comprehension by saying that prices were decided by 'how much it's worth'.

Unreflective and Emerging Reasoning among Children

Schug and Birkley (1983) noted that Fox (1978) found the reasoning of 8-year-old children appeared qualitatively different from that of younger children[104] and their research extended earlier work on the development of economic reasoning. It has as its central purpose the examination of the economic reasoning of young children aged 4–5, 6–7 and 8–9 rather than having these age ranges only as part of a sample. They were the central target. They elicited responses from 70 children randomly selected (25 children 4–5 years, 23 children 6–7 years, and 22 children 8–9 years of age) on seven basic economic concepts. The concepts of scarcity, choice, opportunity cost, monetary value, price, exchange and advertising were selected for investigation. Then by using a code manual they classified the answers into two theoretical categories — unreflective reasoning, characterized by ideas which were highly literal, linear or tautological responses; and emerging reasoning where the participants were able to identify reciprocal relationships, and were less literal and more flexible in their responses.

In analysing the responses to the question:

What do the shop owners do with the money we give them?

Schug and Birkley (1983) found a dramatic shift between the youngest children in the study and the older children, with virtually none of the 4–5 year-olds using emerging reasoning, while at the 6–7 years stage, 44 per cent of the children were using emerging reasoning and by the 8–9 years stage, 82 per cent. Across all the concepts investigated, there were statistical differences in the children's reasoning by age, for five out of seven concepts, those of choice, opportunity cost, price, exchange and advertising. In addition, the pattern of responses in all but one showed an upward progression from the simple to the more abstract forms of reasoning. However, their results indicate that economic understanding varies depending on the children's experiences of the concept and more particularly that some children as early as 4–5 years are already developing an understanding of some basic economic ideas such as scarcity and the purpose of advertising.

Monetary Transactions Related to Roles

Furth (1978–79), using a larger sample of 98 boys and 97 girls aged 5–11 in three primary schools in southern England, focused on the two key concepts of money and societal roles, and the children's image of government and community. He used a free interview to develop questions on, for example:

> The shop concerned with goods: where does the shopkeeper get the goods from?; shop payment: does he pay for them? what money does he use?; shopping: what happens when you go shopping?; change: when do you get change and why?; shop money: what happens to the money collected in the till?; personal expenses: where does the shopkeeper get the money for his home or television?[45]

He constructed a schematic outline of the shop's business. The understanding of the retail shop's transactions was shown to be relatively explicit and easy to differentiate into logical steps.

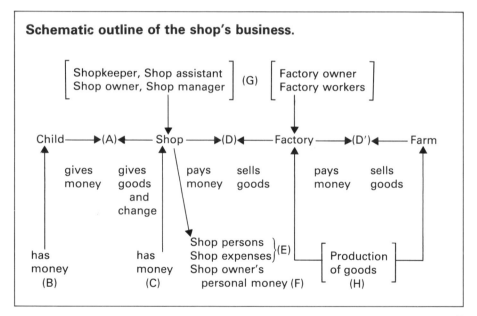

Schematic outline of the shop's business.

Furth 1979[46]

Stages in the Development of Children's Monetary Understanding

The outline was then used as the specific criterion for classifying 122 out of 195 of the children's thinking into one of four stages of monetary understanding:

(i)   no understanding of payment
(ii)   understanding of payment of customer but not of shopkeeper
(iii) understanding and relating of both the customer's and shop-keeper's payment, but not of profit
(iv)   understanding of all these things[47]

(The remaining 73 children were classified on Furth's more general criteria.)

Table 8.2 Stages of societal thinking in 195 children, age 5 to 11, in percentages of age						
Stages	*Age and number of children*					
	5 (16)	6 (34)	7 (25)	8 (29)	9 (46)	10 (34)	11 (11)
I	94	65	9				
II	6	32	72	76	28	15	
III		3	20	24	70	68	64
IV					2	18	36

Furth 1978[44]

His percentages show the distribution according to stage and age. The transitional stages (II) and (III) were observed in the societal thinking of most children between ages 7 and 10, and represent the majority of pupils in primary schools where,

> the concern is with first-order functional relations and partial theories beyond immediately observed events.[48]

A relatively recent study by Armento (1982) was carried out with 355 children aged between $2\frac{1}{2}$ and 16. Noting that Sutton (1962) found little variation in the responses of 85 6–13-year-olds interviewed on economic topics,[110] she, by contrast, concluded that economic questions associated with situations familiar to those children at the younger age range were handled with greater sophistication than those less familiar. Schug's (1983) work with 7-year-olds (Furth's stage ii) also confirmed Armento's findings. The children's responses progressed from being exclusively self-centred to being more objective, from the literal to the more generalizable and from the concrete to the more abstract.[2]

It would, therefore, appear that certain concepts develop at a faster rate in children's thinking, with little difference in responses within the upper years of the age range under consideration, while other concepts develop more slowly and show little change within the younger ages and are more applicable to the later years of the age range.[3]

Armento (1982) raises two further important issues. Firstly, in this type of research where children's conceptualizations are tapped through verbal language only, it is necessary to take into account the child's interpretation of the meaning of the word, the non-equivalence of language ability and conceptual level. Are the responses simply due to the problem of their language development and communication? Secondly, she notes that categorizing children by age and discussing general tendencies for particular age levels tends to mask individual differences and the learning of any particular child.[4]

The two stages in the research programme conducted by the author at Edge Hill College of Higher Education, to support the Primary Education and Industry Project, were designed to replicate and extend the research summarized so far.

The initial study in 1983 was conducted with 120 children aged 7–11 years in fifteen classes in seven schools in North West England and North Wales. The eight children from each class were chosen by the headteacher, in collaboration with the classteacher, so that there were four children of each sex and two children from each of the four quartiles of the class. The teachers were asked to select children who would be relaxed in the test situation. In an attempt to compensate for the equivalence of language ability and noting the possibilities of incorporating children's observable behaviour[36] into the structural interview, an initial stimulus of a television programme describing part of the production process of a product well known to the children was produced by the project team. The children were then questioned individually, while at the same time handling and working on floor mats, specially designed and produced by the project team to illustrate an aspect shown on the television programme. The questions and mats were both designed to assist in eliciting responses concerned with the key concepts of price, added value, division of labour and interdependence as illustrated in the diagram opposite.[125]

The age range considered, (7–11) would appear to correspond to all four of Furth's (1979) stages and therefore it was necessary to present the children with materials with which they could associate and also to plan the materials so that the various substages contained in each stage could be examined.

The structured interview was based on a set of questions (Note A) and recorded on to video-tapes for all the 120 children. This was undertaken in order to judge the applicability of this type of material for more general usage. The interviews informed the researcher as to how the children's ideas of the concepts developed longitudinally, using the same questions

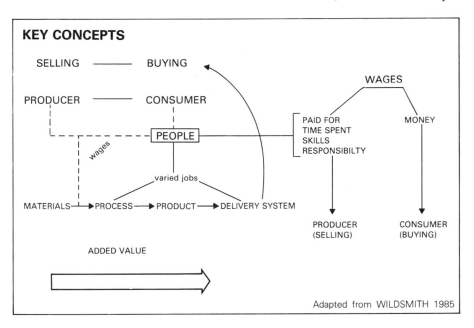

Adapted from WILDSMITH 1985

and materials. The children spontaneously gained new insights in the course of talking about the societal issues to the interviewer. The children's responses over all the concepts showed similar spreads amongst the stages as those shown by Furth (1978) for all four age groups (7–8, 8–9, 9–10, 10–11), with the children in the upper two quartiles in each of the ages generally being at the higher stages.

The greatest spread was observed for those children aged 9–10 and 10–11, where examples were found of children covering the complete range of the stages I–IV. A number of individual children appeared to lie outside their quartile's position for all the concepts. This was particularly noted from the two upper quartiles where individual children were judged to lie in the lower stages. Equally, there were individual children from the lower two quartiles who appeared in higher stages than might have been expected. The reason for individual children being placed by their teachers' in particular quartiles, i.e., mathematics quotient, reading ages and verbal reasoning scores, might not be reflected by their responses to questions based on experiences connected to a product known to them as consumers.

The need to consider individual children was an important issue, as was the spread for the upper age ranges. Of equal concern was the fact that different responses might occur if similar questioning took place using the same producer-consumer model, but in different situations. In order to attempt to expand the research findings, a second stage was conducted in 1985 with 96 pupils. Twenty-four from each of the four ages, 8–9, 10–11, 11–12 and 12–13, with one child of each sex from the top, middle and bottom ability ranges were selected by their teacher in sixteen classes from eleven schools, designated primary, middle, secondary comprehensive, in North West England and Wales. Four products were selected to be purchased by appropriate members of a family of four, brother/can of drink; mother/potatoes; sister/a diamond ring; and father/can of petrol, and questions (Note B) were asked using an interview technique exactly replicating that used by earlier researchers. All the responses were tape recorded. The producer-consumer cycle is affected by different economic factors for each of the products discussed.

The responses received to one specific question from six children aged 12–13 are used to illustrate the level of understanding. The children, on an individual basis, freely agreed to the price they would pay for a diamond ring. The interviewee is then asked:

What did the sister pay £x for?

The six children answered in terms of the diamond — people who mined and cut — gold/silver mined and shaped — jeweller for cutting — wages — skills/what you can do better than anyone else — travel — tax/VAT — jeweller's shop — assistants, to keep the business — precious/hard stone and instruments for cutting. Six children aged 8–9 answered only in terms of the diamond in the ring, although one child added that it was worth a lot of money. Similar qualitative replies were received to the same form of questions for the other three products for both groups of children. Analysis of the results appears to show that by the children's responses to the questions, the majority have not reached stage IV in the key economic concepts before the age of 12–13.

Conclusions

This type of material by its format never can provide an absolute indication of whether or not an individual child has attained a certain selected concept. However, the studies indicate that there are critical periods for the development of economic concepts and that pupils at the ages of transfer are widely spread over the stages of concept development. The research undertaking by the author does suggest that by the age of 12–13, children have reached the highest stage judged by a particular economic model whose focus is directly related to the individual child; hence national and global issues might be appropriate to consider after this age. The research discussed suggests that stages do exist for an understanding of economic concepts and that consideration should be made for the development of these concepts by using a 'spiralling curriculum model'[15;59] over the whole age range 5–13 and for a curriculum strategy throughout the age range. The question remains as to whether economic understanding in pupils aged 5–13 can develop from economic awareness without the knowledge of the development of children's understanding of selected economic concepts being incorporated into curriculum planning,[51;119] or in fact, curriculum materials in general. It is the 'pitfalls of oversimplification'[30] that this chapter has attempted to map.

However, economic awareness for the 5–13 age group must now arise from such things as the curriculum contexts being offered by teachers to their children, the issues the children and teachers raise in discussion and questioning as well as the teacher's knowledge of children's understanding of key economic concepts.

I am particularly indebted to Professor W.A.L. Blyth, Emeritus Professor, University of Liverpool, and Mark C. Schug, Associate Professor, School of Education, the University of Wisconsin-Milwaukee for their assistance and help with my research since 1982.

Notes

A   The main questions included:
> How does the person in the shop decide what the drink will cost?
> What do you think goes into the price of –p for one can of drink?
> What part do the (trucking company) play in our story?
> What are they paid for?
> The (trucking company) pay the driver £x, why was the driver given £x?
> What will the driver use the £x for?
> Who depends on the driver?
> Who does the driver depend on?

B   The questions asked included:
> Why do we give money when we obtain goods in a shop/supermarket/ petrol station or farm?
> and on the *four* articles: where he/she/they got money from?
> Who decides what he/she is going to pay?
> Why is the — priced at £/p?
> What are you paying for?
> What does the person in the shop/farm/petrol station do with the £/p x given to him/her?

Chapter 5

Using 'Adults other than Teachers' in the Classroom

Duncan Smith

Introduction

The tradition among primary schools of inviting people from the local community such as the policeman, nurse, doctor, postman or vicar to talk to the children about their work has long been a part of educational practice. As well as being an important means of linking the school to the community, teachers would claim that not only does it help children appreciate the contribution made by these people to their daily life but also the importance of learning from other people's experiences. In spite of the frequency with which these visits take place, the nature of the practice is nevertheless limited in a significant number of ways. Firstly, the way in which the 'visitor' is used is often quite limited; the short talk, perhaps with slides, followed by questions, is often the standard approach. Secondly, the link between what the 'visitor' provides and what the children have done prior to the visit or will do afterwards, is not always clearly defined. Thirdly, the 'visitors' often come from a very restricted sector of the working population. Finally, the visits tend to be 'one-offs' with little in the way of continuity or progression in the contact with the 'visitor'. It is in these four areas in particular, that schools and curriculum development agencies such as SCIP and SATRO, have been trying to improve practice.

Why Involve People from Industry in the Classroom?

One of the major justifications for bringing people from industry into the classroom is that they are able to provide first-hand experience of a sector of the 'working world' with which most teachers are unfamiliar. This is not, in any way, to deny the experience of work which teachers bring to the education of young children. Attempts to describe industry and commerce as the 'real' world of work as opposed to schools which from time to time may seek to imitate it, are not entirely convincing, as Jamieson argues.[66] Rather, the claim is that industrialists and trade unionists can provide children and teachers with insights into alternative forms of work, different structures and hierarchies as well as different values and attitudes towards work. Children also experience alternative areas and sources of learning which, hopefully, will broaden their understanding of the world in which they are growing up.

Working with 'adults other than teachers', however, is not just beneficial because it contributes to children's knowledge of the 'working world'. It also provides them with another context within which they can develop interpersonal skills. Relating to adults who, for instance, operate in ways which are different to that with which the children are familiar is a valuable experience. Having to phrase requests for information or present ideas to someone whose professional skills and expertise lie outside education and who may, therefore, be unfamiliar with certain classroom practices, is also a challenge for primary school children. The opportunities which such contacts create for children to develop an empathy with people who work in different settings and who may have values and opinions about work which are different from those presented by teachers or parents, are significant.

A further reason for involving people with specific experience of industry and commerce is that many of them bring to the classroom alternative approaches to learning. While it is true that some industrialists will still adopt the old style 'presentation', many more are anxious to use 'active' learning approaches, which involve them working alongside the children. Problem-solving exercises, design and make, case studies, simulations and role plays are just a few of the alternative ways of utilizing the experience and expertise of industrialists.

Introducing children to a variety of 'role models' would also be thought of as a very important part of their education by many teachers. The experience of some children in this respect is very narrow, a point made by Holmes and Jamieson.[56] Many industry topics for instance, appear to rely heavily on the support of people in middle or senior management of companies. Often this is because their work gives them the flexibility to be able to help schools with classroom projects or company visits, whereas it is much more problematical for employees on the shop floor to find time to support such work. The frequency with which schools use women in the role of 'adult other than teacher' for their industry projects is also very small. This would seem to support the view that either schools only look to people in senior management positions for help, or companies only offer help at this level, and the small percentage of women found in these positions in many companies accounts for their non-involvement in the activities. Imbalances of this kind need rectifying if stereotypical attitudes to male and female roles in the workplace are to be changed.

Schools, as part of their broad educational aims, claim to be engaged in helping children make sense of the society in which they are growing up. Industry and work are a part of that society and for teachers not to involve representatives of that sector in the educative process would seem to be something of a contradiction. Having accepted the argument for such involvement, the question remains as how best to utilize these people's experience.

How Can People from Industry Contribute to the Curriculum?

There appear to be three roles which representatives of industry can play in the development of industry education in the primary school.

1. As planners and designers of curricular experiences, in collaboration with teachers.
2. As providers of experiences and expertise.
3. As assessors and evaluators of the experience.

Each of these can, in turn, be divided into a number of different functions, depending on the nature of the experience.

Planning

Aims and Objectives

There is a tendency for teachers planning industrial experiences for children to take on the entire task themselves. They identify the aims and objectives, decide on the teaching approaches and select ways of assessing the learning. Once such a scheme is planned, they then begin to look for industrialists and trade unionists to help them implement it. There are a number of reasons for this, including the fact that some teachers do not believe that industrialists have either a responsibility or the expertise to engage in the process of curriculum design. They see it as their responsibility as professional teachers, with the knowledge of the children's ability and the way they learn, to plan the scheme.

In the case of other teachers, it is not so much a matter of them believing that industrialists cannot or should not help, but a feeling that they are more likely to get the support they are looking for if they have a clearly defined scheme to present at the outset. Other teachers adopt this viewpoint because they believe that industrialists prefer to know the exact nature of the commitment, and having a ready-made scheme is one way of giving them this assurance.

The latter two viewpoints do indeed have some merit. There is a need for teachers to have the outline of an idea before they approach a company and it is helpful to be able to give those who are being asked for help some idea of the extent of their commitment. There is, however, a need to allow people from industry to help shape the schemes of offering their ideas on the overall aims, objectives, teaching approaches and ways of assessing the learning. Such cooperation would, it is hoped, result in a greater commitment on the part of the industrialists to the scheme. In cases where this form of cooperative planning does not take place, problems can arise; for instance, when the aims and objectives of a project are not understood or agreed by those involved in its design. It is important for there to be a reasonably high degree of consensus about what are the expected learning outcomes. Joint planning of a project can also help to identify personal value judgements and attitudes, which, if not fully appreciated at the outset, can give rise to problems, particularly when the project reaches the classroom.

Concepts and Skills

Collaborative planning can also help focus on the key concepts and skills which it is hoped the children will acquire. There may, of course, be some disagreement between the planning team over what the children are capable of understanding, but it is preferable to have these discussions before beginning work with the class.

Holmes and Jamieson[56] identified three areas in which 'adults other than teachers' were thought by teachers to be experts. Firstly, there is the area of 'technical knowledge', details about a particular manufacturing process or market research. Secondly, the area of 'industrial organization', more general than 'technical knowledge', such as the causes of inflation or aspects of unemployment. Finally, there is what the authors call the 'culture of the organization', concerned with attitudes and values such as discipline or accuracy in the workplace.

There is a danger, of course, of making assumptions about the level and extent of these people's expertise. Often teachers may expect industrialists to have knowledge of a very wide range of industrial practice, whereas in reality, their knowledge and skill is quite specific to a particular function of industry. The conclusion to be drawn from this is that teachers need to be specific about the focus of the project.

This process of collaboration in the planning of a project can also have other benefits. Both teachers and industralists, as a result of working together, will have a better appreciation of each other's skills, what each can contribute to the project and where they will need to support one another. They may also gain a clearer understanding of the organization in which each works and thus more easily appreciate some of the difficulties which they face in making the project successful. Ultimately, the value of such collaboration is that a more meaningful, accurate and stimulating experience is created.[108]

Teaching Approaches

The use of experiential teaching approaches has become a feature of many industry-related projects. People from industry, for instance, have helped design case studies, simulations and role plays by providing 'real-life' experiences of the industrial environment which can be used with the children. Industrialists and trade unionists have also helped teachers plan mini-enterprise activities and industrial visits, in the case of the latter giving teachers and pupils some prior knowledge of the organization or process they will be observing.

A number of the case studies in this book illustrate the principle of using 'adults other than teachers' in the planning process. Fitzpatrick at Forsbrook involved representatives from Russell Hobbs and Staffordshire Potteries in the initial design of the project; Clerkin at Manor School spent some time talking with the manager of the workshops at Newham about the way in which the project could concentrate on the manufacturing process. Burleton refers to the initial problems of getting industrialists interested in the primary age group, but the subsequent value in planning particular aspects of the textile project with the company. Finally, Hales spent the initial period discussing the 'We make shoes' project with a number of people in that industry before finally deciding on its aims, objectives and structure. The projects were thought to have a greater degree of authenticity and accuracy as a result of this process of collaborative planning.

Implementation

The importance of using 'adults other than teachers' (AOTs) in the school-based part of a project is stressed throughout this book as is the need to move away from the idea that their role is simply to 'give talks to the children'. Many teachers, and for that matter industrialists and trade unionists, believe that the real benefit to children's understanding has come from the willingness of the AOTs to adopt 'active' learning approaches which involve them working alongside the children. They have adopted a number of roles in this classroom-based work:

1. Leader of the activity making decisions on its organization and framework.
2. Co-leader with the teacher.
3. Adviser/consultant.
4. Participant.
5. Observer.

Leader

An industrialist or trade unionist may take sole responsibility for running an activity such as a case study or simulation. In these cases, the industrialist will explain the purpose of the exercise to the children, brief them if they have roles to play, provide them with various procedures for doing the exercise, deal with the operating problems and finally, decide when the activity will be concluded. This may give the teacher the opportunity to adopt an observer role. Careful briefing of the AOT is naturally vital in these circumstances, involving not only knowledge of the children's age and ability but also an awareness of time and other resource constraints. Working in this way the children may take longer to build up a relationship with the AOT and may initially continue to refer to the teacher for guidance. Allowing the AOT to run an activity on his/her own can often be the first stage in building a relationship between him/herself and the teacher, particularly in those cases where the teachers may have little knowledge of a specific piece of industrial practice. It not only serves to reassure the teacher of the AOT's competence to work with the children, but also increases his/her willingness to collaborate with them in the planning of subsequent activities. Fitzpatrick's early experiences with Russell Hobbs and Creda were certainly of this type, in that representatives of the company ran production simulations with the children, with the teachers there principally as observers.

Co-Leader

Ideally, some form of joint leadership between the teacher and AOT will develop, involving a sharing of some of the tasks. Explaining the purpose of the exercise might, for instance, be the teacher's responsibility, while briefing the children on their roles might be left to the AOT. De-briefing the exercise might well be done by both teacher and AOT. 'Personal style' can sometimes be a problem in these situations with the teacher's way of operating and relating to the children being very different from that of the 'visitor'. Communication issues, such as how to address the children and how they should address the adults, as well as dealing with behavioural problems, need some preliminary discussion.

Adviser

'Adults other than teachers' perform the role of advisers to such activities in two basic ways. Firstly, they can help by providing general advice or insights into industry. If, for instance, children were exploring the theme of technology, they might want general information on how it has affected certain sectors of employment. A project focussing on conservation or care of the environment might include general information on how industry tackles the problem of pollution and the issue of cost set against public pressure or jobs. In one sense this is the more difficult role for AOTs to perform in that both children and teachers may expect them to have substantial experience and expertise on a wide range of industrial issues.

Their other contribution as adviser is specifically concerned with particular industrial processes. In the case of a representative from management, this may be in the form of advice on how a company markets its product or how it is costed. Alternatively, it might involve briefing children on the role of a production manager or financial director in a mini-enterprise. A trade unionist would be able to help children understand what the job of a shop steward entails or assist them in the process of negotiating with 'management' in a production line simulation.

Schools vary in their use of 'adults other than teachers' in both of these approaches. In some, for instance, they try to ensure that an 'adviser' works with all pupils and that consultancy is built into the learning process. Others leave to the children the decision as to whether to consult the AOT, rather than impose it in the form of a rule. Both approaches have advantages and disadvantages. The former guarantees that the children are aware of the expertise which is available and the likelihood of it being used by them is probably higher. The latter allows the children more freedom of choice over whether to seek advice and from which source they should get it. It may be, for instance, that the person who has been allocated specifically to work with a group may not have the expertise it needs, whereas a person working with another group would be of more help.

One of the dilemmas for teachers, industrialists and trade unionists is between allowing the children to make decisions for themselves, even when some of them may be clearly wrong, and intervening and perhaps dominating the work. Achieving a balance between both these extremes is difficult; the 'interventionist' approach is more likely to be the one which needs tempering.

Many of the case studies in the book illustrate the role of the AOT as adviser; Hales' work with the children at Higham on the Hill, Garwell and Anderson's account of the work with the local mines in Gwent and Holdsworth and Murphy's extensive use of AOTs in the project in Eltham, illustrate the range and impact of this dimension on the projects.

Participant

The use of AOTs as participants, particularly in such things as role plays or simulations, is also favoured by teachers. Representatives of senior and middle management, trade unions and, very occasionally, those at operative level, become involved in activities in which they play a role alongside the children. On occasions, the role will be closely associated with their job in the company, at other times they might be asked to adopt a role which is entirely outside their direct experience. Operating in this mode will often help to establish a good working relationship with the children and the label of 'expert' will not be so obvious and intimidating. The need for AOTs to avoid dominating the activity and allow the children to participate on an equal footing is important. Even in circumstances where some of the decision making is not as precise as they would wish, industrialists should try to allow the children to feel that they can share this process with the adults.

The opportunity for children to work with a range of 'adults other than teachers' can not only assist in their understanding and appreciation of industry, but also contribute to the development of their interpersonal skills.

Observer

The role of observer is connected with the assessment and evaluation of the experience. 'Adults other than teachers' can support the teachers in observing both the processes and the outcomes of the learning. Observations, for instance, on the way children tackle problem-solving activities, simulations and mini-enterprises, on the way they use advice and on the feasibility, or otherwise, of their ideas and solutions would help the teachers and children evaluate the experience. Their comments on the use of such social skills as cooperation, negotiation, compromise and empathy could also be part of their assessment of the learning.

Assessment and Evaluation

Industrialists and trade unionists have successfully helped teachers assess the children's learning in a variety of activities. Professor Blyth provides a valuable framework for assessing children's learning in his key chapter. The role of de-briefing, for instance, in establishing children's feelings towards an activity, their understanding of what took place and the key individual and group learning points, is an important feature of experiential learning in which AOTs can take part. Assessing the intellectual and social skills of the children can be done in a number of ways; making a presentation to an industrialist of an enterprise activity, getting children to write their own case study or role play, producing a report on a visit to the company, carrying out interviews with workers using their own design of questionnaire, producing a photographic record of a production simulation or a story book for younger children, are just a few of the methods that the children can employ.

Evaluation, concerned with helping teachers, industrialists and trade unionists make sense of the whole activity, is an important part of the process. Questions related to the preparation of the children, as well as of the teachers and AOTs, the use of industrialists' experience, the organization and management of the children's learning, the range of activities in which the children have been engaged, all form part of the evaluation process. The responses of both teachers and the people from industry to such questions will provide the basis for the future planning of such projects.

Out-of-School Activities

Visits by children and teachers to industry are a key feature of many projects as illustrated by all the case studies in this book. The role of 'adults other than teachers' in the preparation of pupils for the visit, the visit itself and the follow-up work is of crucial importance.

Preparation

A number of the case studies refer to the fact that the teachers visited the company prior to the children making their visit. The discussions between the teacher and the representative of the company helped shape the project's aims and objectives and clarified what was possible within such constraints as time and personnel. Such contacts also helped to build up a working relationship between the teacher and AOT and allowed alternative ideas and suggestions to be put forward.

A visit by a representative of the company to the school prior to the children's is also a strategy used by some teachers. This gives the visitor an opportunity to brief the children on aspects of the organization that they will encounter, as well as providing guidance on safety procedures which they will have to observe. Meeting and talking with someone from the company prior to the visit also helps the children to relax and feel able to ask questions when they make the visit.

The Visit

Much criticism has been levelled at industrial visits on the grounds that children learn very little from this type of experience. The stereotype image of 'crocodiles' of children walking around a company endeavouring to listen to the information being given, in situations which are often not conducive either to listening or understanding, is all too often a reality. Criticism is also levelled at companies for not providing an appropriate visit for the age and ability of the children, often a reflection of the lack of consultation between themselves and the teachers prior to the visit taking place. Teachers are also criticized by companies for not adequately preparing the children, to which some teachers reply that adequate preparation cannot be done without the help of industry. Finally, companies frequently complain that it is not always obvious how the visit will contribute to follow-up work back in the classroom.

The work reported in the case studies in this book attempts to counter such criticisms; teachers and industrialists worked together to plan an appropriate visit, many industrialists managed a visit to the school beforehand, children were briefed and the very close link between the visit and follow-up work is constantly emphasized. Finally, the visits were directly related to a particular idea or theme and the children generally knew exactly what they needed to find out.

Improvements in other aspects of the organization of visits are also obvious from the case studies. One of the ways that primary schools make effective use of parents is by involving them in the visits. In many cases, this is not simply done because of the legal requirement relating to supervision, but because subsequent conversations between parent and child often reinforce the learning. Visits are often organized in such a way that the children work in small groups each with a teacher, parent and employee of the company. The information is then shared by mixing the groups when they return to school. Some companies have endeavoured to use their younger members of staff for these visits, in the belief that the children will find it easier to relate to such a person than someone who is clearly of an older generation.

Follow-up

The variety of ways in which visits have been followed up is quite impressive. No longer is it just a matter of getting the children to write an account of the visit. Situations which the children experienced are recreated in role play, drama or simulation, the information which was gathered is put to a specific use in such things as pricing or marketing a product in a mini-enterprise. Problem-solving exercises in science or design are set up, based on what was seen on the visit. All areas of the primary curriculum have a part to play in developing the experience: art, music, craft, science, language and mathematics.

Often the follow-up work is supported by people from the companies who are able to supplement the information which was gathered during the visit. On occasions, the children have requested a further visit either to gather additional information or check the original. A repeat visit will not always be necessary for all the children, so the class will brief those who are selected to go on what information is required.

Many primary schools make use of such things as open days and parents' evenings to exhibit the children's work. In some instances, these meetings have been transformed into learning experiences for the children, parents and industrialists. Activity-based open evenings have involved the children themselves in developing exercises for the parents. Fitzpatrick in her work at Forsbrook made use of such occasions and in one instance was successful in persuading another company to work with the school on the following year's project.

Other Activities

Work shadowing has become an increasingly popular means of helping young people understand something of the various roles and functions which individuals perform within an organization. In the main this form of experiential learning has been used by secondary schools, but there have been a few instances of children of primary age getting involved in a shadowing exercise. Watts[124] reports on the scheme at Devon's Road Primary School, Tower Hamlets. A project on 'People and Work' with 4th-year juniors involved a visit to a button factory. After a meeting with the chairman and directors of the factory and four members of the production line, the children were allocated to individual 'worker-guides'. A period of observation was followed by a chance to put questions to the individual workers. Follow-up work based on the 'shadowing' experience produced a variety of responses.

Some primary schools have organized 'industry weeks' during which a range of activities such as simulations, role plays and design exercises are run, using people from local industry as advisers. Such schemes have the advantage of allowing quite large groups of teachers, industralists and trade unionists to work together for a reasonable length of time, hopefully without the interruption of other school or company commitments. On the other hand, the one-week activity does not allow for progression and development in learning to the same degree as a structured project over a half or a whole term.

There have been one or two instances of schools developing an 'industrialist in residence' scheme, whereby a representative from industry spends a proportion of time attached to one school. Various time-scales have been tried, one or two days a week for half a term or blocks of two or three weeks. The advantage of such a scheme is that it is an opportunity for teachers, industrialists and children to build up a good working relationship and for individual as opposed to group or whole class interests and initiatives to develop.

Issues

The subject of the preparation and briefing of 'adults other than teachers' prior to their work in schools is one to which there is constant reference in this and other parts of the book and there is little doubt that it plays an important part in the successful operation of a project. Equally crucial is the need for teachers, industrialists and trade unionists to be clear about the aims and objectives of such projects and to share a reasonable level of agreement about the desired outcomes.

The case studies in this book illustrate the wide range of 'adults other than teachers' that schools have used to develop their projects. Even so, there is a need to extend that range to other sectors of the economic community. There still seems to be a problem, for instance, in getting people at operative level into schools; time and money are clearly the major reasons for this. Those schools which have succeeded in this respect have often done so through the generosity of these people giving up their non-work time. Some schools have used the expertise of people who are unfortunate enough to find themselves unemployed or those who have taken early retirement.

A further aspect of this issue relates to the aim of widening children's concept of work. If this is to be one of the goals of schools–industry work, then 'adults other than teachers' who represent those other sectors of 'industry' and 'work' need to be involved in the projects. People who work in the voluntary sector regularly help many primary schools; those people, however, who are self-employed or run very small businesses often find it difficult to give of their time. Teachers, together with people who work in this sector of the economy, need to devise ways of introducing this dimension of the 'working world' to children.

Recent research carried out by the School Curriculum Industry Partnership on the different sections of the community from which AOTs are drawn, revealed that a very small proportion of women and Blacks get involved with school projects. There is an obvious reason for this state of affairs in the tendency for schools to invite, and for the companies to offer, people from middle or senior management and, therefore, the likelihood of the AOT being male and White is very substantial. It is very important if these projects. The danger in not introducing children to these working standing of role models in industry and work, to involve such groups in these projects. The danger is not introducing children to these working groups is that the old stereotypes of the 'world of work' being a White male-dominated activity will persist.

Reference was made earlier to the use by some schools of people who are unemployed. Considerable use can be made of their experience and expertise in spite of the fact that they may not presently be in employment. Some teachers have naturally had some reservations about using people who are unemployed, believing that they may experience some embarrassment, particularly if the children make reference to it in the course of their discussions. Others feel that using people who are unemployed might create an impression of industry which is rather negative, though, of course, those teachers who stress the importance of giving children a balanced impression of industry, see the contribution of such people as essential. One important aspect of this issue is that they are principally being used for their experience of industry as opposed to their feelings about unemployment, though inevitably the latter may emerge from time to time.

The involvement of trade unionists in primary school projects would appear to be growing, albeit slowly. There is still, however, uncertainty on a number of counts about their precise role in such work, doubt about whether young children can fully appreciate the part trade unions play in industry and some concern about the possibility of biased attitudes creating inaccurate impressions in young children's minds. Some of the case studies illustrate the variety of ways trade unionists have been used in schools, helping with case studies, simulations and mini-enterprises, preparing children for visits and debriefing them after the experience. Clerkin in the Manor School case study refers to the contact which the children had with three trade unionists; Fitzpatrick also made use of them at Forsbrook, and Hales' project at Higham on the Hill clearly owed a great deal to the trade unionists.

The question of whether the children can understand and appreciate the role of trade unions is, in one sense, a matter of adopting appropriate teaching methods and selecting trade union issues which can most obviously be related to experiences of the children. The successful use of trade unionists often appears to build on the ideas and curiosity of the children, as illustrated by the Arael School case study. The evidence from the case studies seems to indicate that the children clearly gained an understanding of certain key economic concepts as well as aspects of the organization and structure of a company. Developing their understanding of the role and function of certain aspects of trade union practice, therefore, would seem to be appropriate for some children, particularly those in the upper junior age range.

The fear that children may be subjected to biased attitudes and forms of union indoctrination appears, from the evidence provided by the case studies, to be totally groundless. This, of course, does not suggest that every contact which primary schools have with trade unionists will be totally satisfactory. In those cases where, in the opinion of the teacher, problems of bias are created by a particular individual, whether it be from the management or the union side of industry, then ideally an opportunity should be found to discuss the problem. There have been occasions when such incidents have occurred and as a result teachers have elected not to invite such people back. A discussion of these concerns might overcome some of the worries and allow the relationship to continue. Many of the representatives of unions and management have ensured that their comments and opinions have been presented in such a way that no criticism of the kind mentioned earlier could be made.

The use of 'adults other than teachers' in the assessment of children's learning appears, as yet, to happen only infrequently. The most frequent use of AOTs in this role is following the children's involvement in a mini-enterprise where they have had the chance to present their ideas and a report to an industrialist. This provides an opportunity for the AOT to assess various aspects of the children's learning as well as the ideas on which they have worked. Some schools have used people from industry to debrief case studies or simulations, others have created the opportunity for teachers and industrialists to work together on the design of an assessment procedure.

Some schools invite industrialists to evaluate the whole of a particular project, though the means which are used tend to be quite informal. The commitment to making such an evaluation will depend on the person's involvement in the planning and operation of the project. Commenting on an entire scheme is difficult, particularly for someone outside the school, if he/she has not been deeply involved in its development.

Developing the expertise of 'adults other than teachers' in their various roles is an important consideration and viewed as a priority by many teachers. Such a process involves time and a commitment on the part of both groups. There are signs, however, that such collaboration is beginning to develop and that the outcomes are significant in terms of the children's, teachers' and industry's learning.

Section B
Industry Education: The Practice

Chapter 6

The Textile Industry
Freshfield Primary School, Formby

Sheila Burleton

Introduction

Freshfield County Primary School is situated in Formby, a small dormitory town on the Merseyside coast between Liverpool and Southport. Over the last twenty years a large amount of residential building has transformed Formby from a village of just over 11,000 inhabitants in 1961 to its present size of nearly 30,000 people. It is regarded generally as an affluent area with many of the inhabitants having white-collar jobs within commuting distance of those two principal centres of employment. There is very little of what might be described as 'traditional industry' in the area, but the town is surrounded by agricultural land. Two industrial estates, one large and one small, located to the east of the town, provide employment in the construction and motor engineering industries.

The school has 278 children aged between 5 and 11 years. Until two years ago there were separate infant and junior schools on adjoining sites, but they were merged on the simultaneous retirement of both the junior school headteacher and his deputy. A decline in the number of children led to the two schools being amalgamated under the leadership of the infant school headteacher and deputy headteacher. The policy in both departments of the school has always been to help children, by means of modern educational practices, to develop into happy and independent individuals with a healthy respect for themselves and other people.

The infant department was vertically grouped, while the junior department had a more formal structure with two mixed-ability classes in each age group. The fall in rolls resulted in reorganization into mixed age group classes, where necessary, in the junior department; the infant department, however, retained most of its original organization.

Since 1985, all aspects of the school curriculum have been under review and change. With the older children, for instance, there has been a positive move towards more oral language work and the introduction throughout the school of a new mathematics scheme. All this has been achieved gradually and with regard for the parents who, in the main, have very traditional expectations of educational methods. The work completed in this case study was undertaken by a top junior class consisting of 29 children.

In September 1984, the class teacher attended a two-week in-service course at Edge Hill College of Higher Education, entitled 'An introduction to industry throughout the primary school curriculum'. The teacher's interest had been aroused by the placement in the school of a student from the college who was on final teaching practice. As part of her studies she had been investigating the idea of bringing industry into the primary school curriculum.

Developing the Project: A Curriculum Framework

At the conclusion of the two-week course, the class teacher looked at the curriculum as it related to her class, in particular what was planned for the autumn term, with a view to adapting it, rather than beginning entirely new work. It was decided to use the school social studies scheme which in the top junior year included work on topics from the Industrial Revolution to modern times, and a television programme based on life surrounding a Yorkshire woollen mill at the beginning of the century — 'How we used to live', Yorkshire Television. The project became loosely named 'The Textile Industry' but after preparation of an enormous flow chart it was decided to curb teacher enthusiasm and narrow it down to a study of textiles. It would begin with the manufacturing process of the material in its raw state through spinning, weaving, dyeing, design and making of clothes, to the retailing of children's clothes in chain stores, mail-order catalogues and local small shops.

As many locally-based resources as possible would be used, and all subjects in the school curriculum incorporated. Language work would be developed through such things as interviews, letter writing, drama and mathematics, as well as through problem-solving exercises involving measurement and the collection and notation of facts. Scientific experiments involving the dyeing, wearability and washability of fabrics and the construction of models were also planned. Geograpical and historical insights would also be developed by looking at exports and imports. It was also decided that the entire school year would be dedicated to the project rather than the one term originally planned. The children would be encouraged to develop as many aspects of their skills as possible, including communications, team work and decision making. Work would be recorded not only in written form but pictorially, and by the use of tape recorders. Provision would be made to include individual, group and classwork whenever necessary. Visits to relevant places were planned as often as time and money would allow, and whenever possible people from the world of industry were encouraged to make visits to the children at school. These visits proved to be vital in making the whole project come alive and gave the children a glimpse of the wider world of work.

It was essential that the project was planned in such a way that it would still have meaning even if visits to factories and other establishments could not be arranged. Although industry claims that children should know how the country earns its wealth, it also believes that time is money, particularly in the present economic climate. Companies must also take account of the conditions of 'health and safety at work' regulations. The class teacher knew of a place to visit for the historical background where the children would be able to see machinery as well as the processes of spinning and weaving. It was also felt desirable to visit factories where cloth was dyed, clothing was manufactured and where the final products were sold, so that children could witness all the processes and talk to the workers involved in the various stages.

Making Contact with Industry

A parent of one of the children was a director of a clothing manufacturer in Liverpool. He was approached, and after initial doubts about the age of the children, agreed to a visit but stipulated that it must be during the first two months of the following year. Finding a dyers and suitable retailers was, however, a different matter. Rather a long time was spent in the evenings with the Thompson Directory and writing paper. Many firms did not reply, even when a number of letters were sent; telephone calls were equally unsuccessful. Eventually, two large chain stores situated in Liverpool city centre did reply and stated that an appointment could be made for the teacher to visit, but by the time these replies arrived, it was too late for them to be of any assistance.

On a preliminary visit by the teacher to W. Karp & Son Ltd, a clothing manufacturer based in the centre of Liverpool, it was stated that they were one of the suppliers of children's clothes to the Littlewoods Organization. As Littlewoods are a national company with their head office based locally in Liverpool, it was decided that this would be the ideal company with which the children should form a link, and renewed efforts were made to gain their cooperation. With hindsight it would probably have been better to ask W. Karp & Son for their assistance in making contact with Littlewoods but, as they had already spent considerable time and been most helpful, it was thought prudent not to stretch their goodwill too far. Following a number of letters, telephone calls and an opportune conversation with a member of the school staff who knew someone employed by the company, an interview was quickly arranged with the personnel and training manager.

At the interview, the aims and objectives of the project were clearly stated and after considerable discussion it was arranged for the class teacher to spend two days at the Littlewoods head office researching the background to the company, how the textile buyers operate, merchandizing and the mail-order business. This link had taken tenacity and a number of weeks to establish, but proved that with effort such contacts could be made. The Littlewoods Organization were most helpful and supportive once communications had been established, but they, like many companies, are disillusioned by what they see as teachers making visits without any real objective. Eventually visits for the children were arranged for May and June to the Littlewoods store in Southport.

Children's Perceptions of Industry

Before beginning the adapted plan of work, the class teacher gave the children an informal questionnaire with the aim of establishing their attitudes towards industry. It was intended to put the same questions to them at the end of the academic year to ascertain any change of opinion. Some of the questions were:

> What does industry mean to you?
> What types of jobs are included in industry?
> What conditions of work do you think people have in industry?
> Would you like to work in industry?

The replies were mainly as the class teacher predicted; industry meant factories, the jobs were looking after and cleaning machines, the conditions were noisy and dirty, and they would not like to work in industry. The last answer was surprising as many of the children expressed a desire to become engineers and secretaries and obviously they did not consider these occupations to be in industrial surroundings.

Visits and Follow-up Work in Class

The more formal studies began by discussing the work based on the city of Liverpool, in particular the port, the slave trade, the import of cotton and the associated reasons for these activities. This was followed up with the historical development in the spinning of thread and the weaving of cloth which it was necessary for the children to understand if they were to gain from the television series which showed spinning mules and looms in the factory situation approximately 80 years ago. To illustrate this further, the class visited the Lancashire Textile Museum at Helmshore.

On the museum site stands Higher Mill and Whitakers Mill. Higher Mill is 200 years old and houses a fully operational waterwheel, fulling stocks and other machinery for finishing woollen cloth. Whitakers Mill is a condenser cotton spinning mill which was in operation until 1978. Not only were the children able to see a range of textile machinery in an authentic industrial setting, but were able to interview two workers who had spent 40 years of their working lives in the textile industry. They also took full advantage of the museum workroom and experienced for themselves the difficulties involved in hand carding and spinning using a drop spindle.

The children proved to be very economically minded and surprised the museum teacher with their endless demands to know how much it cost to build, the rates paid, price of machinery, how long it would take to install, wages and general running costs. On returning to school, they expressed disappointment at not having enough time for carding and spinning and for putting other questions to the workers. The museum teacher was contacted and agreed to visit the school, bringing equipment which would enable them to have extra 'hands on' experience and also brought an archive film made as part of a recruitment drive for the textile industry in the 1920s. An arrangement was made for a small group to return to the museum to conduct a taped interview with the two textile workers in order to satisfy their curiosity on the technical and social aspects.

The class visit was so popular that the children expressed a wish to return in the summer term. This was arranged, and on arrival they were divided into groups to undertake various problem-solving activities which led to a variety of classroom work, including model-making using woodwork techniques and Lego Technic for both boys and girls. One group measured different machines, made a scale plan and worked out a logical placing of machinery for a spinning factory. Both visits to Helmshore acted as a stimulus for some excellent creative writing; one of the most charming examples is the following poem, written by an 11 year old girl.

The Lonely Waterwheel

I am a waterwheel
Standing in a mill
I used to make the factory work
And I could do it still

It used to be so noisy
Clanking, bumping, clatter
They couldn't do without me
But I no longer matter.

The owners closed the mill
And I started to decay
My axle rusted solid
My wood rotted away

That's how new owners found me
A few bits of wood
They thought they could repair me
I didn't think they could!

They managed to restore me
To make me work again
Would I again be powerful
To help the weaving men?

But now I'm just a showpiece
A bit of history
A lot of people come here
And stand and look at me

But I still feel lonely
Despite their friendly gaze
I miss the workers, miss the noise,
I miss my working days

Following these activities, the class began their own weaving and experiments to observe natural and man-made fibres and various textiles using magnifying glasses and microscopes. Some children also planned the building of a factory which involved finding out about planning permission, government grants, transport, the services needed for the employees, e.g., canteen, toilets, laundry, siting of machines for work flow and many other aspects. They came to the conclusion that no modern company would be able to afford to build a factory and a small town for the workers as employers had done in previous times.

During the first half of the spring term the class made a visit to the Liverpool Museum and W. Karp & Son Ltd. The class had been discussing the different types of clothing necessary for contemporary life ranging through day and night wear, leisure wear and uniforms, to protective clothing for various types of employment and climate.

On arrival at the factory, the pupils were seated in the canteen and addressed by one of the directors on the firm's background and the range of clothes made. This was followed by an explanation of work study and a description by a young lady recently employed as a designer, of her experiences working for different British companies, including the travel abroad which was necessary to keep abreast of the fashion scene. Prior to the visit, the children had prepared individual questionnaires and many of these were answered during the preliminary talks, but so many questions were asked that the session had to be curtailed to allow adequate time for a tour of the factory floor.

The class was divided into small groups and safety precautions were fully explained. The children had formed a preconceived idea that the factory floor would be similar to that shown in 'Coronation Street'. This conception vanished immediately upon entering the work floor. It was noted by all groups that there were many more women than men, and that the workers did not waste time by talking, but worked extremely quickly and quietly. The reason for this became apparent as the children were introduced to the concept of piece-work, the fact that wages were paid for the amount of work actually completed. They were fascinated by the tour of the factory and the employees were extremely friendly and very pleased to answer questions. On returning to the canteen the questioning was resumed with the children relentless in their quest for facts, often posing questions which adults would regard as too embarrassing to ask. The factory staff were astonished by the maturity of the questions. The following were among many of the questions asked:

The number of people employed
The number of working hours
The age of the building
The cost of the machinery
When was your most profitable year?
When was your least profitable year?
What was the reason for the variance?
What type of security does the factory have?
What sort of accidents occur on the shop floor?
Why does the firm not have its own retail outlet?

Integrating the Experience into the Curriculum

On returning to school, a varied programme of follow-up work began. The class set up its own production line making clothes. It was decided that the whole class could easily be involved in the making of simple dolls' clothes. Group discussion followed to break down the necessary production line into its various components. When a list of jobs had been compiled, each child found suitable employment, though not without argument and debate. A simple outfit was designed and, with great difficulty, patterns were made. Due to lack of skill, the finished article was not a great success, but it was never intended to be a marketable product. As an exercise it helped the children discover for themselves the difficulties involved, including the many complaints that wages were low because of the inability of other members of the team to work quickly enough.

From this experience an informative drama was developed and performed for the rest of the school. It was noted, not only by the class teacher, but by other members of staff, that the children seemed to have placed themselves in the type of job to which the teachers would probably have thought them most suited. The girl who is happy-go-lucky, with no apparent ambition, academic or otherwise, seemed really involved in her chosen employment as a presser and became engrossed in ironing. A boy and girl with artistic flair were intent on being designers and a boy with an analytical temperament was happily engrossed in workstudy.

Two large friezes were made, showing the different stages of the production line at the factory. It was received with much appreciation and amusement by the employees but there was an unforgivable omission; the children forgot to depict the canteen workers! Some of the drawings were enlarged and collage techniques were used to produce figures representing the various stages of design and manufacture for the display on the school hall walls. Written work included accounts of the visit, 'thank you' letters, poems and prose comparing old and new factories and conditions.

The class also designed their own garments and these were displayed on a background of overlapping fashion pictures cut from catalogues and magazines. When this background had been prepared, many of the children noticed that there were more photographs of women's wear than those for men and children. This began a humorous discussion on why this should be and developed into a battle of the sexes. However, it did lead to the compiling of a questionnaire to be completed by their parents to prove their theory that women spend more on clothes, followed by the children, with Dad worst off in the wardrobe stakes. Their findings confirmed that the mothers did spend most, on a wide variety of clothes; the father's clothes were usually individually more expensive but they tended to have fewer and did not become as easily bored with what they wore. On the whole, most of the children had almost as much as the mother spent on their wardrobe, mainly because they were rapidly growing.

Science activities developed from observing textiles to experimenting in dyeing natural and man-made cloth using natural substances. Some children preferred to do this on an individual basis, others in groups of twos and threes. The children provided a wide variety of leaves, berries, flowers and foodstuffs. Guidance was kept to a minimum level with the teacher's aim being to observe how they set about and developed the experiments. They discovered that the best results were obtained when using very hot water/juice in the dyeing process. The first set of experiments was ruined when the fabrics were left overnight to dry and, on return, it was discovered that the classroom had been invaded by ants, much to the amusement of the children and the horror of the school caretaker.

Gradually, the children discovered that by mixing different substances, more permanent results could be obtained even after washing. This led to the concept of mordants and the introduction of alum as a safe chemical to be used in the classroom to perform this function. Experiments on the wearability and washability of various fabrics used in the children's clothing were also undertaken, following an advertisement on television noticed by one of the groups.

Exploring the Retail Trade

Before visiting the Littlewoods store in Southport, the children were able to see a video based on the history and organization of the company, and were informed of the processes involved in the purchase of goods by the stores and mail-order companies. This involved explaining the work of both buyers and merchandisers and the support provided by the various office staff. It was considered unnecessary and unsuitable for the children to visit the head office of the Littlewoods Organization by both the company and the teacher. However, the reaction of the pupils when visiting the store's general office showed that this opinion was incorrect; unfortunately there was no time to rectify the situation.

The children visited the Southport store in two separate groups. The manager and assistant manager had previously dealt with visits by older children, but were happy to accommodate the younger age group. They were very helpful and gave the children a valuable insight into events behind the scenes in a large store. Their reaction to the children's questions was similar to that of other adults: surprise at their knowledge and understanding. The children were amazed to find that there appeared to be more space behind than on the sales floors, how much went on, and also how well the company cared for its employees.

The sophisticated computer system used by Littlewoods fascinated the children with its facility for not only storing information on the Southport store, but, via a link-up with the main computer at the head office, being able to gain access to the information stored at the company's 110 other stores and the six mail-order catalogues. The concept of the electronic mailing system enthralled the children and they were all delighted to receive individual instruction and practise on the computerized tills.

The children had a preconceived idea that the boilers for the heating system would be situated in the basement. They were highly amused to find them on the top floor, together with the air-conditioning system. Whilst inspecting the huge boilers, they were able to interview the store's maintenance man. He proved such a favourite with a variety of stories about his job that he was invited into school and spent a successful afternoon with the class answering more questions. The association with the Littlewoods Organization was most beneficial to the children and the store manager was delighted when, at a later date, a mother made herself known to him, thanking him for his help and stating how impressed she was by the amount of knowledge her son had gained from the visit.

The follow up work, including role-play, depicted problems encountered by the staff in the store; for example, shoplifting and the return of unsuitable goods. The class then began to look at smaller stores and the difference in their technique of merchandizing, their location and catchment area. Several occasions were spent looking at the shops in the centre of Formby. One exercise was dedicated to the mapping of all shops which sold goods with a textile connection and compiling a list of how textiles are used. This led to a lively argument outside one of the florists as to the composition of their artificial flowers, plastic or fabric. The only solution was to enter the shop for a closer investigation; this was achieved in the politest way possible. This incident is an indication of the children's increased awareness of the use of textiles. It was also noted that there was a larger number of shops dedicated to the sale of clothing in the Formby area than the population would probably demand. This prompted the question from the children to a local clothes shop owner as to how they survived economically with so much competition.

Assessing the Experience

For the end-of-year open week at school, the class exhibited their work in connection with the textile industry and the teacher made a display of photographs taken throughout the year recording the children's activities and visits. There was a variety of models, both static and mobile, collage, weaving, painting, drawing, written work and taped interviews. The visitors were certainly impressed by the display. The children developed their own *ad lib* script and the production line was assembled at the front of the school hall. The main aim of the performance was to demonstrate to the whole school how clothes are made in various sections and that team work is necessary for the benefit of all.

The children were also asked for their opinions of the work they had undertaken. It was obvious that they too had enjoyed the year, but like the teacher could happily have spent more time on the project. This disproved the teacher's initial worries about losing their attention and enthusiasm over a full year of work based on one topic. Most children claimed they had discussed school more with their parents and would have liked to develop more of the practical work. The teacher was surprised when a majority said that they had enjoyed the dyeing experiments least of all because they had been 'smelly and messy', though at the time they had appeared to revel in it!

For the teacher, the year was probably the most rewarding of her teaching career. Her own outlook was broadened and there was a rekindling of an interest in industry which began during her time at college but which somehow had got lost in the first few years of teaching. The whole project acted as a stimulus for all areas of language development, art, craft and science. Although practical mathematical concepts entered the project — for example, measurement, money and graphs — time had to be set aside for the more fundamental and routine mathematical work. It was rewarding to find children volunteering to continue to work through break times and after school to complete individual projects. The wealth of 'extras' they brought into the classroom ranged from working models to taped interviews with older relatives and, in one case, a collection of songs from the Lancashire cotton towns. This year's activities were invaluable in observing the personal development of the children and at times there was a wonderful feeling between class and teacher of stepping into the unknown together. In particular, it was rewarding to observe the blossoming of one boy who had previously shown little real interest or aptitude academically, who, as the year progressed, showed a natural practical ability and gained self-confidence. The depth of his questions on visits was astounding.

Chapter 7

'We Make Shoes'
Higham on the Hill Primary School and
Community Centre, Hinkley

Steven Hales

The School

Higham on the Hill, sited at what is thought to be the centre of England, borders the four counties of Leicestershire, Warwickshire, Staffordshire and Derbyshire. The village, which lies between Hinckley and Nuneaton, adjacent to Watling Street, has some 600 inhabitants who form a lively community with 'old' villagers and 'newcomers' mixing aimiably.

As a church and community school, Higham comes under the auspices of Leicestershire County Council. It has 55 children, divided into three class bases with a teacher head/community centre warden and two full-time members of staff. Part-time teaching staff contribute, at the moment, an additional day a week.

The school aims to provide the children with a broad based education which prepares them for a world in which self-esteem, self-motivation and self-discipline are essentials. Children are given opportunities to develop their talents fully. The thematic approach to the curriculum gives opportunities for collaborative learning and a total commitment to 'real' experiences.

A walk around the village, along the cottages, the pre-war houses and the new estate, gives little impression of industrial links. There are, of course, a number of farms surrounding the village, which have been used in the past for educational visits, and there is the Motor Industry Research Association test track at the west end of the village. Some inhabitants are employed as 'outworkers' in the local hosiery and knitwear trade, others in the declining number of local coal-mines, and some in the boot and shoe industry of south-west Leicestershire. In the next village of Stoke Golding, there are a few small businesses. All of these became possible resources to assist the children's learning.

Early Influences on the Project

In April 1985, the head attended SCIP's Primary Schools-Industry conference at Edge Hill College where he was introduced to a range of experiences and examples of practice in schools-industry work, which he felt to be in keeping with many of the aims of his own school. It was at this conference that the seeds of the 'We Make Shoes' project were sown.

Whilst the conference and the SCIP document *Schools and Industry (5–13)* offered many paths to getting the project started, the head had to make certain decisions about the structure of the project. In the period between the conference and the following summer break, he observed local industry and noted the many workshops linked with the hosiery and knitwear trade and the boot and shoe industry. He spent a day in both types of workplace. It was felt to be important to select a product with which all the children could identify and, subsequently, the shoe industry was chosen.

Making Contact with Industry

The first stage in the planning of the project was to make contact with the industry. The Leicestershire SCIP coordinator, and the school industry liaison officer (SILO), helped by providing lists of contacts in the local shoe industry and showed encouraging enthusiasm for the project. The former offered to run a production line simulation with the children and the SILO helped arrange a visit to a shoe shop and also set up a 'play' shoe shop in school.

In contacting the shoe industry, the head felt he had to do more than just send out an initial letter; there needed to be something more substantial. A document, entitled 'Looking at the world of work', and containing a number of articles from the educational press and some of his own thoughts for the project, was compiled. It was hoped that it would prove thought-provoking to those industrialists receiving it.

The initial letter, with the document, was circulated to some thirty companies and organizations linked with the boot and shoe trade in the south-west Leicestershire area. In many ways the results were disappointing, a dribble of replies were received with remarks like, 'It is an interesting idea, but are your children too young?' or, 'We do not accept parties under the age of 14', or 'You can bring a party of ten for a half-hour tour'. However, there were two rays of sunshine: a reply from the local trade union official and the Leicester and County Footwear Manufacturers' Association. Without doubt, these had to be followed up and personal contact was needed, as much gentle persuasion and convincing had to be done.

By this time, the aims and objectives of the project had been identified. It was intended to give the children opportunities to enhance their knowledge of industry, in particular the manufacturing process in the shoe industry. It would also provide opportunities for them to develop certain skills, such as research, and recording and interpreting information and experiences. Finally, it was hoped that the project would create positive attitudes to a work place among the children.

With these aims in mind, contact was made with the local branch secretary of the National Union of Footwear, Leather and Allied Trades. During the conversations, it became obvious that he would be able to arrange a programme of visitors and visits over a period of about three months which could provide the initial stimulation to the children's learning. The head was slightly surprised at his enthusiasm, but felt he would have empathy with young children.

Discussions were also held with the secretary of the Leicester and County Footwear Manufacturers' Association. He showed a degree of scepticism at working with children of this age group, but made a commitment to the project through the 'mini-enterprises'. He, too, had contact with young children and was impressed by the innovation of this kind of work.

It was at this point that sponsorship of the project was mentioned. He had contacts with the large companies and it was becoming apparent that this manner of working could be expensive to both school and parents. It was partly as a result of the generous support, both in financial and material terms, from a variety of individuals and organizations that the project developed such a broad perspective. At an obvious level, it helped provide transport for the children to the various workplaces, but at another level, it enabled them to pursue and record experiences in ways which otherwise would not have been available to them.

Developing Staff Awareness and Expertise

The next task was to convince the staff. Thus far, all they had seen was the head going off to meet a number of people, writing many letters and receiving numerous phone calls, and a number of strangers visiting school.

In motivating the staff, there were two excellent factors in the organization of in-service work in Leicestershire. With pre-planning it was possible to arrange sufficient supply days to organize school-focused INSET. Two days were planned for early November and, for one of these, the staff team, that is the three full-time staff, two part-time teachers and the school ancillary, settled down to primary schools-industry work. There is great benefit to the working of the small school to have as many adults involved as possible to create curriculum breadth.

A number of priorities were set for the INSET day; to introduce teachers to this type of work, to explore its feasibility within the school structure, to investigate a variety of stimuli in relation to curricular areas linking the children's work to the school guidelines. This pattern had already been established in termly projects covering a four-year cycle. The staff team produced a topic web which related to the curriculum areas of language, maths, science, environmental studies, creative arts, religious education and movement. Furthermore, the project work was related to the skills checklist, which encouraged the children to develop skills in researching, recording, interpreting experiences, experiencing and feeling, relationships and positive attitudes. Although the staff were accustomed to working in this integrated way, some doubts were expressed about the expanse of this particular project. It was also stressed that the parents would need to be kept informed of the way the children would be learning, emphasizing how the 'core' areas of the curriculum were being continued. The team resolved to meet again a month later when the final plan would be put together.

In early December, the staff team met again. They identified the concepts they wished to be emphasized, relating in particular to the manufacturing process and the importance of team work. The plan for visits and visitors was confirmed in relation to the programme of work prepared by each teacher. The level of cooperation among everyone involved at this stage was very encouraging.

The Project 'We Make Shoes'

The Visits

The initial aim was to give the children experience of a manufacturing process and the factory visits were planned to give them opportunities to observe that aspect of the workplace purposefully. It was the staff's intention that all the children in the school, except the 5-year-olds, would visit a number of workplaces to give them insights into a variety of manufacturing processes. Three factories, Eatoughs Ltd of Earl Shilton, making ladies' shoes using high-technology, Ortons of Earl Shilton, making men's shoes, and George Ward's of Barwell, making ladies' shoes with more traditional methods, were selected. Each would accept a group of fifteen children on three consecutive weeks, and the group would be divided in half again for the tour of the workplace, with a 'factory guide' and a member of staff or parents. In these small groups the children were able to observe closely the operatives at work and question both management and workforce alike. The welcome extended by each of the workplaces was excellent and their guides were able to give adequate time for the children's questions. Additional insurance for the children was taken out for these visits.

By the time of their third factory visit, the children were able to identify and compare the workplace's approach to the manufacturing process. The design room enabled the children to relate the product to the High Street and high fashion. They were intrigued with one designer whose work went under the name of 'Lady Diana'. The variety of rolls of leather and polyurethane in the store room provided much interest, with the opportunity for sample collecting, while the discerning child could relate to the different quality of products. The cutting or clicking room was full of machinery noise and all children quickly observed how a 'clicker' uses one skin to make a pair of shoes, thus avoiding any possibility of a variation in colour. Many of the children observed how the closing room was a woman's world and the lasting room was comprised mainly of men. The checking of the shoes, particularly the covering of scuffs with wax crayon, gave rise to much discussion, particularly from a group of girls who considered that, for the price, a pair of shoes should be perfect! The speed at which operatives packed the shoes was compared from factory to factory. The children's level of questioning became more pointed as their knowledge of the manufacturing process increased. Their interest was maintained as each factory offered something different. The children travelled to each visit jointly on the coach, and when rejoining the group there was always a variety of stories to be told. There were shrieks of glee at being given the contents of the reject box at George Wards and, of course, the wonders of the computer room and the lemonade and biscuits at Eatoughs Ltd proved popular! The overriding factor was the tolerance of each of the factories and the encouragement given to the children to create positive attitudes.

Classroom-based Work

Back at school the children started the follow-up work. The organization of the school enabled cooperative teaching to take place and the task for the children was to record the story of the manufacture of a shoe. Regular input sessions were held to ensure that the children were able to make the most of the observations they had made and link these to the concepts. The work sessions took place in their own class bases so that the benefits of small class sizes, where individual attention could be given to the children, could be capitalized upon. The display board was used to mount the manufacturing process, using samples collected from the factories. The children used this for reference purposes. The children's knowledge from the visits was sound, reinforcing the advantages of experiential learning.

Alongside this work, group topic work had been started. Children in vertical groups undertook subjects such as the Shoe Museum; shoes through the ages; shoe uses; shoes from around the world; shoe fashion and care of feet. The children were encouraged to develop their research skills in obtaining information from the various resources available and to display their work, a process which encouraged group cooperation.

Links with the retail trade were encouraged for all classes. The older children visited Roy England's shoe shop in Hinckley and the younger infants visited the Loxley Shoe Warehouse. The latter visit was a sheer delight as they visited during early closing. The children had the freedom of the shop and they took on the role of shop assistants while their class teacher and parent helpers were the customers. The shoe shop which the children set up in school, with the schools–industry liaison officer acting as supervisor of the stock room, enabled the children to practise the retail process.

Using 'Adults other than Teachers'

A number of visitors came to school in the weeks following the initial visits. Each visitor followed a similar pattern, in that he/she talked to the main group of children and was then interviewed by the older children. Developing this research skill necessitated the children understanding, constructing and employing a structured interview. They were helped in this process by the visit of a *Leicester Mercury* reporter. The first three visitors looked at a workplace from different viewpoints. The production manager at Eatoughs Ltd talked about management; a local branch secretary talked about the role of the trade union official, and finally a 'clicker' explained his job and the workplace from an operative's point of view. These interviews were fundamental in creating unbiased opinions of a workplace. A gentleman who made special shoes for the disabled was also very well received by the children.

Curriculum Integration

Work in other curriculum areas also commenced. There had been a series of communications with the Shoe and Allied Trades Research Organization in Kettering, but they would not permit a visit. However, they did forward a number of useful leaflets which formed the basis of the science work. It is established practice to work on a science topic throughout the school for one morning a week. The children in each of the classes therefore worked on a variety of tests related to the wear and tear of leather and polyurethane, the wear and tear on soles and heels, the strength of plastics and metals, the strength of solvents and the care of feet. The children were able to hypothesize, plan suitable tests, see implications of change, extend and improve suggested approaches and criticize constructively.

The advisory teacher for English worked alongside each of the class teachers to produce class stories on a 'shoe' theme — 'Sarah and Gavin and the Magic Shoes', 'The Land of the Shoes' and 'The Shoe Store Mystery'. The advisory teacher did not have time to develop these stories fully, but his approach, talked about at the INSET day, gave the staff ideas for further development.

Throughout the project, other curriculum areas were worked on through concentrated 'whole day' efforts, such as the 'Shoes Art Day' and 'Shoes Maths Day'. In the former, all the children worked on two of several art and craft workshops, some used leather and polyurethane to make collages, while others designed shoe wallpaper, an ideal home for 'The Old Woman in the Shoe' and some made cloth 'scruffs' (slippers). In the latter, children worked in their class groups; the upper juniors used calculators to decide whether the Higham Shoe Company could cope with a rush order for Frank Bruno's Sports Shoes, while the lower juniors worked out the area of their feet and shoes, and the infants put their size of feet in rank order. The older children enjoyed participating in the play which the head wrote especially for the project, 'You've never had it so good!' Although it was set in the 1950s, with a number of rock 'n' roll items, it had a relevance to a modern shoe factory with terms like negotiation, redeployment, redundancy, and automation occurring. It certainly helped the children to review factory politics in greater depth and it emphasized the valuable role of union negotiations. The play was peformed as part of a drama festival in Birmingham and at the Open Day.

Developing the Mini-Enterprise

With the mini-enterprise about to start, there was a need to capitalize on the children's experiences in the workplaces with a relevant production line simulation. The SCIP coordinator brought along his 'Lego Car' simulation in which the children in mixed age groups manufactured fire engines and dust carts. Advisers to each group of children came from the High School staff who were on INSET courses. The children interacted with each other as leader, partner or follower in preparation for the mini-enterprise.

The children organized themselves into four companies — the Higham Key Fob Company; The Higham Bookmark Company; The Embossed Table Mat Company; The Higham Picture Frame Company. Materials were provided by the Manufacturers Association, the enterprise grant from the National Westminster Bank, and Malden Timber of Coventry. The groups selected their own managing director, a production manager and a quality controller. They were, however, also involved in the production line. Each company had its own adviser, drawn from a group comprising a YTS trainee, a member of staff, two parents, the branch manager and the sales manager of Malden Timber. The adviser was there to offer help when needed, it was the responsibility of the managing director to get the company working. They were given guidelines on product design, costing, manufacture, marketing and sales. It was agreed that the sale of goods should take place at the project Open Day.

Benefit from these ventures were felt by both the children and the adults alike. One of the original aims was to give the children experiences of teamwork in industry and the children had to participate readily in this joint venture, and develop a sense of responsibility as well as share in decisions about the profits of the sale. The children were highly delighted with the profit made and were involved in the decision to spend it on an electronic keyboard.

The 'Higham Shoe Company'

It was hoped that the children's understanding of the concepts would be brought out in the work of the Higham Shoe Company. Under the managing director, the company was divided into two sections; the sports shoe department and the pop star department, which, in fact the younger and older children developed respectively. Their brief was to prepare a portfolio for a star of their choice which included designs, costings, production details, a marketing campaign and sales information. Furthermore, they had to produce a 'mock-up' of their shoe. The children's choices were interesting. In the sports shoe department the children designed shoes for Barry MacGuigan, Torvil and Dean and Bryan Robson, while the pop star department produced portfolios for Garry Glitter's and Rod Stewart's disco boots. The visit to the advertising agency, where one of the parents worked, gave the children opportunities to talk with the managing director, the graphic artists and the print manager. The children returned to school with ideas for television and magazine advertisements. The children even had the confidence to deal with a rush order for Frank Bruno's running shoes which involved using the calculator.

Reactions

One of the most important aspects, and one with which parents were particularly concerned, was what happened to the 'basic' work when such a project is embarked upon. Certainly, in this school the core work, like maths, reading and spelling continued. However, sometimes parents find it difficult to appreciate the incidental learning which takes place. It is a problem that does not go away, and creating the right public image can overcome such a situation. It was one of the main reasons why the culmination of the project was to be the Open Day. Furthermore, it was an opportunity for the many people who had helped to facilitate the children's learning to view the fruit of their labours. Over 250 visitors, including parents, friends of the school, industrialists and educationalists, attended the Open Day. Many hours were spent mounting the displays and the children were delighted to see their work admired by so many. They acted as 'guides' to the exhibition and conducted themselves with a degree of self-confidence and pride. The project was given coverage in many of the local papers as well as radio.

Looking Back and Looking Forward

The school does have within its system opportunities for the formal assessment of the children's understanding of the concepts, their skill development and their attitude to their work. Staff assessed the children's understanding of the manufacturing process and the use of teamwork in industry, the skills of observation, interviewing and group interaction, and their attitude to group responsibility and working with adults. Their assessment took place on a simple grading system, using A, B, C for understanding and 1, 2, 3 for effort. The grading would be arrived at, particularly with the older children, by the member of staff and the child discussing their performance together. The staff, in fact, are familiar with this type of grading as it occurs at the end of each term and each topic. It serves also as a way of staff assessing their own performance and contribution to the children's learning.

In the final hectic days of the project some appraisal forms were given to the children, the staff, the industrialists and the parents. The head asked the children what they had enjoyed most, who was the most interesting person they had met and what they thought they had learned. Without doubt the children enjoyed the practical activities the most, a real boost for experiential learning! All the people the children met were mentioned as their most interesting person, but the industrialists interviewed and the company advisers to the mini-companies were the most popular. The responses to the final question: 'What do you think you have learned?' were the most interesting:

> I learned how a shoe is made and how expensive materials are. (Douglas, 11)

> That you must look after your feet well. (Maryntje, 8)

> We have learned a lot about factory people, the costing and making of shoes and the running of mini-companies. It has opened my eyes to working in a factory. (Janine, 11)

> I learned about shoe factories and the smell. (Zoe, 9)

> How it is in a shoe factory and how strong plastic beer bottles are. (Heather, 8)

> I learned a lot about running a factory. Mr Brown was a bit like Bobby Robson. (Steven, 11)

Adult reaction was as interesting. They were asked first what they thought the children had learnt from the project:

> They had acquired knowledge of the shoe industry free of value judgements, connected with status and social worth. (SCIP Coordinator)

> A greater awareness of life outside school and valuable experience of the adult working world. (Branch Secretary of NUFLAT)

> To work with others. (Adult helper/parent)

Individuals were also asked what they felt they had gained from their involvement in the project:

> The level of sophisticated thinking in these young adults. (An operative)

An appreciation that it is possible to aim 'high' for learning out-comes with this age group. (SCIP Coordinator)

A total conviction to experiential learning. (Member of staff)

I have also learned that the future for industry is not trying to 'get at' the kids when they are well into senior school, but to involve them at primary level, encourage the development of positive attitudes and capitalize upon these at high school. (Industrialist)

In some ways it was anticipated that the project would come very gently to a close, but now that it has been completed, a number of new developments have emerged. From the school's point of view, further links with industry, resulting directly from the Open Day, are proposed. An 'Enterprise Week' has been arranged for the end of the summer term through Hinckley Workspace, a site where individuals set up in business with funds from the county council. After a visit to Workspace to observe the operation, the children will take part in an Enterprise work experience programme. Further into the future, a project is planned using a contact with a parent's warehousing transport company and a contact made on the Open Day with Thorn EMI; 'We Make Lamps' is a possibility.

Chapter 8

The 'We Make' Projects Forsbrook Infants School, Stoke-on-Trent

Shirley Fitzpatrick

Forsbrook Infants School is situated on the southern suburbs of Stoke-on-Trent. The village is only four miles from some of the area's larger companies including Russell Hobbs, Creda, Staffordshire Potteries and Wedgwood, all of which, over a period of four years, have collaborated with the school. It shares a campus at Blythe Bridge with the Junior and High schools. There are approximately 140 children on roll, five teachers and the headteacher. It was in July 1982 that the schools-industry liaison officer came into school with the idea for an industry-linked project. Being interested in this type of work and with the backing of a supportive head, the class teacher accepted the challenge which led to the 'We Make . . .' series of projects.

Initial Links with Industry

The class of top infants comprising 6 and 7-year-olds had already been introduced to project work lower down the school with topics on The Family, Our Environment and People Who Help. No specific topic on industry had been previously undertaken. The new projects were to involve working alongside local companies, exploring one of their products in depth. Russell Hobbs and Creda share a site which is within walking distance of school and it was the former company, manufacturers of a range of small electrical products, which first agreed to cooperate with the school. It was decided after much discussion to study the automatic electric kettle. Before the project was introduced to the class of twenty-five children there was extensive planning with visits, telephone calls and meetings. The head, the class teacher and the schools-industry liaison officer met with the training officers of the two companies on a number of occasions to plan the detail of the project. The class teacher had a number of ideas which she felt would work with the children, but wanted to be flexible and allow the company to offer its ideas. An important part of this planning process was the staff's visit to the company to see the kettles being manufactured.

After first studying the local environment, both past and present, the company was identified and the product introduced to the children. Shortly afterwards, the children visited the factory and though not allowed on the factory floor, they viewed the kettle assembly area from a balcony and experienced the atmosphere within the factory and saw some of the processes involved.

A production simulation followed shortly afterwards when the children learned more about how the factory worked, as they role-played running their own company. Tremendous interest was shown by the children as the project developed in different directions throughout the spring and summer terms. The project allowed basic skills to develop naturally and practical application helped many of the children to understand the relationships between what they experienced in school and what happened in the work place. Scientific experiments, many and varied, were particularly popular as was the art, craft and design. Written work included accounts of visits, recording and creative writing.

Having contact with many adults in a variety of situations helped the children to become more confident and more socially well-adjusted, and those industrialists who were at first sceptical soon became convinced about the value of the work with the children. Parents who at first experienced misgivings as to the suitability of the project were soon able to relate to the classroom activities and noted the quality of the work produced. (A fuller account of this project appears in *We Make Kettles: studying industry in the primary school*, edited by Ian Jamieson (1984) Longman.)

Assessing the Early Experiences

Many lessons were learned during 'We Make Kettles', not only by the children but the class teacher. It had proved necessary to plan thoroughly and to involve the industrialists both in and out of school to convince them of the value of the work being undertaken. It became clear that industrialists had limited time so it was essential to have concise details of what might be required of them. Sometimes it proved difficult to contact the training officer, the link with the factory, so the teacher had to try to foresee any problems which might occur and endeavour to iron them out at an early stage.

It was a very rewarding year in the teacher's career. It proved to be the beginning of a new stage of personal development in her teaching life. She had always been happy to teach with 'my door closed' but quickly realized there was much to be gained from involving parents, friends, and in this case, industrialists and employees. Until this time she had always felt uneasy with others in her classroom, even though the school had an 'open door' policy towards parents and the local community. It was the enthusiasm of the children and her own enjoyment which produced a totally relaxed atmosphere into which many visitors, industrialists, employees, ex-employees, parents and friends were welcomed.

The Development of the Work: 'We Make Cookers'

Most children urged their parents to come into the classroom to see the latest developments, thus establishing a much better parent/teacher relationship. It was clear that the children were capable of, and enthusiastic about, industry-linked work, so it was not difficult to persuade Creda to allow the school to work with them on the second project — 'We Make Cookers' which began in January, 1984, though planning began in the Autumn of 1983. As the training officer at Creda had been involved with the 'kettles' work, he was familiar with the general approach. He was also aware of the success, capabilities and behaviour of the children and indicated the willingness of the management to allow the children on to the factory floor. A similar approach to work was followed, i.e., to include experiential learning on local industrial premises, to emphasize education through industry, and to involve industrialists in the planning and teaching. Once again discussion and planning produced a plan of action which allowed the project to progress smoothly with the class of forty children.

Three separate visits were made to Creda, allowing the children to view all areas, from the quiet colourful showroom, to the extremely noisy and potentially dangerous press shop. Creda provided every opportunity for the children to learn by encouraging questions to which they gave clear explanations and demonstrations. Once again employees visited school to help the children with their work or to demonstrate their skills. Convinced of the value of parents' help in the previous year, the teacher had no qualms about enlisting their help on factory visits, to supervise art and craft groups, experiments and cookery. The loan of a Creda cooker was much appreciated and volunteer parents offered to come in on a regular basis to supervise children as they began to take cookery, a new area of the curriculum for the top infants.

In September 1984 two classes moved to top infants. A colleague decided, reluctantly at first, to join in an industrial project. Though she was convinced that the children enjoyed and gained from this type of work, she was not sure that she could embark on such a project. During the autumn term, therefore, the two teachers worked with their own classes on basic reading, writing and number, but began preparing for the industry project scheduled to start in the spring term.

'We Make Mugs'

During the 'kettles' open day, local industrialists came into school to see the work the children had produced. One of them, the personnel director of Staffordshire Potteries, was so delighted with the work he saw that he stated his willingness to work with the school should they ever wish to study pottery. After much thought and discussion, the teachers telephoned Staffordshire Potteries and made an appointment with the personnel director. They went with a clear plan of what they would like to do and were introduced to an assistant with whom they would be working. He listened attentively and then rather dashed their hopes as he said, 'Well, you can show a child a brick wall and they will get something from it, but whether it is of any lasting value I don't know.' The teachers were, however, able to convince him to allow the project to develop and decisions were taken on the different areas of the factory the children should see.

With permission given, they went ahead with plans and made a preliminary visit to the factory floor to select the areas of study most suited to the children and to familiarize themselves with the processes involved — in this case some of the most modern manufacturing techniques in the pottery industry. Good communication and planning before the company is introduced to the children pays handsome dividends later. Having laid the foundation for a successful working relationship with Staffordshire Potteries, they began to put their plans into action immediately after the Christmas holiday.

Visiting the Factory

First, the children visited the local Gladstone Pottery Museum to learn about the method used to make Victorian pottery and the people who worked in it. They were fascinated by the bottle kilns, the thrower, and the lady making china flowers. It was at this point that the teachers removed the partition between the two classrooms and introduced team teaching. The implications of this decision were far-reaching for the project, children and teachers.

The two classes then visited Staffordshire Potteries accompanied by teachers and ever-loyal parents. Once inside the factory the children, working in small groups, saw the manufacture of mugs from the basic raw materials right through to packing and dispatch. Employees chatted happily with the children, answering questions and even letting them experience what it was like to do their jobs. The children were allowed to handle the raw clay, put it into moulds, sponge the edge of the mugs, put handles on them, place them on a conveyor belt, test them by tapping them with a stone to hear a 'clear ring' and finally help with packaging. They asked questions about what happened to the waste, how the process, whereby the clay is shaped into a mug inside a mould, worked, how the handle stayed on and whether the employees got bored.

One of the most interested pupils was the very one who in school could be rather disruptive; he asked intelligent questions and was completely absorbed in the processes. Some of the less-academic children suddenly came into their own and this new-found interest later proved beneficial to their all round intellectual and social development. One child had the chance to put clay into the mould herself and understood, illustrated and wrote about what she had done. Success was evident to the children themselves; it was not a case of the teacher having to praise good work or criticize poor effort. As the children learned more about the raw materials used and the various stages of production, Staffordshire Potteries helped by providing an excellent display of their products and a display of raw materials and mugs at various stages of production.

Using the Expertise of Local Industry

Representatives of the company visited the school two weeks after the visit and began to be convinced of the value of industry linked work. They were amazed at the amount of written work done and the accuracy of the accounts. Employees drew lots to find which six could visit the school; they came to see the type of work produced, to talk with the children and offer them encouragement. Some even made helpful suggestions for ways of approaching art and craft work, with the result that this aspect of the work flourished from a very early stage in the project.

Design was an important element of the work as the children hoped to produce one of their own which could be put on a Staffordshire Potteries mug. The children worked on their designs before the visit of the company's chief designer who came to see the completed designs and other work around the classrooms. The teachers took the opportunity to get him to talk to the children about his work. At first he looked aghast, wondering how he could talk to 6 and 7-year-olds. It wasn't long before he realized that he had a most interested and attentive audience who, to his surprise, were most knowledgeable. They had no inhibitions and asked many sensible questions about such things as whether all the designs were the responsibility of one person, or if, for instance, Cadbury's wanted a mug made whether they had to submit the idea to the company. They also wanted to know how it was possible for the company to print so many colours on the mug, but why they were only allowed to use four.

In April the classes did a production simulation game — Forsbrook Flowers. The children took on the roles of workers, quality controllers, purchasing and sales managers, suppliers and customers, whilst the company's personnel director and manager took responsibility for training and management of the two companies. The companies produced folded paper flowers which were coloured with felt-tip pens. The simulation was run on two days with the children taking different roles on each occasion. It was interesting to note the differences in the organization by the managing directors. One thought it worthwhile to take out one folder and one colourer so they could become supervisors. Both introduced a bonus scheme but one gave a bonus after production of ten flowers and the other gave a bonus only after twenty flowers had been made. All the children took their new roles very seriously. Even the customers expressed their liking for certain designs and their dislike of badly coloured flowers.

An innovation was the introduction of a factory inspector and a trade union official. An employee of Staffordshire Potteries, who had been a shop steward but was now part of management, was the factory inspector who commented upon the lack of space between employees, and asked whether the felt-tip pens were toxic. It made the children think about their conditions of work. During the next session he became a trade union official and went among the children explaining how becoming a member of a union could help them. He explained how they could appoint a shop steward who would approach management on their behalf when problems arose. At that particular moment the room was too hot because they had kept the windows closed deliberately! He was trying to put over the other side of the union's activity rather than that which is so often all too obvious on television, e.g., during the miners' strike.

The schools-industry liaison officer questioned the children a few days later and was pleased at the amount they had learned and remembered after the production simulation. It was evident that the children had begun to understand something of the structure of a company, about the interdependence of the various sections as well as such things as the importance of quality, training and the place of profits.

Integrating Project Work

Throughout, the project work on 'We Make Mugs' was not kept as a separate entity but integrated into all areas of the normal school curriculum. As in previous projects, writing became more popular as they wrote accounts of visits, recorded experiments and produced creative writing, e.g., 'I was a piece of clay' and 'I am a mug'. Oral English improved markedly as confidence grew, with the children getting used to questioning, discussing, explaining and just generally chatting to the many visitors with whom they came into contact. Alongside this work the children continued to work through the normal school reading schemes, English, comprehension and language development.

Fletcher Maths work was often reinforced and extended by work undertaken during the project. For example, the children began to handle money as they set up their company (see mini-company overleaf). They had to take money, give change, sort coins of different values and pay it into the bank. Comparisons were made of the capacity of a variety of mugs of different sizes. The height and diameter of the mugs were compared and mugs measured and weighed both before and after firing.

Questionnaires were sent out to find various facts: the most popular shape, size, design, colour, where people purchased their mugs, whether all the family use mugs. Records had to be kept of the number of mugs sold and the number to be sold, and the number of models made by the children. This project was particularly visual as the children produced exciting art, craft and design. The children were introduced to the art of making pottery by using Plasticine. A mother who used to be a flower maker in the pottery industry came in to help the children, first with Plasticine and then with clay. They made clay models with 'real clay', which does not require firing, and which they painted with care so that they would be saleable. Models were made using slip-in moulds. These moulds were taken over to the junior school to be fired. A father came in on Friday afternoons to help the children become more proficient at using the potter's wheel. Towards the end of the year the art teacher at the High School kindly offered his help by showing groups of children how to use the electric potter's wheel.

Crayons, chalk, wax crayons, paints, junk for models and collages were regularly used. Tie and dye, fun dyes, fabric crayons and dye sticks were used as the children produced colourful tea-cloths sporting a Staffordshire Potteries slogan. A friend came in to help the children put lithographs on tiles. To find out what happened when colours were overprinted on the mugs, colours were mixed and results recorded. One child could not at first believe that blue and yellow made green, just as yellow and blue did! Each child produced an original design to be put on a mug, using up the four colours. The designs varied enormously.

Science experiments are always exciting and enjoyable to this age group. They experimented with garden soil and clay, using it alongside prepared pottery clay. They found out the properties of clay and air. They discovered what happened when clay in its 'green' state was immersed in water. They noted the outcome when badly-made modules were fired. Work on electricity included the making of circuits and switches, short circuits, two-way switches and broken circuits. History and geography were combined in the study of the local environment. Pupils learned how pottery making first began in the Burslem area due to clay and coal being readily available. They came to realize the value of a good transport system, beginning with the canal system which was specifically developed to transport raw materials and distribute the finished wares. Maps were used to find out where the raw materials originated and an atlas used to follow the route of mugs as they were exported to many countries throughout the world. Local maps were used to find the best route for the clay being brought from Stoke station to the factory at Meir.

The Pupils Set Up Their Own Company

During the 'We Make Mugs' project the children were asked to produce an original design to decorate a mug. Each child in the two classes working on the project was given a slip of paper cut to the size of the design required. The only restrictions were that they must not infringe copyright and not use more than four colours. Finished designs were mounted and numbered. School staff, children, parents, friends and visitors were asked to vote for the design which they found most attractive. The three designs from each class with the highest votes were forwarded to Staffordshire Potteries where their experts selected the two which they thought would be most saleable.

It had always been intended that mugs bearing the children's designs should be produced to market in school. However, it was not until they were discussing a local enterprise week that it suddenly occurred to them that the children might well be able to run their own business. Discussions with the children followed, during which a great deal of enthusiasm was shown with everyone eager to take part in this exciting venture. The teachers and the children discussed the various roles and positions of responsibility within a company, after which the children were given the opportunity to put themselves forward for election. A secret ballot was held to elect the managing director, finance manager, company secretary, sales manager.

The children took it very seriously and chose a team which the teachers themselves would most likely have selected. Once the management had been elected, they set out to find a suitable name for the company. Eventually, after numerous suggestions, they suggested Forsbrook Infants' Mini-Marketing Company. The Staffordshire schools-industry liaison officer agreed to provide and sign a certificate of registration for the company. The major priority was to raise the capital with which they could purchase the first consignment of mugs from Staffordshire Potteries. When the children were asked to consider how they could get the money, the first suggestion was 'go to the bank', then the headteacher was suggested, but some children thought that she would not have that sum of money to spare. Eventually, one child mentioned the Autumn Fair which is held in order to raise money. They agreed that this was a possibility and a group of children approached the headteacher with a request to borrow £100. She listened to them and agreed to the loan on the understanding that it would be repaid with 10 per cent interest.

Having secured the loan and each child having purchased a 10p share in the business, the next step was for the company secretary and the finance manager to open a business account at the local branch of the National Westminster Bank. Though quite taken aback the staff at the bank accepted their business.

Four hundred mugs were ordered, 200 of each design and then a massive advertising campaign began. Posters were produced by many children and an advertisement was written out and forwarded for inclusion in the parish magazine. Those children in charge of advertising selected the most eye-catching posters to be taken out to shops, building societies and the local library. Many posters were placed in strategic areas of the school. Some children were crestfallen when their posters were rejected because of poor presentation but it made them realize that their work had to improve if they were to be successful.

Production managers made sure that children's clay models, flowers and mould-produced models were plentiful and they had to make regular visits to the junior school where they fired the models. They ensured that the models were painted carefully, for they were to be sold for 5p and 10p each.

With the arrival of the mugs, the 'coming soon' strips on the posters were replaced with 'on sale now' strips. The children had bought the mugs at 25p each plus VAT and decided to sell them at 50p each. This seemed a good idea as the children were able to handle 50p and £1.00 with confidence and it was easy for them to work out the change. When the mugs were on sale for the first time the children were inundated with parents clamouring for them. Sales boomed during the first days but then dwindled. Staffordshire Potteries may have foreseen the large demand as they sent 936 mugs, not 400 as ordered. The finance group sorted and counted the money, made out the paying-in slips and paid the money into the bank. Records were kept of sales and detailed accounts were made.

After the initial demand by parents and friends, sales began to slump. It was at this stage that the children took steps to find new outlets. Katie, the vicar's daughter, persuaded her father to allow a group of children to sell mugs in church after the Sunday morning service. Another child approached the library but they refused to allow mugs to be sold, though they offered to have a poster. A girl went to the local VG Supermarket and asked if they could set up a stall on their car park and they readily agreed. The managing director of the company telephoned Cheadle RDC to find out how they could obtain a stall in the open air market. Other groups of children visited the junior school, the high school and one girl asked if they could sell mugs at play school. Yet another persuaded her father to take four children to the Polytechnic where he was a lecturer. On different days, groups of children set up stalls on the Co-op car park, outside the local grocer and a shoe shop. All children had experience in selling and children of all abilities made excellent sales people. Payment for the first consignment of mugs was made promptly and further orders were placed.

The managing director was a strong character who made sure that the workforce were kept on their toes. The production manager was equally forceful, whilst the company secretary saw that records of sales were kept up-to-date. The finance manager and his assistant paid staff for petrol, signed cheques and paid Staffordshire Potteries. They purchased four dozen plain white glazed mugs so that each child could paint on their own design. They paid the headteacher for coffee, biscuits and plants bought for the industrial evening. Because the children leave at the end of the summer, the company was wound up at the end of June. The children voted to pay themselves a 10p dividend and so received 100 per cent profit on their investment. The final statement showed a profit of £378.79. With some of this money the children bought a Creda cooker for use in school and put the remainder of the money into a building society account.

Assessing the Experience

The three years of industry-linked work served not only to give the children a link with the outside world but also broadened the curriculum. A much more detailed study of the local environment, a far greater amount of science, many different types of art, craft and design, some included for the first time, were all developed. Cookery, purely as a result of the project, now became a regular part of the timetable. Visits, speakers and visitors helped establish a new interest and excitement amongst the children. Those who came into the class shy and retiring often blossomed when they became engrossed in their project work. One example that comes to mind is that of the child who did one of the winning mug designs. Once his design had been selected his confidence grew and so his written work developed. Though shy, he soon developed into a most pleasant child who was able to converse with anyone; in fact he was one of the children who accompanied the teacher to London to give a presentation from the platform at the Royal Society of Arts when the school received the Education for Capability Award.

Parents commented upon the fact that they could now hold meaningful discussions with their children. Frequently, children who would normally have been uninterested in school work were motivated by this type of approach. Children developed a greater thirst for knowledge and a more enquiring mind.

Looking back over the three years, both teachers now realize how much the projects have helped to further their own education, boosted their confidence and above all made them more professional teachers. They have learned that young children are capable of absorbing, understanding and retaining far more than they would have deemed possible.

When 'We Make Kettles' began, other staff were doubtful as to whether the work would be suitable for infants. It was only after three projects leading to the RSA 'Education for Capability' Award that they felt something special had been achieved. Another member of staff now feels that her teaching has been rather dull compared with the work done in the top infant classes, and she has expressed a wish to be involved at some time in the future. There is some evidence that colleagues undertaking projects in their own classroom have learnt from the success of work in the 'We Make . . .' projects and are encouraged to adopt similar approaches.

Chapter 9

Where We Used to Learn
St Mary's RC Primary School, Eltham

Peter Holdsworth and John Murphy

Introduction

St Mary's is a Group 5 primary school. In July 1984 the school moved from Eltham High Street, where the site was split by a public footpath and surrounded by shops and car parks, to a more residential setting half a mile away. Both sites were the property of the Sisters of Mercy. The new site contained a large building in about 3 hectares of open ground and was a far more suitable setting for a primary school.

About 60–70 per cent of St Mary's pupils transfer to the local secondary school. In July 1985 the staff were asked if they would like to select a group of children to participate in a joint environmental project with the local secondary school's first-year pupils and the Divisional Industry Schools Coordinator (DISCO). The mutual benefits of creating such cross-curricula links were thought to be enormous and both schools looked forward to learning from each other's practice and strengthening the bonds that already existed. After looking at a number of possible local issues around which the project might be based it was agreed that the development of the old St Mary's school site would be the most appropriate choice.

Unfortunately, the teachers' industrial action forced the secondary school to withdraw from the proposed project. The staff at St Mary's felt that the opportunity to work with the DISCO presented too many opportunities to be turned down and decided to proceed.

The two fourth-year classes, comprising fifty-five children, were to be involved in the initiative which was planned for the first half of the summer term. It was decided that the children would work in groups of five or six, plan how the site should be developed and present their ideas to a panel of local 'experts' at the end of the project.

Collaborative Planning

Two terms were spent planning the project: the class teachers, deputy head, primary advisory teacher, DISCO and a local council planning officer were all involved. Their first priority was to identify the aims of the project. For the staff an initial goal was to assess the benefits of working on an integrated project which involved collaborative work, active learning and the use of 'adults other than teachers' (AOTs).

Teachers

St Mary's was in the fortunate position of having a deputy head who was released from his teaching commitment for one year to undertake curriculum development. He was, therefore, able to act as organizer and coordinator, working in conjunction with the DISCO and the two class teachers.

The initial reaction to the possibility of working on an industry project was guarded enthusiasm. Fear of the unknown and the fairly formal structure of the school itself created doubts as to the successful outcome of such a venture. Although planning was carried out collaboratively among the whole team, the majority of the work inevitably became the responsibility of the deputy head and DISCO. The two class teachers had a full-time teaching commitment and AOTs were used at this stage in an advisory capacity.

During this phase the deputy head had the opportunity to visit other schools involved in industry projects, observing simulations and methods of debriefing. He was also able to attend a Geography Schools and Industry Project (GSIP) workshop and the School Curriculum Industry Project (SCIP) national conference. Two of the many positive outcomes of these sessions were:

1. Making contact with people who later came into the school to help and advise.
2. A greater understanding and belief in SCIP philosophy.

The interest that was being generated by the project was, however, creating unforeseen pressures on staff. The class teachers were uneasy at the thought of outsiders examining their classroom practice. These fears were faced, tackled and apparently overcome only to re-emerge at later stages. Part of the problem was that they had gradually taken a more passive role in the planning process and were relying far too heavily on the two coordinators. As a result they felt more like the actors in a play than the authors. The school's relatively formal approach to pedagogy reinforced the teachers' concept of the classroom as their own domain. In the top juniors, for example, group work was an initiative in its infancy. There was a need to support and encourage innovative classroom practice without destroying all that was obviously successful. Through working collaboratively, an outcome for teachers was to open classroom doors and acknowledge others' strengths and weaknesses.

Eight pre-project activities, therefore, were planned by way of preparation. The purpose of these activities from the teachers' point of view was to:

1. Become used to AOTs in the classroom.
2. Have an opportunity of observing the children working in groups.
3. Consider the importance and skills required in the process of debriefing.
4. Participate in different teaching and learning strategies.

All these activities proved successful and confidence and enthusiasm emerged as the overriding emotions prior to the launch.

Parents

The scope of the project provided an opportunity to involve a number of parents as well as educational support staff. Groups of children were to be involved in active research outside the classroom for which adequate supervision would be essential.

This was the premise from which the inclusion of parents was planned, though by the end of the project it was evident that they had far more to offer than simply monitorial duties. Both class teachers selected appropriate parents from those who were available to take part, giving each an explanation of the commitment they would be undertaking. All parents and teachers involved discussed the formers' role, how the children's work would unfold and the different teaching strategies that would be involved. One workshop was arranged for parents prior to the launch, although it was soon realized that this was insufficient. Bad planning had left no time for future meetings so parents entered the project enthusiastically but confused over their role and the aims and objectives of the 'professionals'.

Divisional Industry Schools Coordinator

The Schools Industry Coordinator's role was to act as an equal partner in the planning team. Contacts needed to be made, resources acquired, so the DISCO used his time to meet appropriate representatives from the local community and to use networks already established. For example, the project was able to take advantage of contacts already made with the local council planning department. The DISCO also worked with the teachers on the active learning strategies which were used, helped and advised on briefing and debriefing of children, parents, AOTs and teachers, and advised on evaluation strategies. At an early stage the Schools Industry Coordinator also helped run several of the classroom sessions working alongside the teacher. Having another teacher available to support work in the classroom was extremely useful, especially as new methods, including simulations, AOTs in the class and group work were all being introduced.

Through the SCIP in-service provision it was possible for the deputy head to attend a national conference along with the coordinator. This meant that throughout the project both DISCO and the deputy head worked to a similar understanding of the benefits of an experiential approach to learning.

'Adults other than Teachers'

As part of the planning process a variety of contacts were made and by the end of the children's work well over twenty adults had visited the school, some on more than one occasion.

Initially, some AOTs were used to support preparatory work with the children. The Council Planning Officer was able to provide invaluable advice and information and a local architect volunteered to work with the children on topics such as scale, the reading of plans and maps and communication through drawing. These proved to be immensely valuable; not only were children learning something of the techniques, insights and vocabulary that they were shortly to need 'for real', but also gaining experience in the use of these 'experts' as a resource.

On reflection, the use of AOTs in the planning phase helped to broaden the initiative by providing several useful ideas. Perhaps the most important was the suggestion by the Planning Officer that the children should computerize their survey data. Use of AOTs in this way also helped to establish a framework and context for the project that was as close to the real situation as possible.

Objectives and Structure of the Project

The objectives of the project were that all children would:

1. Understand that as members of the local community they have a responsibility for their environment. That there is an active part all individuals can play in the process whereby the local environment changes and develops.
2. Become aware that any local issue is a complex web of problems which involves many different agencies, interest groups and, therefore, arguments.
3. Become aware of the reasons why land use changes.
4. Learn to work effectively in groups.
5. Learn a new decision-making skill.

The preliminary activities were planned to introduce the children to some of the skills they would need for the project. Through exercises such as a 'Survival Simulation', 'Lego — a production line simulation', a Teeshirt production-line simulation and problem-solving activities, the children began to experience the problems of effective decision-making in groups. There was also an opportunity for both classes to improve their interviewing skills and consider the importance of asking the right questions when visitors were invited into school for a 'What's My Line' session.

Structuring the project to enable the children to work effectively was important so each week of the proposed timetable had a main theme running through it:

Week 1: Introduction
Week 2: Data Collection
Week 3: Initial plans
Week 4: Newspapers
Week 5: Preparation
Week 6: Presentation

Within this framework, times were allocated for visits, AOTs and a variety of group sessions.

The Council Planning Officer had provided the school with maps and the official planning brief for the site which made clear the constraints and limitations for developers. A simplified version was prepared for the children without diluting the messages it contained, along with a formal letter from the planning department explaining the task. This was to 'draw up their own plans for the development of the site'. It was felt important that the children should see this as a real task with real problems. During this first week each group also had to decide for which particular area of information they would be responsible and how they would gather it.

During the second week children would have an opportunity to make visits out of school to collect their data. A variety of methods were used such as surveys and questionnaires. At the same time a number of AOTs would be available in the school to act as another resource for the children. It was at this stage also that children began to computerize their information.

By the end of the third week the groups were expected to have initial plans for the site outlined as they had a deadline to meet. This was an interview with a Chief Planning Officer for the Borough. She helped the children to assess their proposals and identify areas where further research was needed. During the planning stage it was felt that the children's enthusiasm might begin to flag by the time they were into the fourth week of the project so it was decided that a focus on writing with the assistance of the local newspaper might provide a new and interesting stimulus. The DISCO, therefore, arranged for the editor of the *Eltham Times* to work with the children on report writing and the devising of headlines. Each group was then invited by the journalists to write their own short report on the work they were doing. These reports were printed, along with a photograph, in the following week's edition. This proved to be an exciting exercise as groups worked to meet their deadline, some were able to experience their work being 'subbed' by a professional sub-editor and finally seeing their own work in print.

The penultimate week was set aside for preparation. Plans had to be finalized using all the information gleaned to support proposals and decisions made on the best method for displaying each group's findings.

The climax of the project was to be the presentation in the final week. The children set up their own exhibitions in the school gym. Two panels of local experts were invited to the school and each group had to present their ideas and justify their proposals. That same evening parents and all the AOTs who had been involved were invited to view the exhibition and talk to the children about their work.

Preparation of the Parents

The parents involved, three in one class, four in the other, were introduced to the children on the launch day. Fears over their lack of preparation were realized in the first session when one parent took over a group and began directing and issuing instructions. It was decided that frequent briefing sessions were essential and these took place as and when necessary.

The class teachers decided to allocate one parent to each group to provide support, stability and continuity of contact. The parents' own enthusiasm and growing interest in the project resulted in their being in school every day throughout the six weeks of the project, something which had not been anticipated or hoped for. Obviously this proved to be an invaluable resource.

All of the parents had children involved in the project and two asked if they could work with their own child's group. Though unforeseen at the time, this did in fact create considerable problems with one group. The situation reached a climax with the son shouting at his mother, claiming that she had been responsible for problems within the group. It was felt that the only way to resolve this situation without causing further offence to anyone was to involve the parent in another capacity. Fortunately, she was an excellent typist and was able to help groups put information onto the computers. Gradually, the parents also adopted strategies the team were trying to introduce, though along with staff they found it extremely difficult at times and admitted to being directive on a number of occasions.

Throughout the six weeks, the briefing sessions for parents with the staff provided a useful opportunity for everyone to express fears and problems. Parents admitted to periods of confusion, despair, frustration and even questioned their own ability to cope and the wisdom of the teachers in undertaking such a daunting task. Their main criticism was that children often did not listen to them, they were just parents not teachers.

Over the weeks of the project, parents did begin to see their role more clearly and were supportive of children and teachers alike. They grew in confidence and by the end of the six weeks felt as though they had participated in something extremely worthwhile. One parent wrote, 'I really did enjoy helping with the project and I feel I have learnt a lot from it, not just from the Industry side but also working closely with children and adults alike and drawing from each other'.

The Launch of the Project

Prior to the launch the children knew nothing of the project's theme. On the opening day the head welcomed the parents and visiting AOTs and the deputy presented a brief outline of the project and how it would work. The children were reminded of the processes that they had been through the previous term during the preparatory activities. A quote from one child was used as a key phase:

To work successfully as a group I must overcome my own personal likes and dislikes.

After this brief introduction, one of the Council's Planning Officers was introduced to the children and presented each group with its own planning brief and a letter explaining the tasks to be undertaken. The groups were now given their first task which was:

1. To choose a name for their group
2. To decide on the rules they needed to help them work together effectively and come to group decisions.

These were put on flip charts and displayed around the gym for each group to see.

During the afternoon all the children were taken back to the old school site to familiarize them with the building and the size of the area to be developed.

The next stage involved the children identifying the areas that needed research and helping them ask the right questions. A simple game had been devised whereby each group was presented with an incomplete map of a fictitious area. The children were told that someone wanted to build a car park with 300 spaces on a site indicated on the map. The task was simply to decide whether the developer would be given permission or not. Four rounds of a game were involved during which one member of each group could ask for a single piece of information from the game organizers. At the end of each round each group had to give their decision, yes or no. The framing of questions was obviously vital as the children were unaware whether they were dealing with a small country village or large urban town. A few groups very quickly realized the importance of the question asked and were able to come to a sensible decision, others were not. The parents also formed a group and took part in the exercise and debriefing which followed. All the staff noted that the adults were by far the most unruly and most difficult group to control!

The session finished with a brain-storming exercise during which the children had to identify the main areas to be researched and the key questions that needed to be asked in order to reach a sensible decision about the development of the site. These areas for research included shoppers, residents, car parking, traffic, listed buildings, shop keepers.

Flip charts were again used to display all the information. A negotiation session followed which enabled groups to each work on one specialist area. However, it was made clear that all this information would need to be shared eventually with each group.

Key Learning Strategies

From the start of the planning phase, those involved had identified certain key learning strategies which were to be used throughout the six week project. These were: collaborative group work, active learning, the use of 'adults other than teachers' (AOTs) and the use of micro computers.

Group work

As has already been mentioned, the preparatory sessions provided an introduction to group work both for teachers and children. During these initial activities it was evident that boys often tried to dominate and that individual children were unhappy about collaborating with others. The Lego production line exercise revealed several children who would far rather have made their own truck than share with others in the group. Another problem was involving all children in the decision-making process. The quiet or reserved child was all too ready to go along with the rest. On occasions, there was direct conflict between two dominant children. The debriefing of children was used as a strategy to pull out the learning from these activities and to encourage participants to identify problems, solutions and learning, for themselves. The use of small groups for debriefing children proved to be an effective process throughout the project in a variety of situations. Ideally, far more time should have been set aside for these sessions, though to be fully effective they are costly in terms of teachers' involvement.

Active Learning

Rather than a teacher-directed project, the emphasis was on the children taking responsibility for their own learning. Active learning not only involved the children in working inside and outside the classroom on practical activities, but also in the organization of the work and the decision-making. However, the groups were provided with a structure and framework within which to operate. There were procedures for ordering resources, planning sheets and diaries to fill in, notices advising on visitors in school each week and information sheets available to provide advice. The children had to take responsibility for these operations and the class teacher acted as facilitator rather than director. At times this proved to be extremely difficult; teachers, on occasions, did take a directive role, sometimes it was vital that they did. When children and teacher were under pressure with deadlines to meet then there was always a tendency to slip into a more teacher-centred approach.

Using 'Adults other than Teachers'

Throughout the six weeks the individual groups had access to 'experts' via an easy booking system, which was explained to them at the start, with simple guidelines on using this resource. The visits of most AOTs were arranged for the first three weeks, thus concentrating on the information-gathering stage of the project. A notice board was set up showing who was to visit and their particular specialism. Groups would then 'book' to see the relevant visitor via a simple pro forma which was handed to the class teacher. If the visitor was not already fully booked, the group was given the time of its appointment which it was expected to record. During each session with an AOT, normally timetabled for 20–30 minutes, the children were responsible for using the time as they thought best. They interviewed the experts to elicit information or advice, they were never talked to by the adults. Initially, there was some uncertainty as the children confused various AOT's roles, perhaps misunderstanding the difference between architect, planner and landscape architect. However, this was generally overcome by a little more explanation beforehand and through the briefing of the AOTs themselves. This briefing was considered a key component in the process. The AOTs, many of whom were visiting the school for the first time, were given a résumé of the project itself and an overview of objectives and teaching strategies. The fact that the children were reponsible for each session was also stressed and it was interesting to observe that all the visitors appeared to find this approach less threatening and far more productive than working with large groups in a formal setting. Many commented that they would be happy to be involved again and several provided groups with further resources such as maps, videos and statistics from their own sources.

Throughout the project an individual group might, on average, have conducted eight of these interviews. During this time the children themselves learnt much about the skills needed to discover information, the framing of appropriate questions, the recording of the information received (most groups used tape recorders), the management of their time (groups began by involving all members in these sessions but often decided at a later stage to send only two or three members) and coping with a range of responses. The children soon learnt, for example, that different AOTs had very differing views on the same subjects. Some children initially found this extremely confusing and, on occasions, distressing. The fact that there was not one right answer to the problem and that so many differing issues were involved provided a wealth of real learning and decision-making potential for the groups.

Micro-Computers

The use of computers was a new initiative in the school. A micro was available throughout the project in each class and proved to be invaluable in processing the vast amounts of data the children collected. As most groups were involved in at least one survey, the information to be computerized came from a range of different sources. These included local residents, car drivers, shop keepers and shoppers themselves. One survey involved delivering over 200 printed questionnaires to shops in the High Street and their collection two days later. The group achieved over a 90 per cent response rate and that piece of the survey work itself provided a considerable range of information and views which could only have been used realistically with the help of a computer. Although the children had not had access to the hardware previously, they soon became quite expert in using the data and word processing packages. They also had considerable support from the authority's computer advisory team. One advisory teacher spent a whole week in the school working with individual groups at the start of the project. A spin-off has since been that the school has purchased its own computer and will be introducing this work further down the school.

Visits

As with AOTs, the use of visits by the children was another key process during the project. The children were given the opportunity to work outside the classroom collecting a variety of information to help them with the task. At the start of the project each child was given a timetable which showed when groups were able to make these visits. The identification of specific times enabled the planning team to organize teacher supervision well in advance and also introduce a further element of planning and organization for the children. The type of visit was not stipulated, that was another decision for the children to make themselves. There was also no obligation for all group members to be involved with each piece of work outside school. A simple booking system was used so that groups could arrange to make a visit on a specific day. This involved filling a request form which was handed to the class teacher to confirm whether the particular visit could go ahead. All work outside school needed careful planning, cover had to be provided in school if a class teacher was accompanying a group and, of course, each group required a teacher to supervise it. Advisory teachers, coordinators and even inspectors were asked to help and parents provided extra supervisory support.

The main purpose of these visits was to enable the children to collect information about the site and its development. As has been mentioned, all children visited the old school buildings on the launch day and many were affected by the vandalism and general decay of the site. In the following weeks, groups became involved in their survey work using a whole range of techniques, personal interviews, questionnaires and the inevitable traffic count. Groups also used visits to measure car parks, take photographs, draw townscape views and analyse shopping provision.

Arrangements were also made during the course of the project for one group to visit a local supermarket and another a leisure centre to ask questions and collect information. For example, the visit to the leisure centre was used by a group planning a similar centre for their own proposal. They were interested in the range of facilities available, the amount of space required for certain activities and questions of access, cost and construction. Obviously, the type of visit could not be pre-planned and teachers had to respond quickly to demands made by groups who had some specific need.

During the course of this work the children soon learnt how to use the time effectively, how to administer a questionnaire and meet the public. The stress was always on their taking responsibility for their own work. Many groups initially devised totally inappropriate surveys and, after trying them out, discovered that alterations needed to be made. After more careful preparation a second trip was booked to collect the information they required. By the end of the project some groups had become quite experienced in collecting specific data they needed to support a decision already made. As a Borough planning officer commented on the presentation day — 'Some of the groups have developed a nice line in biased questionnaires!'

Presentation

After five weeks each group had undertaken an area of research, collected and shared their information and made a decision on how they thought the old school site should be developed. The presentation was planned in two phases, an afternoon and an evening session.

For the afternoon of the project's final day, two panels of local dignitaries had been invited. These consisted of Borough planning officers, local councillors, representatives from SCIP and GSIP, a college lecturer and authority inspectors.

In the school hall each group of children had their own area to display work and findings, plus the use of a computer. Groups took it in turn to meet one of the panel, present in a fairly informal setting their proposals and explain how and why they had reached their decisions. The panel's brief was to ask questions and extract more information from the groups ensuring that they involved every child. Each group had thirty minutes with the panel. For teachers and children alike this was the high spot of the project.

The 'professionals' reported back to staff, provided many constructive comments on the work and felt that there were many exciting things to be shared with other members of the staff. The project was thought to be an excellent springboard to develop the strategies across the rest of the school.

The evening session enabled children to present the findings to their parents and all the AOTs who had been involved. The adults were particularly asked to talk to the children as the display was regarded as secondary to the information and understanding the children had gained about their environment and the people who work in it. It was also emphasized to parents that it was the process rather than the product that was important.

Outcomes

It is never easy to assess the learning outcomes from a piece of work such as this. Certainly those involved, the children, teachers, parents and the AOTs all learnt a great deal. However, analysing the outcome in detail is particularly problematic, there were so many variables.

Comments made during the feedback session by members of the presentation panel all seemed to stress the children's understanding of a range of often sophisticated, political and economic ideas. These included concepts such as the listed building, townscape and the differing views represented by a variety of local pressure groups. The children certainly began to work far better in groups. By the end of the project several mentioned the importance of collaboration and compromise. There was a significant improvement in a variety of skills, including the ability to plan time effectively, to select and make use of relevant information to support an argument, the sorting of data and a variety of methods involved in recording such information. Many children became extremely competent in presenting their ideas and decisions both in written and oral form. There was certainly a greater need to concentrate on concepts of size and to lay more stress on the analysis of data. The teachers also become more aware of the traditional tendency for boys to dominate some groups and the decisions made.

Throughout the six weeks there were many comments about adults learning more than the children. Certainly the teachers learnt much about the benefits of active teaching methods, of providing children with greater responsibility for their own work and operating in a less directive way. During the actual project the teachers' management skills were tested to the full, coping with an endless influx of AOTs including experts, interested parties and inspectors, constantly supporting the parents and managing the resources in the classroom as well as adopting new teaching strategies and a class of lively children.

Prior to and during the project the teachers had the support of primary advisors and subject advisors as well as the DISCO and deputy head. There were times, however, when the pressure and workload seemed endless, times when real euphoria over the children's progress and understanding took hold. Every week during the project a debriefing session was held to monitor the progress and air complaints and frustrations and to plan future sessions.

There were problems. Children not used to working this way initially panicked or wasted time, lacking the skills to organize their own work. However, the children very quickly learnt and used appropriate strategies to overcome these problems. Teachers also learnt much about the benefits of using AOTs in the class; the importance of briefing and the value of debriefing sessions. Using experts from the world of work and local community gave the whole project so much more impact and relevance in the eyes of the children. It also had considerable effects in terms of motivation and access to a wide range of resources.

The two terms spent in the planning stage were vital and the preparation work completed with both classes before the project proper commenced, helped to acclimatize both staff and children. The value of parents' work in the classroom has already been mentioned. However, all agreed that more time should have been spent briefing those involved prior to the project launch and that more thought could have been given to their involvement with specific groups. Initially, the school had some reservations about involving parents directly in the curriculum. The project has given the school a different perspective to the value of parents; in the past they have been used purely as support in a monitorial capacity. The staff have now been made more aware of the expertise parents have to offer and will seek to provide further opportunities for them to contribute to the learning experience of children.

Perhaps the most significant outcome for all was the realization that children of this age are often capable of far more than teachers are prepared to acknowledge. We are all too ready to protect rather than challenge them in the manner which this particular project attempted to do.

Chapter 10

Linking with a High-Technology Industry
Daisyfield County Primary School, Blackburn

Mrs Sandra Cross

Introduction

Daisyfield Primary School lies on the edge of an industrial estate in an old and somewhat deprived area of Blackburn, where unemployment levels are extremely high. There are 320 pupils in the school, 95 per cent of whom are of Asian origin. The school has fifteen staff. In an earlier project, in time allocated to topic work, the teacher had used the Blackburn Coat of Arms to trace the history of the textile trade and its effects on the town. Some of the parents of children in the school had been part of the skilled labour force which had contributed to the growth of that particular industry.

The children made visits to two local textile museums where they witnessed the traditional skills of spinning and weaving. A visit was also made to the local Technical College to see students experimenting with colour on cotton and wool.

The children learnt, however, of the slump which occurred in the textile industry in the 1930s, resulting in large numbers of people being unemployed. They also discovered that it was at that time that the Philips group built the Mullard factory (later to be known as Philips & Dupont Optical UK Ltd) in the town, because the skills of the textile workers were valuable in the process of valve assembly. It was from this initial investigation of the development of the Mullard factory that the idea to make the company the focus of another industry project was born.

Developing the Link with Philips & Dupont Optical UK Ltd

The first contact with Philips & Dupont Optical UK Ltd was made in 1985 when one of the classes in the school had been involved in the Domesday

Project. The factory was located in the area the class was surveying and an added incentive to maintain the link was that the company had been commissioned to produce the Domesday disc. In addition, the class teacher had previously worked in the personnel department of the company and so was aware of some possible ways of developing such a project. While realizing that the company had a policy of not allowing young children into the factory, the teacher felt that it was worth perservering to try to get permission for them to see the Laser Vision department.

The company eventually gave their approval for a visit by the children, who so impressed members of the management by their behaviour and the standard of work they produced as a result of the visit, that they agreed to a visit by another class the following year.

Prior to the children's visit, the teacher spent some time herself in the company, finding out about its history and in particular about the founder of the company. She was also given some of the early valves made by the company as well as other components which provided an initial stimulus for the children.

Aims of the Project

The project was developed with twenty-seven second-year junior children over twelve weeks and the overall aim, as perceived by the teacher, was to help them appreciate the importance of the factory to the community and understand something of what went on inside the buildings.

One of the initial objectives which the teacher identified for the project was to help the children gain some appreciation of the scale and size of the factory. The first experience for the children, therefore, was walking the two-mile perimeter of the factory. The children were accompanied by the Public Relations Officer who explained the purpose of some of the buildings, as well as the reasons for their particular size and design. During their second visit, the concept of scale was further demonstrated to the children by the fact that there were traffic lights and pedestrian crossings controlling the flow of vehicles inside the factory grounds! Some of the children were clearly overawed by what they witnessed.

Using the Visits as Stimulus for Follow-up Work

The initial visit stimulated a great deal of discussion among the children who were able to recall a range of features such as the cleanliness of the site with its shrubs enhancing the appearance, the Goods Inwards Department, the Medical Department and the Security Office.

The second visit began with the children clocking-in at the factory, something they had done at school during the previous week. This exercise had not only pointed up the need for punctuality and shown how employees' wages were calculated, but had also helped them with their understanding of the 24-hour clock.

The teacher also wanted the children on this occasion to see the production line which produced the video discs and the polishing process. The investigation of this latter process involved the children in talking to the operatives about the important job of polishing of discs and with those who were responsible for quality control. The children also met some of the scientists who worked on the research and development of the product.

For this visit the class was divided into three smaller groups so that the children could hear what was being said by their guides and see more clearly the various operations involved in the production of the disc. This form of organization for the visit also encouraged them to put numerous questions to the guides. The children particularly wanted to know how the information was put on to the disc, a concept which the teacher initially found difficult to explain to them. It was suggested that one way of introducing the process was by getting the children to press a coin into Plasticine and from the mould make a plaster cast. From this, the idea of a 'master' from which all the other copies were made was explored. This helped the children understand the process whereby information is transferred on to disc and how thousands of copies are then made from the original.

Following this visit, the children wrote about their experiences and also began reading the novel, *Charlie and the Chocolate Factory*. The story contains a reference to a special key used to open the secret department in the factory and recalled, in the minds of the children, the special blue key used to unlock the doors of the high security Laser Vision department. Some of the signs and symbols on doors and walls which the children had seen in the company were recalled when similar examples were referred to in the novel.

A third visit to the company was set up for the children to discover more about the production of the video discs; in particular they saw the plastic granules being melted down and made into discs, they were told how the discs were stamped out and were helped to understand the resilience and durability of a disc. The children also went into the demonstration room where they watched programmes on video disc and saw a new development on touch-screen tuning and data-selection. Finally, they visited the packing department to watch the discs being stored prior to dispatch.

The children also had an opportunity to talk to representatives of the company about such things as the cost of a disc and the number sold in a year as well as the more personal questions about wages and holidays. Some of these questions, in particular those about sales, were answered when the children visited the computer room and saw this data presented on the large display screens which the company has in many parts of the building. The children also made a visit to the North West Electricity Board showrooms. They were shown all the appliances sold by the Board together with the prices and the countries in which they were made.

Developing the Experience within the Primary Curriculum

The teacher endeavoured to relate the experience to as many areas of the primary curriculum as possible. A great deal of language work developed from the visits, particularly in view of the fact that the factory was very much a part of the local environment. Discussion work, which had always been a feature of the teacher's approach to language development, received a tremendous stimulus from this project. The children got into conversation with people in the town about the company, they watched the advertisements for the company's products on television and much of this became the basis for classroom discussion. Written work also featured in all elements of the project, whether as write-ups of the visits, or letters to people in the company, or accounts of the setting-up of the company.

The clocking-in at school and the children's observation of this process in the factory gave the teacher the opportunity to do some work on the 24-hour clock. Some historical and geographical experiences were also incorporated into the work as the children spent time looking at the origins of the company in Holland and at Anton Philips, its founder.

Art work was done in pairs, illustrating aspects of the visits such as holding a disc, a forklift truck loaded with boxes of discs, the production line, and the conference room where they met the company's secretary. Music and movement was used to represent the movement of a particular piece of machinery seen in the company and later the idea of a spinning top was represented through the same medium.

The teacher produced a simple simulation to represent aspects of trade and finance, in particular those relating to the trade in electronic equipment. Two groups of children were identified, one representing Great Britain, the other Japan. Each group consisted of a Minister of Trade, four workers and a manager. Each Minister was issued with twelve coins and each manager had ten television sets. Great Britain used ten coins and bought all ten televisions. Only three televisions were sold to Japan, the remaining five coins were used to pay the four workers and manager. The group discussed the fact that Japan had fifteen coins with which to pay their workers.

Setting up an Enterprise

Arising out of the experiences which the children had at the company, the teacher decided to experiment with the idea of allowing the children to set up their own enterprise. Her aim was to give the children the opportunity to experience working as a team to produce a product which bore some resemblance to the laser disc. She also wanted them to be aware of the different jobs involved.

The mini-enterprise consisted of a production line, a packing department which made the containers and a design department working on posters, labels and logos. One of the processes involved making a 'sproo', a piece of plastic to be attached to the spinner; this process involved the 'workers' clamping the 'sproos' into a vice and preparing them for the top.

The mini-enterprise was run on six half-days and the 'workers' rotated around the various jobs. Both the teachers and the children soon encountered the problems: complaints about tiredness and strain, about the poor quality of work from some children, the lack of help and support from those given responsibility for managing the enterprise, in particular the adequacy of the training, poor personnel skills resulting in members of the management team publicly criticizing a member of the workforce. Solutions to many of these problems were worked out and agreed by the workforce and the management; no reprimands, for instance, were to be made in front of other workers.

The children also had to adjust their working practices to fit the prevailing conditions, in other words they needed to be helped to adopt a flexible attitude. Management, for instance, was asked to carry out the tasks of the workforce in the event of a particular problem arising. Elsewhere, 'workers' were taken off production because of the large number of tops in stock and moved to the packing department.

A secretary for the company kept records of how many hours the children worked and whether particular workers qualified for bonus payments. Payment was made in the form of sweets. Bonuses were, however, lost if the 'worker' was responsible for a rejected top. At the end of the week the secretary issued the clock cards to the 'workers' and they checked whether their 'payment' was correct according to the hours worked and the bonuses or stoppages. The job of secretary was one which the children particularly enjoyed.

In all, the company produced 200 tops, and a sales promotion of posters and announcements together with a stall in the school hall, resulted in the sale of 169. The remainder, apart from five complimentary tops, were sold to the 'workers' at a special discount. The children had encountered the idea of discount in the visit to the Electricity Board showrooms, where they discovered the prices paid by the public and compared them with those paid by the staff of Philips & Dupont Optical UK Ltd. The data provided the stimulus for a mathematics lesson. The price of the top to everyone else was 3p, a figure arrived at in a brief discussion between the teacher and children when consideration was given to what it was thought their 'customers' could afford. The figure of 10p was thought to be too high.

Responsibility for handling the finances of the enterprise was shared among the children. There were very few overheads, of course, because much of the material had been given to the school. No form of book-keeping, therefore, was employed in this particular instance. The sum of £6 which was made from the sales was put in the school fund.

Learning Outcomes

The teacher felt that the children's understanding of what was involved in the production of a product was greatly enhanced, both as a result of the numerous visits to Philips & Dupont Optical UK Ltd and from running their own enterprise. The children were able to appreciate the many different roles that are performed within a large organization.

The links between the various areas of the curriculum such as mathematics, science, English, literature and music and the working environment were also valuable.

Finally, the project enhanced the children's range of social and interpersonal skills, not only through their having to work together in their own enterprise, but through meeting and talking with 'adults other than teachers'. Such skills as listening, observing, interpreting, interviewing and analysing were all employed, as well as the social skills of cooperation, negotiation and compromise. The teacher observed the growing confidence and maturity with which the children approached various aspects of the project.

Chapter 11

The Tourist Industry at Tintern Catbrook Primary School, Chepstow

Robert Richards

Introduction

Catbrook Primary School, Chepstow, is situated two miles above the picturesque Wye Valley. What industry other than agriculture could there possibly be in such a rural area? The children are nearly always the best starting point. A discussion of work and work-places revealed we lived in a commuter belt. The old village families had been replaced by mobile groups who travel to Bristol, Newport and Cardiff. But other points, which seemed less important at first, emerged: 'my mother does surveys, she interviews visitors to Tintern Abbey'; 'my mother picks grapes for Mr Rogers at the vineyard'; 'my mother works as a waitress in the evenings at the Hotel'. The momentum derived from this discussion resulted in the class of twenty-two junior chidlren, aged 7–11, under the guidance of their teacher, setting out to study the tourist industry at Tintern in the Wye Valley.

The School

Catbrook is a two-teacher primary school built in 1876. There are three classrooms, one for the junior class, one for the infant class, and the third is used as a library, office and television room. The children are drawn almost entirely from the village, which now is comprised mainly of professional people who commute as far as Bristol to their place of employment. Only two of the original village families are left.

The characteristic problems of a small village school include providing work at different levels for the various abilities, the imbalance between different year groups, the dual role of the teaching head creating a tension between teaching and administration and the inability to delegate curricular areas because of a lack of expertise to draw on. On the other hand, there are advantages in an all-age classroom; the children tend to use each other more than in a single-age class and the older children seem to take on a more responsible attitude towards the younger children. No previous work with industry had been undertaken, though the head had, in his previous school, been involved with a project with local firms.

The Environmental Studies Programme

An environmental studies programme of work with an historical, geographical and scientific core had been written, designed to develop the child's linguistic, mathematical, scientific, social and study skills. At the same time, the programme seeks to develop powers of creative expression and sensitivity. The chosen topic allows for an overlap with the children's interests and provides work at a level appropriate to their ability and relevant to their experience. These criteria suggested an inter-disciplinary approach, in which children apply knowledge and skills learnt in one situation to another. Independent learning is encouraged with the opportunity for the children to raise their own questions as well as providing answers. They represent and communicate this information in a variety of ways. The overall aim of the programme is to develop the child's conceptual knowledge of the world, the world on this occasion being the world of work.

The children work in various group sizes on tasks within the project and individuals are assigned responsibilities by those groups. Problem-solving is usually one element of the project; in the past, for instance, they investigated animals' preferences for light and darkness in the study of a pond. Visits are also regular features of the work and, for these, parental support with transport and supervision is sometimes required.

The parents were invited to an evening during which this approach to environmental studies was discussed and slides of previous industry work were shown. They were initially sceptical and wanted to be convinced that there would be meaningful learning taking place.

The 'Industrial' Dimension

The development did not, however, stop there; specific dimensions related to the study of an industry were identified. The overriding aim of the project was to encourage a better understanding of the tourist industry, its essential role and service to the community. Three objectives emerged from this aim:

> To give the children a better understanding of the working world, its opportunities and problems.
> To understand the needs and interests of people in different working situations.
> To experience meeting people outside the peer group, family or teachers.

It was obvious that the children could not possibly study the complete field of the tourist industry and so the project looked at three selected branches:

> A place where tourists would visit.
> A place where tourists would stay.
> Tourists not only today but in the historical perspective of the past.

Starting the Project with the Children

Place yourself in your imagination as a tourist. What do you do when you book a holiday? — look at the brochures?; that hotel looks nice; what can we visit if we stay there?; your selection is finally made; the travel agent books the accommodation. That was the starting point, the accommodation. In this instance the travel agent was the headteacher who agreed to write to the hotels.

The letters written by the head to the four main hotels in Tintern produced no replies, so they were followed up by telephone calls. As with any local travel agent, certain choices were not available; one, for instance, had no accommodation facilities. But, initial disappointment was soon replaced by smiling faces. Embassy Hotels, the owners of the Beaufort Hotel had the right dates and time available for the head to explain the aims of the project and arrange for the pupils to make a visit. It was an ideal choice as the site of the hotel was outside the walls of Tintern Abbey.

After the dissolution of the Abbey in 1537, the site was granted to Henry, Earl of Worcester, and then to his descendants, the Dukes of Beaufort, who handed the care of the Abbey over to the Ministry of Public Works in 1902. The name of the hotel was linking past work in school to the present.

The manager agreed that the children and teacher could visit the hotel under the guidance of the assistant manager and a trainee manager. They were asked to take the children through the hotel as tourists, in two groups. Parents helped transport the children to the hotel.

The Children's First-hand Experience of a Hotel

On arrival at the hotel the children registered at reception. The registration card requested surname, forenames, address, nationality and signature. Once completed, the children were checked in by the receptionist and two room numbers issued, a single room and a double room. The children were handed the keys and waited for the assistant manager who explained that guests usually went straight to their room, so the children followed his advice. The facilities available to guests in each room were explained. They had an en-suite bathroom or shower, and coffee and tea making facilities; an information pack about the hotel, leisure facilities and places to visit was available. The internal telephone system was explained and a call made to reception requesting an early morning call.

Having unpacked, changed and freshened up, it was explained to the children that some guests might wish to order a cup of tea in the lounge, while for others more energetic there was the chance to play snooker in the games room. But time moves on and the chef was preparing the meal in the kitchen.

The chef and his assistants explained the buffet they were preparing for lunch. One child noticed the chef's hat had holes in the top and he explained their hats were made of paper and needed holes for ventilation. If the holes were not there his hair would fall out! The children left the kitchen proud possessors of a chef's hat. What became of the hat? It is still used by the infants when cooking in their classroom.

A meal was soon to be ready. What about laying up the tables? A table was ready for the children to set and silver service was explained. Two 'guests' from among the children were asked for their choice for dinner. They chose from the children's menu. 'Wine, sir?' The children were taken to the wine cellar, a bottle was selected and duly prepared for the table. The children made ice in the ice-maker and placed this in the bucket with the bottle of wine. The name of the wine incidentally was Tintern Parva, Medium Dry, a link with the later visit to the vineyard. This was a fitting end to an enjoyable visit and the children had no doubt in their minds that they would like to be pampered as tourists staying at this hotel.

Follow-up Work in the Classroom: Simulating the Experience

Following the visit, two classroom simulations were set up. The caretaker, a trained silver service waitress, explained table layout and serving. In a corner of the classroom the children set up a table for one and chose a guest, a waiter and a wine waiter to act out the scenario. The meal and accompanying wine were selected and the guest served. After the meal a bill was duly prepared and presented to the guest, who checked it and, if correct, paid and left a tip. The calculator came into its own, especially to calculate the VAT.

Children studying the menu were often puzzled by the terminology used to describe the dishes offered. What is Lobster Thermidor? My mother said 'Mayonnaise is like salad cream'. The dictionary and cookery books brought in from home were the providers of the answers. The mysterious delights of the menu were revealed to the children, teacher and parents through the child's curiosity. The hotel menu had a new meaning. Parents came in on Monday morning saying, 'I tried Sauté of Lamb Sweetbreads on Saturday night, it was delicious'.

The overall aims had been to help the children understand how menus are prepared and what was involved in looking after guests at mealtimes. In terms of the skills which the children used, the importance of listening skills was understood, some mistakes were made and wrong items were brought. Recording skills were used; the children, for instance, developed techniques for abbreviation which nevertheless had to be understood by those preparing the meal. Mathematical skills were also evident in the various calculations which were required and the use of the calculator improved. Social skills were involved in dealing with the 'guests' and with the other 'staff'. A number of the children felt that a waiter's job was rather repetitive.

The second simulation involved the reception area. The headteacher's office was renamed 'Catbrook Hotel Reception'. The children agreed that in exchange for the use of the room part of their duties would be answering the telephone and dealing with other enquiries as receptionists for one day. Every morning for one week, normal registration and dinner numbers were replaced by hotel registration. Each child on entering school filled in a form with surname, forenames, address, telephone number, date and signature. A box was ticked to indicate whether the child was having a dinner or sandwiches. After completing the registration form the child was handed a room key which corresponded to the number on the register. Even teachers, cleaning staff, canteen ladies and peripatetic teachers were registered and handed a key. On leaving the building at break-times or at the end of the day the keys were returned to reception. At the end of the week the children were handed bills for their week's stay at Catbrook Hotel. These were checked by each child. At reception there was a visitors' book, every visitor whether postman or plumber was duly asked to sign on the dotted line.

The simulation helped the children understand the nature of some of the jobs available in hotel work, as well as the need for efficiency and accuracy. They also saw the importance of being tactful and polite in dealing with people, even in situations where the 'customer' behaves in an unpleasant manner, as happened on one occasion.

The Children Design their own Learning Experiences

This enthusiasm triggered off a new avenue of work and the well prepared plans for other follow-up work were abandoned. The children set about devising board games. After discussion it was decided that they should involve a tourist visiting a hotel, a souvenir shop and a tourist attraction or leisure activity. The class was divided into groups of two, three or four, according to age. This was felt to be important as the older children could produce more sophsiticated games, a fact borne out by the finished product. The younger children's games involved throwing a dice to land on a square. Sometimes a simple instruction, e.g., 'You have lost your purse, move back two squares' was placed on a square. The winner was the first to arrive at the last square. An alternative version involved placing objects on the squares, i.e., keys, plates, souvenirs. The winner was the child who collected the most objects on their journey along the board.

The most sophisticated game, 'Touring Tintern', was created by an 11-year-old girl. This is a game for six players, and begins at the hotel reception. The 'tourist' throws a dice to determine a key number and is given a key. On arrival at the bedroom a room card is chosen. The 'tourist' then proceeds to either the lounge, games room, dining room or bar. Following this an activity card suggests a visit to the Abbey, old Railway Station or a walk. Finally, a visit is made to the souvenir shop before returning to the hotel.

The players begin with £125 each. From this they deduct the price of the bedroom. For the selected room, tourist activity and souvenir shop, there are prices marked on the board. The throw of the dice determines the price paid on each occasion. This expenditure is also deducted from the total amount. Whilst travelling, if a counter landed on the coloured squares marked on the board, a card of that colour is selected, e.g., Win £2 on the fruit machine. The amounts are added or deducted from the original figure. The winner is the tourist who completes the course with the least expenditure.

These games provided the opportunity for problem-solving activities. They provided work at a level appropriate to the child's ability and relevant to their experience. The exercises helped the children develop group working skills; compromising with others in order to make progress on a task, testing the ideas out, assessing the result and then making the necessary changes, accepting and responding to criticism, were all important learning experiences. The production of the games involved artwork skills, as well as language and numeracy skills; the rules for one of the games for instance were re-written five times!

The games also increased some of the children's understanding of the economics of tourism, particularly the cost of a day out for a tourist and the idea that tourist attractions should provide value for money. More startling, it made them aware of the cost to their parents for a day's outing.

The Visit to the Tintern Vineyard

Ask any tourist who has visited the Wye Valley about its tourist attractions and the first place that springs to mind is Tintern Abbey. In the course of previous study of the Abbey it was discovered that the Cistercian monks made wine at Tintern 500 years ago. In 1979 a vineyard was planted at Tintern Parva on the site thought to be that of the original vineyard. Two mothers who had helped to pick the grapes at the vineyard made the initial contact and Catbrook School became the first school to visit the vineyard.

The request was to be shown around as a tourist party. The tour began with slides in the wine cellar, showing the establishment of the vineyard, the work in a calendar year and the pressing and bottling of the wine. After questions about caring for the vines, the picking of the grapes and storage, and a look at the cellar, the children walked out to the hillside where the vines were at various stages of growth. The mature grape was nearly ready for picking. No visit to a vineyard would be complete without a taste of wine or soft drink, and this was one occasion when the children really did wish they were adults!

The work on the vineyard was undertaken by the owner and a full time assistant. The children followed through their jobs by looking at the planting of the first vine in 1979 to the first picking in 1983. This involved correct planting procedure, pruning and training the vine along wire supports. Protection from disease was achieved by spraying, and rabbits were deterred by the use of plastic bags, and badgers by electric fences. They are helped by two dogs who pollinate the grapes by running up and down the rows. The owner employs twenty casual workers for picking the ripe grapes and when picked they are sent to Newent in Gloucestershire to be crushed and bottled. The bottles are returned for labelling, storage and marketing, a task undertaken by the owner, his wife and an assistant. The children thought that all this and taking tourists around must be very hard work. This sort of employment did not appeal to them.

The children set about asking questions with enthusiasm: how was glass made for the wine bottles; did cork really come from a tree; did egg really stick the labels to the bottles?

A collection of wine bottles from wine-producing countries was quickly put together, as a result of which it was discovered that the shape of the bottle and the colour of the glass provided a lot of information about the wine in the bottle. This prompted the children to remember messages being sent in bottles. The children's stories with these messages had intriguing titles, such as 'Mayday, Mayday' and 'Torpedo• Attack'. A message was prepared for a bottle and put in the River Wye at Tintern. The children wait in hope for a reply.

One reply they did get was from a French connection. A girl had a godmother who lived on a vineyard in France and so a letter was written together with a questionnaire to Chateau de Montresor. To the children's delight, a reply arrived back a fortnight later. A vineyard in France could now be compared and contrasted with Tintern Parva. The children compared the output of the two vineyards, discovering that the French vineyard produced twice as much as the English one, and learnt that the French vineyard belonged to a bottling and processing cooperative, unlike the Tintern operation. The children also learnt about comparative climates as well as the different types of wine produced.

An Historical Connection

A further connection developed, this time historical. The port of Chepstow once had a flourishing wine trade with France, Portugal and Spain. Sailing boats full of wine arrived from Bordeaux, Oporto and Cadiz. A visit to Chepstow Museum revealed a display of corks, barrels and vintners tools. A tour of the town revealed cellars and almshouses built by the vintners. The oldest inscribed gravestone in Chepstow Church is that of George Braban, a vintner.

This visit and the subsequent work suggested to the children the need for a Wye Valley wine trail, which they set about writing. Language skills were also enhanced by this exercise, the children finding, for instance, that in compiling a trail, pictures, a map and the minimum of vocabulary is the best format. Perhaps one day an enterprising person will organize a trip to Chepstow Museum and town trail, before taking the Wye Valley to Tintern and the vineyard, followed by the sampling of wine over an authentic monk's meal. Fantasy perhaps, but an idea put forward by the children.

The children found biblical connections with wine. A miracle often related is turning water into wine at the wedding at Cana in Galilee. Could the children turn water into wine? The answer was a resounding, yes. 'My father makes wine, he uses a gallon of water', was a child's reply, so they proceeded to make red and white wines. The children carefully followed the instructions and recipes; weighing, measuring, siphoning were skills developed. The importance of sterilizing, yeast, yeast nutrients, citric acid and other active ingredients were discussed and noted. The final bottling was an important day. The children had made labels with polystyrene and lino cuts; the best were selected and used to label the bottles. Yes, egg did stick the labels on. What about drinking and storing the wines? The children, with the help of a parent, made wine goblets, coasters and coolers from clay. A corkscrew was needed to open the wine; Legotechnic came into its own. Whether these will be adequate to open the wine now maturing in Catbrook cellars remains to be seen.

The work in this section of the project was subject-orientated with a measure of integration. An historical, geographical and scientific core emerged. The children developed their own personal and factual writing skills, particularly now that they were writing for another audience. The letter and questionnaire to France, for instance, was initially attempted by everyone; later the children chose the most appropriate form and questions using the information provided by the owner of the Tintern vineyard. Art and craft developed the children's skills in making things which were functional and useful.

Interviewing the Tourists at Tintern

The third area of study involved the tourist today and in the past. It was decided the children would interview tourists arriving at Tintern Abbey. After a brain-storming session with the children, a questionnaire was devised. This had eight questions with boxes for the children to tick. The questions ranged from whether the individual was on holiday or a day-visit, their country of origin, the length of their visit to the Abbey, and their means of transport to the Abbey and other places they would be visiting in Tintern.

As the days for the interviews drew near, the children became rather nervous and apprehensive; nerves soon melted, however, after the first few interviews and a repartee developed between the adults and children. Sixty-eight questionnaires were completed and the information was stored on a computer database system. Important facts emerged; for instance, 25 per cent of visitors came from a foreign country, the majority of whom were North Americans. This showed the importance of catering for the tourist from abroad. One fact noted by the children was that the recorded cassettes giving information at the Abbey were in English, French and German. Only 20 per cent of the visitors knew of other tourist attractions in Tintern. The children suggested that the other facilities should be better advertised. If, however, more people knew about and visited them, they would become overcrowded and ruined for others; the children had discovered a double-edged sword.

Eager for more information, the children wrote to Gwent County Council for information on a survey they had carried out at Tintern Railway Station. The children were amazed at the similarity between their own questions and the ones used in the County Council survey which related to the various activities undertaken by the visitors. This information was too varied to be stored on the computer, so the children produced a booklet interpreting the information.

Tourism: Then and Now

Tourists visited Tintern in Victorian times. William Giblin, Viscount Torrington, William Wordsworth, Lord Tennyson and Turner completed the Wye tour. The children, through reference to copies of old documents, followed in their footsteps. As William Wordsworth, Edward Davies and John Blackwell wrote their poetry a few miles above the Wye at Tintern, so did the children. An anthology, 'Old Poems for New', featuring the old poets and the class, group and individual poems of the children, represents this work. In those days it was fashionable to take the Wye tour and write of your experiences. Today that tradition remains in the prose and poetry written to express the children's experience. The last six lines of the children's poem 'Tintern Abbey' captures the mood perfectly:

> As the sun rises it gleams on the Abbey
> Changing it to an untold place of happiness
> The sun goes down all is still
> The Abbey stands with a hawk's eye
> Hearing the echoes of the rusty past.
> A jigsaw puzzle waiting to be put back
> together by a Queen

How important is the tourist industry to Tintern? — a question asked by more than one child. A suggested answer was to mark on a map of Tintern the buildings connected with tourism. A group of children recorded information in each area. The buildings were divided into four categories

— residential, places to stay, places to visit, other shops and facilities. Tintern Abbey, Chapel Hill, River Tintern and Tintern Parva were combined to form one large information map of the buildings. 25 per cent of the buildings were found to be connected with tourism. The answer to the original question seemed to be 'very'. Shopkeepers and publicans were interviewed about their facilities for tourists, how they set about attracting visitors and the seasonal nature of their trade. Their views supported the answers suggested by the survey.

Learning Outcomes

This work has shown the value of 'active learning' in the development of social and communication skills. The children learnt to interpret information they had gathered and information supplied by a third party. The children also interviewed the custodian of Tintern Abbey, during which they presented their own survey results. He agreed that their findings were similar to his own department's survey, a fact which provided further evidence of the quality of the children's work.

What did the children learn? They learnt a body of knowledge relating to the study. The children needed to understand the meanings of words they read and heard. Their vocabularies were certainly extended. But what was more valuable was the processes by which the children acquired the data and what they finally did with it; the development of skills of observation and collection of information, the interpretation and classification of data, and the representation and communication of that information by a variety of means.

The aim of the project was achieved: the children gained an insight into the tourist industry. They saw and proved its essential role to the village and way of life of Tintern. It provides a service locally, nationally and internationally. The objectives too have been realized. The children became self-reliant, showed initiative and developed a sense of responsibility. The basic requirements of working together as a team were appreciated. Children co-operated well with others, they acted as leaders in some situations and at other times responded to leadership demands. They met and interviewed a variety of people outside their peer group. This in turn developed important aspects of communication skills. Problem-solving is apparent in the games invented and hypotheses tested. The needs and interests of people in different working situations have been explored. Finally, the children now have a better understanding of the working world, its opportunities and problems.

Chapter 12

Exploring the Mining Industry and the Theme of Conflict
Arael Primary School, Abertillery

John Garwell and Janice Anderson

Introduction: The Nature of Conflict

The focus of this study is on the concept of conflict. The concept was deliberately chosen in order to enable the teachers to explore a wide range of situations in industry and compare them with others in which the children might have personal experience.

The aim of the work was to discover whether children would respond to a conceptual approach in a positive manner despite the fact that the concept chosen seemed to involve negative emotions. That conflict is inherent at various levels of industry seems incontrovertible. At a global level it is argued that there is conflict between employers who own the means of production and workers who depend for their sustenance on selling their only asset, labour, to the employers. A prime objective for the employer will be the maximization of profits, which will involve, for instance, keeping down costs. Workers, on the other hand, seek the maximization of their rewards both in the form of income and in pleasant working conditions. In highly competitive situations some employers have argued for the need to cut down on labour costs to stay in business, thus leading to an even sharper conflict with the workers.

The recent strikes in the mining industry have reflected this conflict very clearly in that British Coal have cut costs by closing non-profit-making pits, reducing the labour force and resisting the miners' claims for large wage increases. Many children in the class studied are related to miners and therefore have had a personal experience of this conflict.

At a more local level, conflict between groups in industry arises when, for instance, two groups of workers lay claim to the same job. In the steel industry, for instance, the workers at Ravenscraig, Scotland, might feel that those in Llanwern steelworks in South East Wales, were being preferred when investment plans were being made. In the coal-mining industry dispute there was conflict between striking and working miners. Children are most likely to understand conflict when it is localized and at the micro level, between individuals or small groups.

Whilst it was thought too much to expect the children to understand the whole gamut of conflict relationships it was felt that it would be possible to allow them to work through their own and other people's experiences in order to develop a more adequate, rational conceptual framework about the reasons for conflict and the ways in which it could be resolved.

The School

Arael Junior School is in Six Bells, Abertillery, Gwent. This is the western valley of the county with coal, in its upper reaches, as the backbone industry. Ten miles to the south of Abertillery lies Newport which is the gateway to both the eastern and western valleys and one of the foremost coal ports for the Welsh mining valleys of the eastern section of the coalfield. In company with most of the valley towns, Abertillery has suffered a sharp decline in coal output. The miners in this area were deeply and loyally involved in the year long (1984–5) miners' strike. There were a few miners who returned early to work in this area but the vast majority awaited the general return to work. Loyalty to their union was the dominant ethos.

The school is the result of an amalgamation between two schools; the one which was closed was in the neighbouring village of Aberbeeg. Some would claim that the school, in reality, serves two distinct communities whose members find some difficulty in working together, even in support of the school. It may be too strong to suggest that there is hostility between the two communities, but there are signs of some rivalry between them at both adult and child level. There are 114 children on roll in this junior/ infants school of which 14 are in a nursery department. There is one head for the whole school, with five assistant teachers.

As a result of the appointment of a new headteacher, the policy of the school has changed markedly. More informal, child-centred methods, with an accent on social and environmental studies are encouraged, although the older staff are deeply wedded to a more formal approach. The twenty-six children in the class which took part in the project were aged between 9 and 11 years. This wide age range was a necessary consequence of falling rolls brought about not just through a fall in the birth-rate but by the exodus of many young families in search of work.

When the present teacher took over the class in 1983 she found a mainly passive group of children who appeared like 'little robots'. None-theless, the children responded well to the greater opportunities to partici-pate in the running of the class and in oral work, though the maintenance of discipline became a more complex problem in her more open and informal regime.

Whilst the new headteacher has been very supportive of the class teacher's new methods, some of the other staff still remain to be convinced of their value. On the whole the teachers in this relatively small school still see themselves as autonomous in their own classrooms, so what went on in the class involved in the project was not typical of the other classes.

The Development of the Project

The teacher has been teaching for fourteen years. She was a secondary school teacher, specializing in geography, but switched to the primary age range partly because of her conviction that many of the learning difficulties she noticed in her secondary school pupils had their roots in the primary stage. She therefore wanted to make her contribution to the earlier development of children in order to discover whether some of their learning difficulties could be avoided. She felt that children need to be stimulated and allowed a greater participation in the decisions about their own education.

When the newly appointed head proposed an environmental studies approach, she suggested to her class that they study a place of work. After some dicussion, it was decided to approach the management of Six Bells Colliery, the most important place of work nearby. Many of the children (26 per cent) had relatives in mining, some of whom were pleased to cooperate with the teacher in devising a programme of work. The teacher hoped that the project would provide a 'strong motivational force and a general improvement in the children's attitude to learning'.

The objectives of the project included the acquisition and develop-ment of skills in the mathematical, scientific, artistic and broadly creative areas of the curriculum. During the implementation of this work the teacher sought the advice of the member of staff at the Gwent College of Higher Education most closely involved in school-to-industry work in the Faculty of Education. It was he who suggested that the teacher should focus on the idea of conflict in the project. She was intrigued, but felt the proposal needed some thought. Firstly, Six Bells miners had just emerged from the 1984–5 miners' dispute. Whilst most miners had supported the union throughout the strike, some had not and the consequent ill-feeling in the community was only just subsiding. By reviving memories about this very real conflict, the children might become involved in a process which they could not control. Secondly, there had been some rivalry between two groups in the class which had expressed itself in gang hostilities in the playground and out of school. The staff had succeeded in alleviating this conflict but felt that it could recur under the impetus of a close study of conflict.

The teacher believed that if the work was tackled in an open and relatively objective manner, the children would be helped to see the concept in its broader perspective. Such a perspective, it was hoped, might lead to a less emotional and partisan involvement in their own and their parents' conflicts.

To ensure that the theme of conflict featured in the class project, a member of the school-to-industry research team based at the College wrote a role-play exercise for the class. As a highly active member of a trade union in the iron and steel industry, he was asked to provide lively material about the world of work which would appeal to young children. He wanted 'to let the children know about the role of unions in looking after the interests of their members in view of the managers' concern for shareholders and customers'. He wished to show that trade unions could help to overcome conflict in order that 'the enterprise can operate and prosper to the benefit of both employer and employee'.

Three students on the College's IT/INSET programme were also involved in the work and so there were six adults participating in the 'conflict' project, each with different motivations and perspectives but each expected to interact with the children in an exploratory and relaxed manner. To augment this group towards the end of the project, five parents attended a morning's lesson to take part in discussions about a play that the children had performed about their experiences and perceptions of work. This group all had different messages to impart. Some wanted to encourage the children to go further in their educational careers than they themselves had done; some wanted to put the 'record straight' about the role of the unions in the strike; a policeman wanted to listen and learn as well as put the case for the role of the police, not just in the recent strike but as servants of the community.

What the Children Did

The children's activities can be divided into nine episodes, listed below:

1. The visit to Six Bells Colliery.
2. The visit to Big Pit, Blaenavon.

3. The visit to the Mines Rescue Station, Crumlin.
4. The visit to Marine Colliery.
5. The children's play — The Ammonite tells his story.
6. The role-play on industrial conflict.
7. The children's stories on conflict.
8. Class discussion on conflict.
9. Parent-children discussions and work on conflict.

1. Six Bells

The teacher arranged a visit to the local colliery, Six Bells, only a few minutes walk from the school. Prior to the visit a detailed questionnaire was drawn up and presented to the management. Because British Coal does not allow children to go underground, the visit was restricted to the surface. It was conducted by the Safety Officer who encouraged the children to talk freely to the miners. Amongst the topics covered were the different kinds of jobs involved in mining, the changes in manpower in the industry including its run-down and the introduction of early redundancy. The concept of division of labour, unemployment and above all, change, were thus implicitly covered. Perhaps the most significant discovery made by the teacher was that the 'concept of a union being a representative of the workers was new to the children and aroused considerable interest'. It was obvious that during this visit the children were able to develop certain skills that they would have had difficulty in developing within the class-room, in particular, observation and questioning. They were able to apply these directly to an industrial context and, as they gained in confidence, they were able to draw out comments from both management and workers about the recent, highly emotionally charged, strike.

Once back in the classroom the children set to work recording, interpreting and presenting the information they had gleaned. They expressed themselves in various ways, including writing about a day in the life of a miner and drawing, painting and weaving pictures about work in a coal mine. A topic of special concern was safety, especially as there had been a serious disaster at Six Bells in 1960 when many lives were lost. Many of the children's own relatives had been killed in that disaster. In order to reinforce their experiences at the pit head, the teacher invited the chairman of the school governors, who is also a county councillor, into the classroom to be interviewed by the pupils. As a prominent member of the National Union of Mineworkers he answered the children's own, previously compiled, questions, and gave details about mining conditions both in Britain and in tropical climates. The children discovered that training for all miners was an important way to secure not just efficiency but safety and that one outstanding feature of life underground was the comradeship which mitigated some of the hardships and dangers of working underground.

The children had by now listened to two distinct points of view about mining: that of the workers and the management. They learnt that at least on one aspect both sides spoke with one voice — the importance of safety and the necessity of securing it through discipline. Whether this discipline was due to an externally-imposed set of regulations laid down by management, or arose out of the loyalty and comradeship built up after years of shared trials and tribulations, was a matter well worth exploring. However, at this stage the children were only beginning to understand some of the more concrete manifestations of such abstractions as loyalty, solidarity and discipline — concrete in the sense that they could be attached to the home and now the colliery.

2. Big Pit, Blaenavon

The children were now clamouring to go underground to experience at first hand what it was really like to work under such conditions. Fortunately, one of the pits which was recently forced to close because its coal reserves were, by general agreement, no longer economic to mine, had been converted into a mining museum.

The children experienced the rapid descent into the bowels of the earth and genuine excitement prevailed as the museum guides, all former miners, regaled the young visitors with stories about pit-children terrified of the dark, the dread of fire-damp, rats, sudden death from explosion or cave-ins, lingering death from pneumoconiosis and the 'miners' songs' to maintain morale. The children heard about exploitation and heroism, heat and cold, absolute darkness and the blinding light when surfacing in the daytime.

The children brought back to the classroom the concept of the exploitative nature of the truck system. To bring the idea to life they constructed a company shop wherein they could re-enact some of the transactions which could have taken place 160 or so years ago. In the process they consolidated and furthered, amongst other things, their mathematical understandings.

3. The Mines Rescue Station, Crumlin

Safety became a byword in the project and its meaning was more fully captured by two separate visits to the British Coal Mines Rescue Station in Crumlin, about three miles from the school. The welcome given to the children was quite extraordinary as they heard from the deputy superintendent about the role of the rescuer and the training links between the station and the colliery workers. The spate of colliery closures in South Wales had, it was disclosed, cast doubts on the future of the rescue station. The highlight of the visit was when the pupils crept through a maze of training galleries. The possibility of providing a simulated rescue exercise involving the children was deliberated at great length only to be rejected due to insurance problems and the desire of the rescue teams to maintain their traditional low profile.

4. Marine Colliery

So eager were the children now to learn about the whole process of coal-mining that they supported the suggestion of one of them to visit Marine Colliery, where, as a result of pit amalgamation, the coal mined at Six Bells was brought to the surface. The children toured every part of the surface, initially feeling some alarm at the excessive noise. They were pacified when the safety officer explained that such conditions were a normal part of the working environment. They summoned up sufficient courage to scale a 150-foot ramp, where they observed the processes for loading the coal, and the transport of coal to its markets was explained. To the children's delight they were allowed to keep their protective clothing which has served as a visible memory of the warmth of their reception at the hands of the workers.

5. The Ammonite tells his Story

During their study of the coal industry the children were introduced to the fossils found within the coal measures. This aspect of the project led to creative activities centred around the dramatization of the imagined life story of a fossil, an ammonite. The whole class participated in a public performance of the dance which was well supported by the parents. The themes underlying the story symbolized imprisonment and suffering as the fossil was weighed down under layer upon layer of new rock and subsequently freed from captivity by the miners. It was but a short step to find parallels between this allegory and the contradictions in mining itself, the production of a valuable commodity through suffering and hardship. The often frenzied movements of the children, the declarations of their narrators, the stirring sounds of Kachaturian's music, seemed to move the audience of miners and their wives. After the performance many parents expressed their admiration for and pride in this display of the children's imagination.

6. Role-playing the Theme of Conflict

Whilst it could be argued that the Ammonite's Story reflected a creative, emotional, but possibly sub-conscious response to the rigours of mining, the role play exercise that the children undertook was intended to develop more cognitive processes. It was designed for pupils to experience problem-solving in the field of industrial relations by acting out the roles involved. It was suggested that the children should be encouraged to think about the way in which small incidents can sometimes escalate into serious problems in the workplace.

The children were told that in a quarrel about a coat that had been lent to a friend (Julie) at work, Julie had accidentally torn it, repaired it and apologized to the lender (Susan). However, Susan was not satisfied and in the ensuing argument in the car-park after work, Julie hit Susan just as the manager (David) walked past. He saw the incident, which under factory rules can lead to dismissal. However, he agreed to see the shop steward (Jenny) before taking disciplinary action. The children were asked to take on these four roles, and to answer a number of questions such as 'Why do you think the factory manager needs the power to discipline the workers?'; 'Do you think this power is unlimited or restricted?'; 'How do you think the company's power is restrained?'; 'What do you think would happen if Julie was not in the Union and had no one to support her?'; 'Do you think it is right that Julie should be sacked?'; 'How else would you deal with the situation?'; 'Can you think of similar types of discipline problems at school?'.

The teacher was advised to draw the children's attention to several points of enquiry, e.g.

(i) the concept of management power and the need for discipline on such matters as attendance, punctuality, accepting orders;

(ii) the role of the shop steward/trade union in the simulated conflict; and

(iii) the position of the individual in conflict with authority and the influence of a collective approach to negotiation.

In spite of a great deal of preparation both written and oral, the children who played the roles lacked conviction. The manager was played by a boy who could not project an aura of authority, the girl who played the shop steward tended to defer to the manager and put up only a feeble defence for a member threatened with the sack. In the subsequent discussion it became apparent that the children had, on the whole, very little idea of the roles of either the manager or the shop steward and lacked understanding of what a union really was. However, the teacher seemed successful in clarifying the concepts of power and authority when she likened the role of the manager to her own. The children agreed that they could not challenge her authority and could see why they should not challenge that of the manager's either. They regarded the maintenance of order as essentially his role.

Although the role play exercise did not appear overly successful, the children's interest was sufficiently aroused for them to agree to write their own stories about conflict.

7. The Three Children's Stories on Conflict

The class was divided into three groups, each of which undertook to write and present a play about conflict. One group wrote about a girl who lent her beach ball to a friend. The ball was kicked out to sea and lost. The injured party, Stephanie, was not sure whether it was kicked there by her brother, Harry, or another boy, Tom. The children agreed to toss a coin to decide the issue and the boy who had actually kicked the ball into the sea won and did not have to buy a new beach ball.

In the class discussion the children agreed that the toss of a coin was not a satisfactory way of settling the argument and suggested thorough investigations of the circumstances. Some children believed that it was not Tom but the brother, Harry, who was lying because he was afraid of his parents or his sister and he had a grudge against her. Many children saw the incident as leading to a conflict not only between Stephanie and Tom but between Stephanie and her brother. They also saw the underlying tensions between children and parents. The children felt that fairness was an important criterion in settling disputes, although some did admit that if they were the wrong-doers they would 'cover up for themselves'. From further discussions it became clear that the children applied a higher standard of morality to others than to themselves. For instance, they argued that if they had lost a ball they would be constrained to buy another one because the loss was insignificant. However, when pressed about the loss of their own ball they would insist that it be replaced by the offender.

The second group wrote a story about a factory worker attacking his supervisor. The supervisor had previously been one of the workers with a reputation for laziness. He had been promoted, it is suspected, because he was a cousin of the manager. Once he became a supervisor he decided to impose changes in working practices much to the chagrin of the shop floor workers, convinced that their current working methods were more efficient. The new supervisor started 'nit-picking' until the atmosphere became so tense that one of the workers, noted for his very good workmanship, struck him. The supervisor reported the incident to the manager. The shop steward was called in and put the worker's case. The manager, possibly realizing his own contribution to the breakdown in relations, admonished the supervisor on his poor handling of his men and asked him to improve his approach. He then summoned the offender, warned him that any future misconduct could lead to the sack, and gave him a rise on account of his good workmanship.

8. Class Discussion on Conflict

In the class discussions a number of points emerged. The idea of a convenor or shop steward who could stop the aggression was thought to be an advantage. It was felt that the aggrieved worker should have gone to the manager rather than fight the supervisor and that it was better not to hit the boss because the assailant might have lost his job whilst the supervisor, being a cousin of the manager, might have got away with it. Some children thought the shop steward should have gone to the manager to state that the workers refused to continue working under the supervisor. The children agreed with the pay rise but insisted that the other workers should also have received it, otherwise there could be further conflict, this time between the workers and the manager. To prevent any future violence the children suggested a series of ballots, firstly to elect the shop steward, secondly for strike action involving only peaceful picketing and thirdly for the election of a supervisor. The shop steward was expected to be a peacemaker whilst the supervisor had to be a hard worker and liked by his workforce.

The third story was about an incident on the miners' picket line where a group of working miners tried to cross and go to work. As the men confronted each other, the working miners argued that they could no longer afford to stay out on strike because they had families to support. They stated that the pit would close if it were not re-opened soon. The pickets countered that if they did go back they would be defeated and their jobs would be threatened. There was no agreement. Eventually the working miners tried to force their way through. A policeman stepped in and separated the two sides. The scene ended with all the miners and the police asking each other 'What's it all about?'.

That the children were prepared to leave the question open showed a high level of tolerance of ambiguity, considered to be one of the main aims of teaching social science in primary schools (Lawton, 1971).

That the children had made a marked progress in their understanding of conflict and its ramifications was noticed by all the adults who had watched the plays and had discussed them both in small groups and with the class as a whole. With the benefit of hindsight it was agreed that it might have been better to introduce the concept of conflict by referring to situations with which the children were familiar, such as the home, the playground and the classroom before dealing with industry. However, in the end, the order of presentation did not seem to matter too much as the children themselves introduced material from their own experiences such as the beach ball incident. The sketch about the attack on the supervisor indicated a surprising level of sophistication.

The following diagram might help in furthering children's understanding of conflict; the connections in these children's minds were, however, more tenuous than the diagram suggests.

It would be too much to expect children to be able to construct such a

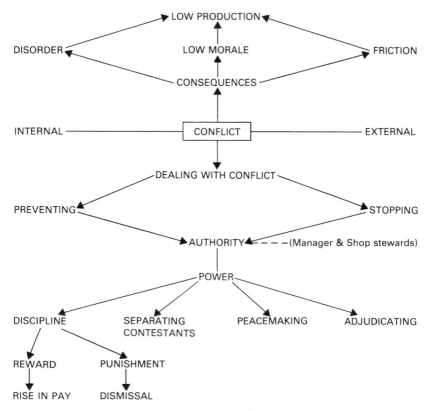

web from cold, but it could be a useful guide for the teacher approaching this topic, and could provide the kind of vocabulary which would enable children eventually to see conflict in a number of different ways and so make their own connections. The teacher could, for instance, gradually construct such a web as she discussed their ideas with them. In this way the children's often monosyllabic suggestions could be developed into a more meaningful structure.

9. Parent–Pupil Discussions

As the project progressed, many of the parents became increasingly involved. Some had helped in the display of children's work, and many had seen the play 'The Ammonite tells his story', and had expressed their support for the changes in teaching method and content made by the class teacher.

It was agreed that the teacher should invite a few parents to join the children's groups for a morning's session. She had already, during the project, discussed the visits and plays in groups of seven or eight mixed age and ability groups. Five parents accepted the invitation and after a short briefing four discussion groups were formed so that there was at least one parent and one teacher-trainee or research worker with each group. The topics to be covered included the play the parents had seen and the nature of the work they were or had been doing. One of the parents was a policeman, two were miners' wives, one of whom was a nurse and the other a former telephone operator. Another was a children's supervisor at the school. It was hoped that the children themselves would raise matters involving conflict.

The group discussions lasted about one and a half hours, interrupted by the mid-morning break of twenty minutes during which time the adults discussed amongst themselves what had transpired. Forty minutes before lunch each group had to report back to the whole class through one of the children elected by the group.

The group discussion proved very lively. Two groups considered the miners' strike with arguments both for and against being freely exchanged. The following extracts not only illustrate something of the range of viewpoints, but also the intensity with which they were held:

Nobody would stop me crossing the picket line, I would hit them.
Q — Why would you hit them?
A — You can't let people push you around or tell you what to do. My Dad punched the councillor who called him a scab. Unions are no good, they are always on strike.

The above is from a boy whose father worked during the strike.

> Q — If you had a problem in work, who do you think you should see
> to help you, the manager or the union?
> A — (Boy) The manager, because he is the boss.
> A — (Girl) The union, because they look after you.
> Q — What about the manager?
> A — He's only interested in making you work and getting profits.

One group discussed the way a 'difficult' child had severely disrupted one of the classes two years ago and how a group of boys had ganged together to deal with him. They admitted that neither the previous class teacher's efforts nor those of the children seemed to work. The child had been equally destructive at his own home and when he visited his classmates' homes. The group did learn that after being placed in a different location away from home and school and after treatment by a psychiatrist, he had improved considerably. However, the class had not been told about his treatment and when he rejoined them, the class, for a brief period, ostracized him. This inevitably led to a regression in his behaviour. It could be argued that if the discussion this group held had taken place at the time of crisis it might have been highly productive in helping to overcome the conflict within the classroom.

Another group, fascinated by the policeman's role, was able to glean from him some of the technical details of the work he performed, such as breathalysing and taking fingerprints. He was somewhat taken aback when one of the children asked him how many people he had arrested who 'had done nothing'.

Throughout the discussions a range of issues related to conflict were couched in what everyone agreed was a sophisticated manner. The parents were particularly surprised and gratified by their children's grasp of complex ideas. There were, however, some lapses from this sophistication. One child, when discussing the miners' dispute, burst out 'It's all Mrs Thatcher's fault!'. The parent insisted that to bring party politics into the discussion was not her intention. Again, one of the spokespersons claimed that her group felt that 'the immigrants are stealing our jobs'!

Some critics of this approach might argue that such statements underline the dangers of freely and openly discussing social problems of this kind. On the other hand, it has to be recognized that even if such matters are not openly aired the children will still pick up and repeat grossly misleading and dangerous simplifications. By dealing with them in a well-structured but relaxed classroom discussion, prejudices and narrow viewpoints can be challenged and placed in broader perspective.

Key Issues

Whilst the children did not at first have a very sophisticated idea of conflict, the adults had some understanding of the concept and gradually, through interaction between adults and children both in the formal classroom situation and in some homes, many of the children seemed to become clearer about the ramifications of the term. Both adults and children learnt how to bring their understandings closer together. That the class periodically split into small face-to-face groups, often, but not always, with one adult to each group, and that the atmosphere was at all times relaxed, helped to stimulate a full spate of ideas from the children was well as from the students who, in more formal circumstances, would have felt less at ease. A sign of this relaxation was the way the children moved ever-closer to each other and to the adults, some even lying on the desks.

An impressive number of adults were, at one time or another, involved in this project. Whilst this involvement was welcomed because it opened up so many vistas on the world of work, it is not an essential element in any one lesson. The class teacher was able to make good progress with her project even when adults other than teachers were not present by giving the children the responsibility of directing their own work in small groups in the classroom or by negotiation with their parents at home. The success of these child-led small group activities was particularly noticeable in their creative activities, including their sketches of the conflict situation.

The teacher had already encouraged the children to become more participative but found that the project considerably accelerated the process. In addition, certain undercurrents of domination and tension were brought to the surface and handled more effectively. At one time the writer noticed a big heavy boy holding a smaller boy in a wrestler's grip, threatening to 'break his neck'. The altercation was nothing more than a joke, but it did enable the writer to indicate how, even as they discussed conflict and violence, it was present in the classroom. The participants as well as the onlookers seemed especially attentive when this matter was raised. It was especially noted that the children associated conflict with violence. Eventually, however, the children started to seek non-violent solutions and towards the end progressed from seeing the solution in terms of individuals to collective action such as trade union action, conferences and social institutions such as ballots. Diagrammatically the increasing complexity can be summarized as follows:

How to Stop a Conflict
Physical Separation (including further violence)

Pacifying Contestants
Resolving an Issue by Tossing a Coin
Full Investigation of the Circumstances
Listening to Each Party's Case Before Deciding
Balloting
Peace Conference

In the relatively short period of the project on conflict (March–May 1986), it was not possible to develop all the potentialities of teaching through this concept. However, enough seemed to have been achieved to form a basis both cognitively and emotionally for further work in a variety of areas including language, history, creative work, social studies and mathematics.

Conclusion

Both Blyth and Ross have argued elsewhere in this book that if children are to develop a critical awareness of society as autonomous learners then an emphasis on concepts is highly desirable. What this work seems to have demonstrated is that this aim of autonomy can only be achieved after a lengthy period of preparation. Gradually the teacher weaned her classes from an undue dependence on her initiatives and directions until they were making progress towards autonomy. Indeed, for the project itself, she made the first moves, but once she had caught the children's interest and confidence she was able to delegate increasing responsibility to them.

Though the teacher had no specific concepts in mind at the start, she had drawn up a skills-based plan for the topic. What she did find was that during a critical stage in the project, when the children might have lost interest, the introduction of the concept of conflict created a new surge of commitment. In fact, at no point could it be said that the interest of the children was lost and the teacher was of the opinion that the project could have continued into the third term. Both teacher and children seemed to grasp more clearly the meaning of what they had been studying about the coal industry. They could see the need for profitability in general but had to face the dilemma that, in the present circumstances, it could only be brought about at the expense of jobs in the mining industry. The teacher did not tell the children what to think; they retained their own differences of opinions but seemed to be able to tolerate views contradicting their own, or possibly their parents' views.

Blyth asks, in his chapter, what is it that is desirable that children should learn about industry in particular and society in general. The answer offered in this work is that what the children learnt is not so important as how they learnt. They were free to share their ideas with both peers and adults. Adults did not surrender their authority as final arbiters on procedures, nor did they belittle the authority they possessed by dint of age or experience. They were prepared, in the parent-pupil discussions, to argue through their own differences, as was clearly shown in the discussion where the former striking miner and the policeman took part.

During this project the teacher deliberately moved from a didactic to a developmental model of teaching (Garwell, in Jamieson, 1984). That this approach seemed to work was evidenced by the surprise expressed by the parents about the ability of the children to talk so freely and well about both abstract and value-laden issues. Not only was their oracy patently improved but their attitude towards written work became significantly more positive. As the teacher had noticed, the children were less fussy and more willing to settle down to the written work connected with the project. She could not claim that the standard of written work had improved but that might be too much to expect after such a short time. 'Notin front of the children' seemed to be replaced by a genuine attempt to build a cooperative learning enterpise.

references

Lawton, D., Campbell, J. and Burkitt, V. (1971) *Social Studies 8–13*, Schools Council Working Paper 73, Methuen Educational.

Garwell, J. (1984) 'The Gwent School to Work Project', in Jamieson, I. (ed.), *'We Make Kettles'; Studying Industry in the Primary School*, Longman.

Chapter 13

Exploring the 'Working Community' Ascension and St Phillips Primary Schools, Salford

Elizabeth Benfield

Introduction

> Why do we need industry in primary education, haven't we
> enough to do with reading, language, number and events like
> Christmas, aren't there enough topics to choose from anyway
> without including areas which demand so much from the teacher
> as well as the child?

These are the sorts of questions that primary school teachers might ask
when first faced with the idea of basing work on industry rather than on
more traditional topic areas such as the Vikings, water, or people who help
us. Those topics have a lot to offer, they are fun, they give the children lots
of knowledge, but how much of this knowledge is relevant to today's
children? There is a place for those sorts of topics but there is also a place
for looking at areas which are directly related to the children's immediate
environment. We live in a society which is industrial and will remain so. It
is the society that primary school children will move into at the end of their
school career. It is a society about which they have some understanding
from snippets in the media, from hearing adults talking about redundancy,
trade unions, wage rises. The information they pick up, however, is in
isolation and, sadly, at the moment, of a negative nature.

There is a vast resource around us which is largely untapped, the
world of industry, the world of people working. It seems wrong not to use
this resource to introduce children to the positive side of work, to the idea
of pride in a product or service, responsibility to one's self and one's
workmates, to something more than 'work is what you get paid for'. Of
course, the negative side is there now more than ever, but surely it is
selling children short not to try to develop something more than an
automatic expectation of unemployment.

To some people, teachers and people in industry, primary school children may seem too young to be exploring such ideas. Shouldn't they still be playing kings and queens, or writing 'a day in the life of a spaceman'? Of course, they still need imaginative play situations, a fantasy element in their lives, inner city children perhaps more than most.

Primary age children have a curiosity and openness about almost everything, but these are qualities which often get submerged in the pressures of an examination-orientated secondary curriculum. Cynicism about work and even life in general sets in very early; there is a feeling among people concerned with industry-based education that there is much value to be found in introducing an industrial element into primary school education. The aim is to introduce children to the working world and economic concepts at an age when their minds are enquiring and open.

Ascension Primary School: Links with Agecroft Colliery

From the first planning of this project for the top infant children at Ascension Primary School, one big drawback was obvious: British Coal would not allow any children, let alone 6 and 7-year-olds on any part of the colliery site. At first this seemed a good reason for looking elsewhere for an industry-based project. The children would not be able to benefit from experiencing the real work situation and meeting the people who worked there. The colliery, together with the Agecroft Power Station however, are such landmarks to the children and the subject of coal such a rich one that it was decided to go ahead. The power station and the colliery are interdependent in that much of the colliery's coal goes over the road on a conveyor belt to the power station.

Children's Images of the Coal Industry

The project was developed on one day a week with the class divided into two groups. It was decided to begin with where the coal came from and the history of mining. The project would concentrate on the industry today and Agecroft Colliery in particular. A visit to the Buile Hill Museum of Mining was arranged and the personnel manager from the colliery visited the school with some of his staff.

Although most of the children knew what coal was, very few of them had seen any and no one had an open fire at home. It was interesting to see that they had nearly all picked up Agecroft Colliery and the coal industry generally in the media coverage of the previous summer's miners' dispute.

They had no clear ideas about coal or miners beyond, 'they're all dead dirty, miss!'

The idea of jobs in the coal industry was introduced with particular questions about what they would be like, what they knew about the nature of miners' work and what further information they would like to collect. The pupils played charades, drew pictures and thought of some questions; this they found difficult. It was not an activity with which the teacher was happy; the time restriction made it an isolated activity and a small input every day would have been much better to get them used to thinking and talking about the work. Some children showed confidence and maturity, but many did not have the social skills needed to work in pairs or groups. This idea, however, was to lead to the experience of interviewing, an area of industry work which might well prove to be generally problematical, especially with younger children and certainly with inner-city children.

After the brief session on the early days of mining, the days of bell pits and women and children working underground, the pupils began to look at 'our mine', Agecroft Colliery. The problem of not being able to go on to the actual mine premises was partly overcome by finding a playing field and a piece of wild ground which overlooked the colliery and power station complex. Because of the vantage point the children could see each part of the colliery in the landscape, the River Irwell which supplied its water, and the cluster of houses which had grown up around the pit. The connection between the colliery and the power station was also clear; they could see and hear the conveyor belt carrying the coal over the road and the enormous wagons carrying the residue away from the power station.

Back in school the pencil drawings were transferred on to sugar paper in charcoal. They were surprisingly detailed and several were extremely mature. The trip was so successful that a second visit was made to look at the entrance where the size of the building was even more apparent. Work on 'winning the coal' was now more meaningful to the children and they began to use technical language as a matter of course. The children also absorbed a great deal of quite complicated detail and began to pick up on references to coal and miners in the media. Safety and the responsibility of each man to the others with whom he was working were also discussed. The children wrote stories about mine rescues and experimented with different techniques, rubbings, wax-resist scratch pictures, to produce atmospheric drawings and paintings.

As the end of the project grew closer the pupils began to look beyond the colliery to what the coal is used for. In this situation it meant changing the coal into electricity, which was a difficult concept tackled with only the more-able children. The children very quickly grasped the basic principle behind the process, drawing parallels from their own experience, for instance, 'that turbine's like a windmill really, but not wind, steam instead'. Their grasp of the language involved was quite impressive.

The Visits

A visit in October to the classroom by the personnel manager of Agecroft Colliery brought a real-life dimension to the work. He brought with him his training officer fully kitted out for working underground and so the children were able to talk to people who really knew what it was like to work in that environment. Although a visit to the colliery itself was out of the question, a trip to the Museum of Mining in Buile Hill Park was arranged. This is not a conventional museum for it has a reconstruction of underground workings which are approached through pit head buildings, the manager's office, the blacksmith's shop and the lamp room. The children were taken in two groups, each group seeing first a film which showed the progression of the industry, especially the conditions for miners during the past fifty years. The children then went underground and it was impressive to see the way in which the children applied the knowledge they had taken in at school to the practical situation. They named things correctly and worked out how machinery operated. Although there could not be a substitute for the real thing, this ran it a very close second.

Eight children were taken to Agecroft Power Station. It was a first for all concerned; the manager of the power station had never had such young children on the premises before and certainly none of the teachers had visited such a place. The children were overwhelmed by the size, noise and activity. The small size of the groups meant that the children could see what was going on and hear their guide's explanation, and yet they were very controlled, an important factor in such a potentially hazardous situation. The children clambered up and down iron staircases, saw the pulverizing mills, the control room, the turbines and the cooling towers. Best of all for the children was the furnace. Peering through an inspection hatch they saw the coal dust blowing in and igniting instantaneously at 2000 degrees centigrade. The huge volume of materials involved in the process meant little to them, but the roaring blaze and the vibration of machinery made a vivid impact. As Phillip said on the way home, 'You'd never think it, miss, when you turn on the stove'.

The last visit was also unusual for infants, possibly even frowned-upon by some people, but it served its purpose. The whole class went across to Broughton High School where they spent the morning in one of the science laboratories. The exercise was concerned with burning — in other words, what happens to coal when it is burnt in different forms. Working in groups of three, the children learned how to control the Bunsen burners and heated the coal in trays on tripods and asbestos mats. They observed closely and found things to comment on at each stage of the experiment. The smell of the burning coal and the taste left in their mouths as they went back to school was a vivid example of what Salford would have been like before anti-pollution measures were taken. This activity was not one which could have been undertaken so successfully in school. The fierce heat of the Bunsens was needed to ignite the coal quickly for the children to see the changes taking place.

St Phillips School: The Textiles Project

The textile industry seemed an obvious place to look for industry-based work with the 4th-year junior class at St Phillips. For many years, Salford was the centre of the textile industry and though its prominence has long since faded, there still remain many links with that industry, although nowadays the emphasis is on the garments side. Street names such as Flax, Cotton and Silk recall the past, but instead of weaving sheds they are now filled with small businesses, many of them still connected with textiles. Many children in the area have parents, especially mothers, who work as machinists or cutters, and yet the children are largely unaware of the industry's connections, past or present, with their immediate envirornment.

The Plan

The class teacher was enthusiastic about the idea of industry work, though she had not considered a project specifically linked to industry before. Initially it was decided to divide the class into two groups to tackle the historical background and situation today, using J. Milom, a company producing karate and judo clothing as the main industry connection. The historical side was considered too interesting and relevant to the area to miss out. J. Milom itself is situated in an old mill building, but the intention was to emphasize the industry as it is today. The link with the industry lent itself to art and craft work on a large scale as well as to science activities. The initial outline soon changed however, after a chance social meeting with an importer landed the teachers with a massive supply of fabric samples.

    The first response was to use this for collage and weaving, but while the children were sorting through the boxes, discovering the variety of weights, colours and textures of the samples, they began discussing what the fabric might be used for. Gradually the idea of using the fabric to produce an article began to emerge and B & B Textiles was underway.

Integrating the Experiences within the Classroom

The early weeks of the project were taken up with sketching, trips to look at the remnants of mills along the River Irwell and trips to the local history library to read contemporary accounts of the lives of the mill workers and their families and to see old photographs of the area as it was. Time was spent discussing work situations, what jobs they would like to do, what they expected them to be like, what jobs their parents did, or in many cases used to do before becoming unemployed. This led into interviewing as a means of finding out about peoples' jobs and the children practised their skills on each other and others in and around the school, such as the headteacher, the rector and the caretaker. They tried note-taking and recording, which were difficult tasks; children do not question constructively very often, but the teachers were anxious that they didn't waste the contact time with industry at Milom's by irrelevant remarks. In the event their own involvement in production line work made their questioning in the industrial situation both pertinent and revealing.

They looked at how modern fabrics had developed and labels were read to discover how they were constructed. The children began weaving and collage, delighting in the range of effects they could get using the fabrics they had been given. The simulation of a production line had not been considered at the outset of the work, but as the children began to hazard guesses as to whether a piece of fabric would be big enough for a skirt, or the right type for handkerchiefs, the possibility of creating a factory situation in the classroom began to come out.

Simulating a Production Line

The decisions about what could be made and how, were all taken on the basis of class discussions. At first these were chaotic, but gradually as they realized the necessity for giving each other time to speak without interruption, the confused ideas became clarified and decisions were taken. The discussion which led up to the choice of product was prolonged and rambling, beginning with ambitious rag dolls and dresses and including handkerchiefs and towels, before finally choosing bags. All the talk was useful, as it pushed the children into discussing things like suitability and texture as well as the look of the thing; for instance, would chiffon make a handkerchief? The decision was made to make drawstring-top bags of various sizes and fabrics which could be used for pumps, pencils, purses or anything else that could fit in them. These were chosen because they were simple and yet involved several processes before completion. None of the children had used a sewing machine, however, and few had any needle-work skills.

A second product was planned, rag books for infants. The suggestion came from a reticent member of the class who had noticed that several batches of fabric had letters, animals, and simple drawings on them. Her idea was to link different batches together with colours, for example, a red book with sections of the red fabrics which had a simple design on them which someone could talk about to the child. This suggestion illustrates one of the most interesting and potentially rewarding aspects of education industry work; that is the opportunity for the generally non-achieving child to shine. When asked to think about a new situation outside the regular school experience, she applied a skill which had not manifested itself before.

There were other examples of children unexpectedly displaying hidden talents in the project. Having established what was to be made, the class moved on to who was to do what. Auditions were held for machining, so that everyone who wanted to had a turn. It was a slow business and the needle broke, the machine became unthreaded, the seams were wobbly, until Jason had a turn. He was a boy of very limited academic ability who had worked hard at getting a 'troublemaker' label. He sat down at the machine and produced seam after seam absolutely straight, perfect in every detail. When it came to choosing jobs, the class was unanimous: Jason must be the chief machinist. For perhaps the first time in his school career he was a total success.

Jenny became the second machinist and the children regarded these as the glamour posts and once they were settled, moved on to the next most desirable, that of manager and tea lady. Equal opportunities changed this to tea person very quickly and David was in charge of milk and crisps at playtime. Other jobs were similarly allocated: designer, cutter, threader, finisher, quality controller, packer, machine mechanic and cleaner, as well as advertising and pricing, and selling, were all taken on. Stuart suggested someone to complain to if you weren't happy, so a session was spent discussing the trade union movement and Jeanette became the union official.

The children had decided to aim at the market close to home, the pupils at the school and the Christmas Fair. Although the group had acquired the fabrics, it still needed cotton, card, and ribbon to thread through the tops of the bags, as well as bags in which to pack the finished product. The children considered bringing in money themselves but the idea of a loan to set up a business was introduced to them and they decided to apply to the headteacher for a loan from the school funds. This involved the writing of a formal letter to explain the intention of the company and ask for an appointment. The loan was duly obtained and four children went into the town to buy thread and any other items they thought would be needed. The class had decided on 'B & B Textiles' as the company name and so production began. Of course, there were many snags and more disagreements. Jeanette, the union official, was run off her feet. But things settled down, bags were made, checked, packed and sold. The advertising made sure of a high profile in the school.

Support of the Work through Industrial Visits

It was possible for all the class to visit two factories and the children were split into two groups for each visit. The first was to J. Milom, situated on the banks of the River Irwell in an old mill whose buildings were grouped around a cobbled yard. This visit gave the children something of the feel of earlier working conditions, while introducing them to a place producing a very contemporary article: karate and judo gear. Their interest was caught from the start and the staff were exceptionally tolerant and good natured with the children. They had never had primary children visit before, although secondary careers-linked visits were common. The children's enthusiasm was infectious as they wandered all over the manufacturing floor and were allowed to try out different machines and processes. Worries about interviewing proved groundless as they explained 'their factory' to the staff and questioned them on their work.

The same enthusiasm and response came from the staff in the second work visit, to A & B Cutting Services Limited who also had never had children of this age before. They seemed to enjoy the experience as much as the children and were very willing to repeat the experience.

Although the production line was a new way of working for the children and succeeded in capturing their enthusiasm and interest, it was the visits to actual work situations and the contact with people making their living in the industry which put flesh on the bones of the project.

Other Work

Although the setting up and working through of the production line was the largest part of the project, it did not, of course, occupy all the children for the whole of the time. While things got underway and during the slack moments there was time for research into the historical side of the industry and into modern manufacturing techniques. The children found out about the history of clothes and the properties and production of a whole range of yarns, both natural and man-made. They carried out experiments to test different fabrics for waterproofing, windproofing and fireproofing, and also tested the strength of different fibres. They looked at different clothing for different jobs; for example, safety gloves, surgical masks, plastic macs and a fireman's uniform. Towards the end of the project, contact was made in a different context with the local branch of the TSB. On hearing about the work, they offered advice on accounting and one of their staff came to the school and helped the children responsible for the financial side of the business set out and keep their accounts. She also introduced ideas which the class had not considered; for instance, how much time the children spent on each item in relation to the price. The children later visited the bank in small groups to see how it was run and to meet the people involved.

Some Conclusions

It is easy to be put off initially by the term 'industry', perhaps the world of work is a better expression. It overcomes the immediate reaction of many, if not most, people that industry is factory chimneys, production lines, and heavy machinery. It is the first hurdle to overcome when trying to interest people, especially teachers, in industry-linked work. It is important to clear this hurdle as the enthusiasm and involvement of the teacher are vital, partly because of the out-of-school time they will inevitably have to put in, but also because of the need to transfer this to the children. This applies to most, if not all, school work but especially so to industry work. Almost the biggest benefit of the work is the children's enthusiasm and insatiable curiosity. It is an opportunity for teacher and children to learn together and it seems only fair that their interest level should be equal.

One of the major problems encountered was that of time. To get the most benefit out of industry-education, the teacher has to put in a good deal of work, both in the setting up of contacts and visits and in the amount of time that is spent on the school day. Another aspect of this time problem relates to the opportunity for cross-curricular work, for instance, mathematics, science and craft. Some areas in the projects were touched on but by no means exhausted, another reason why the teacher considering industry work needs to think widely about the curricular context.

Talking about the manufacturing processes and economic concepts involved in industry and introducing oral and observation skills to the children is not straightforward and should not be rushed. A little and often is a useful guide to introducing these new ideas and skills to the children. Industry work so often throws up the unexpected opportunity and the teacher needs to seize the chance as it arises.

Care is needed in choosing the industry. The big company is not always the best choice for children. It is worth spending time wandering around the locality to see what might be available before approaching companies. Service industries should not be overlooked. The passions and fashions of children can give useful pointers, for instance, pop records or roller boots. If the teacher thinks widely, the choices are endless.

A very positive benefit from industry work is the learning resulting from it. The children are being exposed to the different skills that experiential learning offers. The setting up of a production line, the solving of problems relating to industry or even the trying-out of techniques in factories are very different learning experiences to those gained by just reading a book or watching a video. There is also the social aspect to consider, meeting and talking to adults, welcoming them into the classroom and being welcomed in return to their workplace. These are valuable experiences for any child, particularly those of the inner city.

The teacher coming new to industry work may be surprised, or even alarmed by the sort of work produced by the children. It can vary widely, depending on the activities developed. For example, the work on textiles at St Phillips produced a minimal amount of written work but a great deal of discussion and practical work. The Agecroft Colliery project on the other hand, had a strong drawing element.

The use of industry in education is still developing — there are many issues to be considered and problems to be resolved. What age is right to begin, do you or don't you introduce trade union studies, how will parents react? For industrialists and trade unionists working with such groups, the experience has also been valuable. They have appreciated more readily the issues and problems involved in bringing industry to the classroom, or in extending pupils' and teachers' views of the classroom to include industry and commerce. On some occasions the groups have become a forum for the discussion of the broader educational issues facing schools, such as the role of assessment, of profiling pupil performance and of in-service provision for teachers.

Chapter 14

The Manor School Municipal Industries Project
Manor Primary School, Newham

Ciaran Clerkin

Introduction

Manor, a mixed junior and infant school situated in a social priority area of the east London Borough of Newham, caters for 240 full-time pupils. A further 60 are part-time nursery pupils. In the summer term of 1985, the school mounted a small industry project in association with Newham Municipal Industries, a local authority workshop manufacturing furniture on a commercial basis. The workshop employs 40 workers, most of whom are blind or partially-sighted, and 11 managerial and supervisory staff.

Origins of the Project

The initial stimulus for the project came from the head's attendance at the Primary and Middle Schools Industry conference at Edge Hill College in April, 1985. Although he had long recognized the value of children's learning being closely related to their own local community, the conference provided a significant opportunity to examine the specific aims and objectives of schools-industry work for 5–13 year-olds. As well as case studies of practice presented by teachers and industrialists to illustrate industry's contribution to education, time spent at the conference on games, simulations and role-play exercises helped to focus attention on the potential for development in a primary school. Equally important were the sessions where small groups worked on ideas for class projects, using industry as a resource.

On reflection, what was probably most useful was the time spent deliberating the educational purpose of this kind of work in school, together with the experience of examining the management of industry schemes in the classroom. It began to be obvious that far from being something grafted on to the primary curriculum, industry education could become a substantial component of the whole curriculum, capable of being consistently developed throughout the primary years. As children today have to grow up in a rapidly changing industrial society, such an approach could clearly offer an invaluable way of learning about technological achievement as well as other concepts linked to the world of work.

The school had in the past made visits to local industries, the local fruit market, a shopping precinct and a timber yard. This work had been carried out within the context of project work and the data gathered in such things as shopping surveys and customer and employer interviews was the stimulus for further work in the classroom. Occasionally, some of the people from the organizations came into the school to help the children develop particular elements of the topic.

Getting Started — Or First Find Your Local Industry!

Before discussing a potential school project in any detail with the staff, the head began to look around for a suitable industrial link, rooted, if possible, in the children's own environment. A variety of options were considered, both in the manufacturing and service sectors, including the local building society with whom the school already ran a savings scheme.

Quite by chance, at that time the school was ordering some new units of furniture from the Blind Workshops, as they are known locally. The manager of the workshops was known to the head and a meeting between the two, at the factory, was arranged to outline some ideas. Although the manager was not entirely enthusiastic at first about the relevance of primary school pupils visiting a factory, he was prepared to give the idea a try, providing certain assurances were forthcoming, particularly about behaviour.

During the first meeting the head also learnt a great deal from the manager about the history and development of the factory from the early days. Until the mid-1960s the workers produced baskets, brushes and mattresses in dreary surroundings, using archaic methods. Today, thanks mainly to the vision and pioneering zeal of the present manager, the factory produces high quality, up-to-date products at competitive prices using sophisticated industrial techniques.

Careful records of the factory's development had been kept over the years and the manager kindly loaned many interesting documents, including annual reports, photographs and press cuttings. Although there was sufficient for a full-scale social studies' programme on another occasion, this material provided a worthwhile introduction to the project later in the term. Discussion also centred on ideas to help the children become more aware of the range of products which Newham Municipal Industries (NMI) manufactured and which might be found in their own homes or at school. A visit by the children to the workshop might, it was felt, help them to appreciate more fully the role that visually handicapped people play in industry, given adequate training and support.

Discussing the Project with the Teachers

The head was of the opinion that, where possible, curriculum innovation should normally affect a range of staff across a school in the interests of balance and continuity. However, it seemed sensible on this occasion to concentrate attention on a few staff to try and get something started.

Two experienced teachers, whose approach to curriculum development already reflected the attitudes which would be required once a project got under way, were chosen to launch the project. The head believed that it was important to have teachers capable of looking beyond the immediate environment of the school for stimulating learning experiences. He also thought it was necessary for them to be sensitive to the traditions and authority structures in another organization, and so considered interpersonal skills very important. One was a full-time teacher in her third year of teaching in charge of a mixed-ability class of 10-year-olds. The other was a member of the authority's 'English as a Second Language' team based at the school for a term. She had been working with the class teacher for about two half-days per week, mainly on developing a relevant programme for ethnic minority pupils.

The two staff were initially rather wary of the idea, particularly as they felt unsure about what the children would gain from such work. There was also a concern about implementing someone else's, in this case the head's, ideas and meeting expectations. The head had no desire to leave the teachers with the impression that they were being 'told to do the project'; it was more a question of convincing them that it could contribute significantly to the children's and teachers' learning about industry and about their own skills. After discussions with the head, however, both approached the project with enthusiasm.

The head met both staff and they discussed the project during the latter half of the summer term. The head was prepared to support the teachers by preparing background information, arranging meetings at the factory and co-ordinating the necessary release-time to plan and undertake the visits. He also identified the following as the overall aims of a schools-industry project:

To encourage collaboration between industry and teachers on ideas and teaching approaches which will help children to gain a better understanding and appreciation of work.

For industry and schools to develop a better understanding of each others' organizations.

For industry and schools to explore the ways in which each others's structures and organization can best accommodate the aims of the projects.

The staff accepted the proposal and agreed to run the project.

The Teachers' Plan

The staff visited the factory in order to familiarize themselves with the organization and draw up a programme which was acceptable both to themselves and the manager. They decided to set aside a block of time each Friday morning for four to five weeks to be devoted to activities connected with the project. They agreed to use a combination of team teaching with the whole class as well as group and individual assignments. Three broad aims were identified:

To provide a link between the school and local industry.

To give the children an introduction to the world of work in a factory.

To increase the children's awareness and understanding of handicapped people.

Preparing the Children

To introduce the project the teachers first talked to the children, a class of 10-year-olds, about being blind. Although most of the later discussion would be focussed on work, they felt it was important that the children should relate to the people they would be meeting as normal adults doing worthwhile jobs. The class discussion indicated a high degree of sensitivity about blindness. A considerable number actually knew a relative or friend who was blind or partially-sighted. One child, for example, was able to share his experience of playing games specially made for the blind with his cousin. No doubt due to the proximity of the workshops, most pupils had also seen blind people travelling to and from work on buses and trains.

A display of books about guide dogs and Braille was organized by the staff and various experiments were undertaken to help the children appreciate more fully the difficulties blind people face. The history of the workshops was also discussed, with some time being devoted to examining photo-copies of the historical documents lent to the school by the factory manager.

The Visits

The class was split into three groups for the three consecutive Friday morning visits with each one accompanied by a teacher. The group was shown around by a supervisor and given an opportunity to see the different stages of production. The children asked questions, took photographs and talked to the workers individually both about their work as well as their personal lives.

During one of the visits, the group interviewed three of the workers, including the only woman in the factory, all of whom also happened to be particularly active members of their union. This was an opportunity to raise a variety of issues which had featured in previous classroom discussions. The children asked them about their work and whether it remained the same each day. They questioned them about the unions in the factory and what happened if there was a dispute. Wages and bonuses were also discussed, but no direct question was put to a worker about how much he or she earned. The children also asked why there were so few women working in the factory.

Within the borough of Newham equality of opportunity had been treated as a very important issue and the pupils were well aware of the various ways it affected people's lives. It was significant, therefore, that they took up the subject in the workplace. They also looked at the various ways in which health and safety measures were implemented for the handicapped workers.

A high spot on each occasion, of course, was a trip to the kennels to meet the dogs. This experience led to further discussion with the owners and produced a few useful column inches of copy for the school magazine as well as a number of attractive photographs.

Follow-up Work

The visits were followed up with discussion, writing and other language work together with art, craft and science. As well as creative writing, the pupils used drama and role play to re-create some of the situations they had witnessed in the factory, particularly the idea of conflict at work. The visits helped the children with other related skills such as note-taking, interviewing and presenting. They interviewed the head, for instance, about his choice of the workshop for purchasing school furniture, as illustrated in the following brief extract:

How many units are there in school?
I don't know exactly. There are units in the two staffrooms, the secretary's room, and some in the nursery. There are some in the two community rooms also. So you will have to count them!
(Answer after counting — 29)

Why do you buy from NMI instead of MFI?
Well, I buy from NMI for these reasons. Firstly, they are better value for money. Secondly, because they are made by disabled or handicapped people.

Do you know anyone else who buys the kitchen cabinets?
Yes, I do. I know lots of people locally who buy them for their own houses. In the houses being modernized across the road from the school all of the new kitchens have been fitted with NMI cabinets.

Are you pleased with the product?
Extremely pleased. I think they look smart. The drawers slide in easily. The tops are not difficult to clean and the colour is very attractive.

The pupils also surveyed the amount of NMI furniture in the school, in their homes and in a new housing development next to the school. They also tried to find out more about the tools used in the factory. Experiments were conducted to experience what it was like to carry out a task without using their sight.

At the same time, elsewhere in the school, another group was working on an issue of 'Manor News', a half-termly bulletin for parents and governors. It seemed obvious that the NMI project could well be presented as a 'special edition' of this journal, a technique used on previous occasions to provide an account of such things as school journeys. The idea was discussed with the staff, both of whom found it an attractive proposition which they felt would help structure future classroom activities. Later, pupils were advised about the intention to publish.

The prospect of getting into print provided considerable motivation and enthusiasm among the children which was useful as the end of term approached. To ensure standards were kept as high as possible, it was agreed that first and second drafts would be submitted and discussed with the teachers. The children chose to work mainly in pairs, researching, writing and doing illustrations on topics which particularly interested them under the following headings:

— History of the workshops
— The visits
— Production
— Special features on the workers
— Stories about blind people

The following extract was produced for the magazine:

The History of The Newham Municipal Industries and its Workforce

The workshops were officially opened on 11th April 1938 by the Mayor of West Ham. A bronze plaque was unveiled.

At that time there were boot-repairing, mat-making, broom- and brush-making departments.

Mr Hudson took over as manager in 1969, made the factory more modern and put lights in.

He changed the products to kitchen units about 13 years ago and the name was changed from Blind Workshops to Newham Municipal Industries.

Since then the Industries have got more and more orders and they are now very successful.

There are 36 workers in the Industries, most of the workers are blind but they have special tools to help them. There is only one lady worker in the factory. Her job is putting in screws in the hinges of the cupboards.

On the ground floor a worker cuts the wood into pieces with a special machine. Then the pieces of wood are taken upstairs to the Assembly room. Other workers put the cupboards together. They all do different things.

Some workers travel a long way to get to work. They come by train or bus. At least five workers have guide dogs to help them.

The factory is specially designed for handicapped workers who cannot work anywhere else.

The printing of the special edition of 'Manor News' did not go exactly as planned. The children could have participated more fully in the production at the final stages. Due to unforeseen technical and economic difficulties, some work had to be omitted at the last minute, including drawings and photographs taken by the children. It was to their credit, however, that despite the uncertainty about a publication date, the children maintained an interest and enthusiasm about the project until the magazine eventually arrived in November! As a result of this initial learning experience, the children played a much more active part in subsequent editions, fulfilling the roles of sub-editors, lay-out and design specialists, collators and distributors.

Outcomes

What the Children Learnt

While it is not easy to measure the effects of a 'one-off' activity of the kind described in this chapter against any conventional yard-stick, the commitment of both pupils and staff together with the examples of work in the school magazine indicate a significant level of achievement. From their own observation and recording the children clearly made considerable progress towards a fuller appreciation of the complex relationships within an industrial organization.

They developed, for instance, a greater understanding of the manufacturing process. They saw the raw materials arrive, saw them transported to the appropriate parts of the factory by fork-lift truck, observed various stages of the manufacturing of the furniture, and finally witnessed the products being dispatched. Some knowledge of the managerial structure of a small industry was gained by interviewing the manager, the charge hand and three of the workers. In the case of the charge hand, the children discovered how the training and supervision of handicapped workers was carried out. They acquired insights into the division of labour and work-patterns in a factory, into the marketing and distribution of goods and learnt something about production costs, including wholesale and retail prices. Some information on costings and price was also given to the children by the manager. Observing blind people doing demanding jobs emphasized the importance of perseverance to achieve good results.

A significant improvement in social skills was noted by the teachers because of the need to relate positively to adults in a setting outside the school environment. This was reflected in the children's general behaviour as well as their attitude to school work across the curriculum.

The teachers noted a greater willingness on the part of the children to work more cooperatively, in particular in discussing their work with one another as well as with the teacher. There were signs of greater tolerance of each other's attitudes and idiosyncracies, something which the teachers felt was significant, since normally this was something the children did not find easy to handle. The skill of negotiation in relation to tasks and deadlines also carried over into the relationship between the children and the teachers.

The examples of children's written work in the magazine indicate the development of a more realistic awareness of blind people who, despite their handicap, can take up skilled work, given adequate support and training. They also show how much the pupils gained from direct experience together with careful observation.

By way of showing their appreciation to the people they met at the workshops, the children organized a collection of milk bottle tops, ring-pulls and stamps. These were used to raise money towards the purchase of a guide dog for the blind. A class assembly, based on the topic, was also prepared. As well as generating a sense of prestige and self-esteem, this meant the children could share their work with the rest of the school in an interesting way.

In the classroom, the importance of appraising each other's work was realized more fully, bearing in mind that it would be read in magazine form by a wide audience, including the workers in a special Braille edition. Furthermore, the children gained considerable practice in collaborative discussion and writing because they were dealing with live issues which genuinely interested and concerned them.

What the Teachers Learnt

Although they were already aware that important learning can take place out of school, neither teacher had previously considered that a local industry could provide such a wealth of learning resources for primary pupils. Despite the fact that they were initially rather unsure of what was expected, the success of the visits together with the earnest way in which the children tackled their work was most encouraging and rewarding.

Both teachers were pleasantly surprised at the degree of interest the children took in the daily work and life-style of blind people together with the depth of genuine discussion this engendered in the classroom. They also appreciated more fully the importance of children writing for a purpose about their own experience in order to achieve motivation and commitment. In their own words:

> We were stimulated by the attitude of the class, both towards the topic and their work within it. The project developed a common bond of interest and concern among the children. It created an enjoyable learning environment in which we were able to pursue a variety of other educational aims across the curriculum with less-able as well as average and more gifted pupils.

Reflections

Curriculum development depends for its success on a variety of factors: the headteacher's encouragement and managerial skill, the staff's capacity for change, efficient organization and planning and the support of agencies external to the school. Quantifiable improvement in teaching and learning is of necessity a gradual process to be measured in years rather than months. But in the short-term, for the headteacher supporting new initiatives, the problem remains of how to sustain and improve what has been achieved in a pilot scheme.

The approach to curriculum development adopted during the term offers a worthwhile model for further work of this kind. Moreover, the process involved in compiling this case study has in itself created a non-threatening point of departure for an analysis of the key elements of school/industry links. It has helped staff to stand back a little from the pressures of day-to-day events in order to tease out judgements about problematic situations which arose during the activity. At the very least, this experience should be of benefit in ensuring that future contacts between the school and industrial concerns are developed in a more systematic way.

Chapter 15

The Staffordshire/Shell UK Project
An Alternative Model for School–
Industry Cooperation

Roger Carter

Much attention within SCIP has centred rightly upon the problems and possibilities of establishing contact between individual schools and particular industries or industrialists, usually within a local area. The Staffordshire/Shell UK Project offers a different model for school–industry cooperation which might be seen as providing an additional strategy to achieve the same aim of developing in children an awareness of industrial society in its widest sense. It is an example of collaboration between a Local Education Authority and a major company.

Staffordshire LEA has long held a commitment to the development of industrial awareness in its children. Through the school-industry liaison officer there have been a number of curriculum initiatives in recent years. Currently the authority is a significant participant in the Geography, Schools and Industry Project, which is jointly sponsored by industrialists and by the Geographical Association. Additionally, there was an early involvement in the TVEI initiative in which Staffordshire was one of the pilot authorities. Work on the SCIP Project is also well advanced in the county.

In its turn, Shell UK has a long record of liaison with schools and the world of education. For over thirty years it has provided an education service which has distributed free educational materials to schools. Its support for the Goldsmith's Industrial Fellowship, and sponsorship of a wide range of educational initiatives, and projects such as SCIP, all bear witness to the level of the company's commitment in this sphere. The Goldsmith's Industrial Fellow was to play a big role in the development of the project.

The collaboration between the authority and Shell UK arose because of Shell's projected programme of onshore drilling which took the company to a number of Staffordshire sites during the summer of 1984. Here was an opportunity too good to miss!

Early discussions considered using this opportunity to involve local schools in the production of a teaching pack based on onshore oil exploration designed for the 14+ age range. However, after some deliberation, and taking into account the time of the year, the school-industry liaison officer expressed a stronger interest in a project aimed at the middle years of schooling, in particular the top junior age range. It was also thought important that the project covered as many areas of the curriculum as possible. In March 1984 a meeting was set up to establish the aims of the project and a strategy for developing it. The four aims reflected both the separate and the shared aspirations of the two parties.

Aims:

1. To develop an approach to the study of onshore oil exploration as a vehicle for introducing children to:
   (i) the role of major companies like Shell UK in creating wealth;
   (ii) the concern of such companies to protect the environment;
   (iii) the technology of the onshore oil industry.
2. To assist the development of appropriate levels of industrial awareness among children at the primary stage by proceeding from the specific to the general, from the familiar to the unknown, and from the concrete to the abstract, using at every stage active rather than passive approaches to learning.
3. To demonstrate how the primary curriculum can be enriched by developing teaching materials, experiential learning, and adults other than teachers, in conjunction with a major oil company.
4. To identify and introduce through such materials, a range of ideas, skills and attitudes appropriate to the age and ability of the children.

Apart from the intentions for the children, teachers and schools directly involved in the work, the end product would be a teaching pack, based upon direct experiences, which would be distributed through an in-service programme throughout the county and beyond. Shell UK would fund the programme, and teachers in the contributing schools would be withdrawn from the schools at certain points to produce the materials.

The timescale was to prove difficult because the company would only be operating in the area for a few weeks. The planning strategy involved:

1. identifying six primary schools in the vicinity of the rig site, and then classes and teachers within these schools who would be part of the project (most children involved were in the 9–11 age range);

2. briefing the teachers as to the process of onshore drilling and providing for them an on-site visit;
3. encouraging teachers to identify broad areas of classroom development which they would pursue, and providing them with current Shell UK materials for them to use and evaluate;
4. developing project work in the clasroom;
5. evaluating the range of work in order to identify good practice that is transferable and extracting successful teaching materials;
6. producing the kit;
7. disseminating through an in-service programme.

Most of the problems relating to this strategy resulted from the very short time available to push the programme through.

The drilling site was seen as the centre-piece of the project. A visit to the site was arranged for the project teachers, which produced some very excited reactions, and plans were put in train for visits by the children. There was some apprehension amongst company staff about these visits but a meeting of the SILO and a representative of Shell UK Exploration and Production went some way towards allaying these misgivings. It was agreed that children would visit the site in small groups of about fourteen, accompanied by two teachers and the SILO or Goldsmith's Fellow where possible. The high proportion of adults to youngsters was desirable for safety reasons, though not always easy to arrange in practice, and to allow evaluation of the visits. Each group was subdivided into two parties during the visit which lasted about an hour.

Children were supplied with diagrams of a drill site layout, a rotary drill rig and an exploration well to help with preparations for the visit by the teacher concerned and with identification of site features during the visit itself. The SILO arranged transportation of the children, who wore old clothes and wellington boots, the company providing safety helmets. One other requirement was that the SILO would have to ring the tool-pusher, the Shell employee in charge of the site, immediately before each visit to obtain his consent for the visit to proceed. The possibility of last-minute cancellations was always there, but never actually happened.

The original intention was to arrange for the visits to take place as quickly as possible in order to provide an exciting start to work on the project. In fact, the first visits took place at the end of May and two visits per week became the norm. The programme of visits was not completed, therefore, until mid-July. Fortnightly changes of personnel on the site provided an added complication, requiring negotiation of the schedule of visits at regular intervals. Some schools delayed work on the project whilst waiting for their visit to take place, creating further pressures on the timetable.

Nonetheless, all 150 pupils visited the site eventually and there was no denying the impact of this experience on these young people. While they could not grasp a lot of the technicalities of the drilling process, they could understand the broad sweep of what was involved. The immediacy of the experience, the power of the images it provided had a profound impact on them. This was evidenced, for instance, by a desire to know what happened in the weeks succeeding their visit, a desire expressed by more than one group of children. Some children produced powerful creative writing as a result of their visit; many parents spoke to their child's teacher of the impact of the visit on their son or daughter.

What helped to make the visits successful in terms of children achieving an understanding of the processes of onshore drilling was careful briefing before the visit and debriefing afterwards. The teachers' visit to the site was obviously important here. There was also a feeling that the later the visit in terms of the project timetable, the more successful it was. This can be accounted for in two ways:

1. by the time of the later visits, pupils had been working on the topic of oil in a variety of ways for some weeks;
2. the handling of the visits by site staff was better towards the end of the project than at the beginning.

Site staff were, in fact, very willing to help but, inevitably, they were tentative in their approach to the early visits. The staff who conducted the final visit in the series were noticeably more relaxed and confident in their dealings with the children. This visit lasted an hour and a half as opposed to an hour for the early visits; children were given small samples of drilling mud; a box of rock samples was produced for the children to handle and examine. These additions to the nature of the visit illustrate the care the site staff gave to the visits and their growing commitment to the Project. This impression was reinforced by their expressed wish to see the work produced by the children in their schools.

Whatever the problems, the impact of the visit upon the children was marked. The scale of the operation, the sheer size of the rig, the noise, the heat, the pace and the physical nature of the activity, all influenced the children and gave rise to some most impressive work at a later stage. Parents become involved because the children were so enthused. One parent, an architect, came into the school to help design a rig plan to be used in the construction of a balsa wood model. A computer programmer was involved in the production of a short program. Other adults in the area were invited to become involved as the project work developed. One school had contacts with the proprietor of a petrol station which was being rebuilt and small groups of youngsters were able to visit that site at various stages of its construction. Again, great flexibility was called for as visits sometimes had to be arranged at no more than an hour's notice. During these visits children had contact with a range of work people; not just the proprietor of the service station, but also a tanker driver, builders and a Weights and Measures officer. In another school the Local Planning Department were consulted as to the planning procedures relating to the establishment of an onshore rig.

Another benefit which became very apparent was the effect of the visit on the children's vocabulary. Words such as derrick, pusher, geologist, sedimentary, anticline, drill string, were all being used by the children naturally and with confidence. Whatever the long-term benefits of the final kit, there could be no doubt as to the impact upon the children and staff directly involved in the project.

At this stage the project work in schools was not too prescriptive, although broad areas of development had been outlined at an earlier point. All schools included group work, making use of simulations and discovery learning. Basic skills were being developed throughout. However, individual schools tended to concentrate upon particular themes and approaches, so that visits to particular schools would have revealed at times:

— science work on the properties and the uses of oil (viscosity, lubrication, strength of plastics);
— the transmission of sound waves;
— the design construction and testing of structures;
— group research on the history of oil;
— design of logos;
— creative writing, dance and drama;
— ideas relating to spatial patterns, mapping and man–land relationships;
— role play simulation of a planning application;
— traffic counts and the use of questionnaires in the field.

Towards the end of the summer term, teachers were released to assess their work and distill the best of it as a group in order to prepare for a rounded project pack which would reach into all areas of the curriculum. It was at this stage that the teachers experienced an important benefit in having the opportunity to design and produce a substantial teaching pack from first principles. The necessity to think this through in terms of aims, objectives, learning materials, approaches and assessment imposed a rigour on their deliberations, as did the collective activities of discussion, compromise, and negotiation. The team was aware that any materials which they would produce for others to use would necessarily lack the impact which they had enjoyed of a site visit. They decided therefore, at an early point in their deliberations, that an introductory element would be needed in the pack which would essentially concentrate upon creating stimulus. This element would include sets of colour slides, plans of the rig, suggested Lego and Balsa wood models, and a good range of booklet and poster material provided by the company. Subsequent units would focus on broad curriculum areas, reflecting the work done in the classroom, but structured in such a way as to provide a variety of routes through the pack for teachers and children to follow in their pursuit of particular themes. The pack was designed to provide an ideas framework, suggestions and resources for teachers to use, whilst retaining maximum flexibility in the development of the topic within the classroom. Diagram 1 outlines the structure of the pack and identifies a number of possible routes through it.

Diagram 1

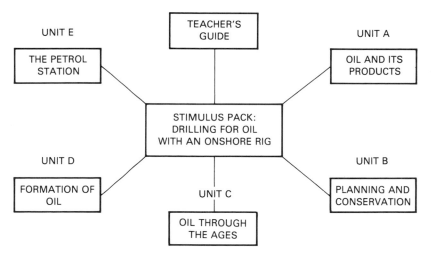

STRUCTURE OF THE KIT

Possible Routes Through the Pack Using the Stimulus Pack as Common to All

1. THE RIG – D (Formation of oil) – E (The Petrol station)
    THEME: Origin — Transport — Delivery
2. D(Formation of oil) – THE RIG – C (Oil through the ages)
    THEME: Continuity and Change.
3. A (Oil and its Products – THE RIG – B (Planning and Conservation)
    THEME: The need to match demand with responsibility.
4. B (Planning) – THE RIG – B (Conservation)
    THEME: The process of drilling from start to finish.

Brief details of the kit contents are outlined below:

Stimulus Pack: This is designed to give information relating to an inland oil rig which will provide the stimulus for the development of a range of themes. As well as a number of booklets and posters produced by Shell UK, the kit contains instructions for the construction of two rig models, one of Balsa wood and one using Technical Lego; details relating to the rotary drill, a set of slides taken on site, with attendant notes, and a set of line drawings taken from the slides which may be used in a number of ways.

Unit A: Oil and its Products: This unit gives some suggestions for practical activities that can be carried out by children individually or in small groups to test ideas relating to the properties and products of oil. All the activities can be safely done in classrooms with simple, every-day equipment under the guidance of a non specialist teacher. For experienced teachers with laboratory facilities, more sophisticated activities are detailed at the back of the unit. Experiments involve mixing oil and other liquids, looking at the thickness of liquids, the rate of flow of liquids, comparing the way things float in different liquids, and ways of making toys go better (lubrication).

Unit B: Planning and Conservation: In this unit a hypothetical map shows the location of three possible sites for the location of an oil rig. A number of roles are identified and children use the roles to simulate a public meeting in which the choice of location is discussed. Through the activity the children come to recognize the factors involved in a public enquiry, and the concern for conservation and protection of the environment which is shared by those involved in such an enteprise.

Unit C: The History of Oil: Within this unit an attempt is made to develop in children a sense of empathy, the ability to extract information from a variety of sources, and to weigh evidence. Because of the world-wide distribution of oil, there is much scope for atlas work; because of the nature of man's relationship with oil, which extends back into the mists of antiquity, there is plenty of scope for imaginative speculation and writing. Centrally though, the unit is concerned with the development of study skills associated with history.

Unit D: Oil through the Ages: In one of the schools an attempt was made to introduce 10 and 11-year-olds to some quite difficult concepts relating to geological time and process, through a range of practical activities. Among the aims of this topic were:

(i) to provide the children with a perception of geological time;
(ii) to relate geological features to a perspective of time;

(iii) to understand that weathering and rock formation are a continual process;

(iv) to differentiate between rocks by their formation;

(v) to show how oil is formed and trapped;

(vi) to show how oil can be found.

The work done on this Project forms the basis of Unit D.

Unit E: The Petrol Station: The planning team felt that many schools might regard the petrol station as providing a concrete point of entry to work on onshore drilling where a visit to a drill site is not possible. Two lines of enquiry are suggested, the study of a petrol station as a service centre within which a varied range of activities takes place and as an amenity which is used by the public and which therefore has range, threshold and other locational characteristics. Opportunity is taken to provide for field work and traffic survey activities.

All of the activities included in the pack have been experienced by the pupils and teachers; in fact the pack is very much a reduction from the sum total of experiences. There is infinite variety and scope within the topic and the contents represent no more than a range of suggestions as to what has been tried and found to be successful.

Dissemination

The completion of the teaching pack brought the project to the dissemination stage. The project was released in Autumn 1985, after a press release through a number of in-service familiarization sessions at the county's Teacher Centres. A competition was organized within the county which encouraged imaginative development of the materials. The Advisory Service was involved in the dissemination process, as were the teachers from the contributing schools.

Conclusion

From the point of view of the authority, the project acted as a catalyst among the schools, some of which were very small, in terms of promoting curriculum development through cooperation. The schools worked together, but equally each gained a sense of working directly with a major company in its own local environment. There can be no doubt as to the benefits to the children and staff directly involved. For other schools, there can be no substitute for the first-hand experience of a site visit, but at least they will have access to what we hope will be a very useful teaching resource, one which results from first-hand class-based work which has been trialled.

It would be for Shell UK to draw its own conclusions from the project. The one observation to be made is that many companies spend large sums of money producing material for schools. Often, and this is not a criticism of Shell UK, the materials are less useful than they might be because, despite the quality of the productions, they have not been trialled in schools, or written by teachers. Sometimes the language used is not suitable for the target group and often the presentation is not of a style that readily lends itself to use by the teacher. Consequently, the materials are often under-used and consigned to the cupboard. The project described above indicates a possible approach from a large company's viewpoint which might result in a better return for capital in terms of teacher usefulness.

Chapter 16

Conclusions

Duncan Smith

Four common themes stand out very clearly in the case studies presented in this book; those of the enhancement of the children's learning through such projects, the opportunities which have been afforded to teachers to try new teaching approaches, the value of the experience of working with people from the community and finally, the teacher's own professional development.

In all the case studies, reference has been made to the ways in which these projects have enhanced the learning of the children, in terms of their intellectual and social skills. In particular, however, the teachers affirm the value of such work in developing the children's basic skills in such areas as language and numeracy, something which many teachers and parents are concerned should not be sacrificed. What these projects have clearly achieved, however, is a broadening of the contexts in which those basic skills can be acquired. Furthermore, they have provided a degree of relevance to the acquisition of those skills; in other words, the skills have not only been learnt but they have also been applied by the children in a range of different situations such as enterprise, industrial visits, role play and business games.

The opportunity to give the children more responsibility for their own learning has also been a key outcome from all these projects. Some of the teachers clearly approached this idea with a degree of uncertainty, wondering whether children of primary age were capable of taking decisions about the shape and direction of their own learning. Clearly, the evidence suggests that over time this goal has been achieved. It is surely no coincidence that alongside such an approach, the teachers also reported on the children's obvious enthusiasm and commitment for the work. Another frequent reference made by the teachers was to the unexpected learning outcomes which these projects produced. The link between this 'unplanned learning' and the children having a greater degree of autonomy in planning their own learning is an obvious one. It was also interesting to note how such an approach also produced the unexpected response from particular children. A number of instances are reported of children who

were thought of as 'low achievers' and 'reluctant learners' making significant progress through being given the opportunity to make decisions for
themselves and, in some cases, for the class.

Two statements from the case studies are worth recalling in respect of
the children's learning: 'we saw it as an opportunity for the teacher and
children to learn together', and 'it was stepping into the unknown
together'. This collaboration between children and teacher in the learning
was a strong theme in many of the projects. The teachers did not cast
themselves in the role of 'experts', in some cases they couldn't! They
shared in the opportunity of being 'learners' which, for the children, was
very valuable in helping them relate more closely with the teacher, as well
as for the teachers themselves, who more readily appreciated the learning
experience from the point of view of the children.

The value of working alongside members of the local industrial and
economic community is a theme which is constantly stressed throughout
the book. For the teachers, the value was in the way in which such contacts
produced a rich and varied resource for the curricular experiences. While it
was important that the teachers set out with some clearly defined aims and
objectives for the project, it was the dialogue with the industrialists and
trade unionists which often helped to expand and refine the ideas in ways
which would not have been possible without those contacts.

There were also numerous occasions when the teachers reported that
these links, 'throw up the unexpected opportunity and the teacher needs to
seize the chance as it arises'. In this sense the collaboration between teachers
and industry sensitized both groups to the increased possibilities for developing work with the children. It was certainly true that the industrialists
learnt a great deal about what it was possible for this age group of children
to understand and appreciate. This learning for both groups resulted in
subsequent work being planned with greater awareness and insight and
with thoughts of progression and continuity.

The enhanced professional development of the teacher was also mentioned regularly in the case studies. Clearly this emerged in their greater
understanding of the capabilities of the children, in their use of more
experience-based learning approaches and in their contact with people
from industry. Reference was made to the way in which such projects
developed the management skills of the teachers, organizing, for instance,
the links with the companies both on their premises and in the school,
organizing the resources for the children and, finally, managing their own
skills in the role of both 'facilitator' and 'learner'.

Over the next few years, these schools will continue to develop their
expertise in managing these projects with industry. In the process, not only
will both teachers' and children's understanding of industry and work have

been developed, but through such collaboration the philosophy and pedagogy of the primary school curriculum as a whole will be enhanced.

Bibliography

1. ALEXANDER, R.J. *Primary teaching.* Holt Saunders, 1984.
2. ARMENTO, B.J., Awareness of Economic Knowledge: A Developmental Study, March 1982. Paper, *Annual Meeting American Educational Research Association, New York City, pp. 8–9.*
3. ARMENTO, B.J., 1982 (*op. cit*) p. 9.
4. ARMENTO, B.J., 1982 (*op. cit*) p. 8.
5. ARMSTRONG, M. *Closely observed children.* London Writers and Readers Co-Operative, and Chameleon Press, 1981.
6. BARNES, D., *From communication to curriculum*, Penguin, 1976.
7. BIRDEN, K., TAYLOR, G. and MORGAN R.F. *A Study of the Perceptions and Attitudes towards Careers in Industry among Fifth-Year Secondary-School Pupils in Lancashire*, STEEL, Preston Polytechnic, 1977.
8. For a consideration of the meaning of 'process curriculum', see BLENKIN, G. and KELLY, A.V. *The primary curriculum*, Harper and Row, 1981; also Blyth W.A.L. *Development, Experience and Curriculum in Primary Education*, Croom Helm, 1984.
9. BLYTH, W.A.L. *Development, Experience and Curriculum in Primary Education*, Croom Helm, 1984.
10. BLYTH, W.A.L. *English Primary Education, Volume 2*, Routledge & Kegan Paul, 1965.
11. BLYTH, W.A.L. *et al.*, *Curriculum Planning in History, Geography and Social Science 8–13*, Collins/ESL for the Schools Council, 1976.
12. BLYTH, W.A.L. *et al.*, *Curriculum Planning in History, Geography and Social Science 8–13*, Collins/ESL for for the Schools Council, 1976.
13. SCHOOLS COUNCIL,*History, geography and social science 8–13.* See Blyth, W.A.L. (Ed.) *Place time and society 8–13: curriculum planning in history, geography and social science.* Glasgow and Bristol, Collins/ESL Bristol, 1976. (Now available through School Curriculum Development Committee, Newcombe House, 45 Notting Hill Gate, London W11 3JB).
14. BROADFOOT, P.M. *Assessment schools and society.* Methuen, 1979; also *Selection, certification and control: social issues in educational assessment.* Falmer Press, 1984.

15. BRUNER, J.S. *The Process of Education.* Harvard University Press, 1960.
16. BURLETON, S., Chapter 6.
17. BURRIS, V.I. *The Child's Conception of Economic Relations: A Genetic Approach to the Sociology of Knowledge,* unpublished doctoral dissertation, Princetown University, 1976 (Microfilm thesis) pp. 96–98, Table 5.1 p. 76, Table 6.3 p. 124.
18. CAMPBELL, R.J. and LAWTON, D. 'How children see society', *New Society, 16,* 425 (19 November 1970).
19. CENTRAL ADVISORY COMMITTEE FOR EDUCATION, *Children and their Primay Schools* (The Plowden Committee), HMSO, 1968.
20. CLERKIN, C., Chapter 14.
21. See for example COOPER, K.R. *Evaluation, assessment and record keeping.* Glasgow and Bristol, Collins/ESL Bristol, for Schools Council, 1976. (see Note 1 above.) The present author is engaged in further work in this field.
22. CROSS, S. Daisyfield Primary School, Blackburn, Winners of the SunLife of Canada N.W. Regional final of the National Primary School and Industry Competition 1986.
23. DALE, E. *Audiovisual Methods in Teaching,* Holt, Rinehart and Winston, 1969 (3rd Edition) Ch. 4 'The Cone of Experience' pp. 105–135.
24. DANZINGER, K. 'Children's Earliest Conceptions of Economic Relationships' (Australia) *Journal of Social Psychology,* Vol. 47, 1958, pp. 231–240.
25. DEPARTMENT OF EDUCATION AND SCIENCE *A Framework for the School Curriculum,* London. HMSO, 1980.
26. DEPARTMENT OF EDUCATION AND SCIENCE *Primary Education in England,* a survey by H.M. Inspectors of Schools, HMSO, 1978.
27. DEPARTMENT OF EDUCATION AND SCIENCE *The Curriculum from 5 to 16,* Curriculum Matters, *2* pp. 20–21.
28. DEPARTMENT OF EDUCATION AND SCIENCE consultative letter *Economic Awareness in the School Curriculum* 22.3.85 sent to interested parties.
29. DEPARTMENT OF EDUCATION AND SCIENCE letter to SCDC. *Economic Awareness in the School Curriculum,* 22 April 1986.
30. DEPARTMENT OF EDUCATION AND SCIENCE, 1986 (*op. cit*) 22 April.
31. DEWEY, J. *Experience and Education,* New York, Collier-Macmillan, 1963.
32. Terms from DEWEY, J. (centre of gravity) (*op. cit*), FOX, K. (knap sack) (see ref. 41), HARLEN, W. (critical periods) (unpublished research paper).
33. DOE, B. 'Awareness of industry "cannot start too early" ', *Times Educational Supplement 3613,* 27.9.85 p. 13.

34. DONALDSON, M. *Children's Minds*, Fontana, 1978.
35. DOWNTON, D., 'A new dimension in social studies for junior pupils', *Times Educational Supplement*, 3 January 1966
36. EASLEY, J.R. 'The Structural Paradigm in Protocol Analysis', *Journal of Research in Science Teaching*, 1974 p. 284.
37. EDGE HILL COLLEGE OF HIGHER EDUCATION *Primary Industry Education Project*, unpublished, Report to Department of Industry, Jan. 1–Dec. 31 1981.
38. For an interesting and relevant treatment of problem-solving in primary Industry Education, see *Problem-solving: science and technology in primary schools*. Engineering Council, 1985.
39. Letters, Alan Evants *EDUCATION* 20 September 1985.
40. FITZPATRICK, S., Chapter 8.
41. FOX, K.F.A. 'What children bring to schools: the beginnings of economic education', *Social Education*, October 1978 pp. 478–481.
42. FURTH, H.G. *The World of Grown Ups*, The Chidren's Conceptions of Society, Elsevier, 1979.
43. FURTH, H.G.. 1979 (*op. cit*) p. 10.
44. FURTH, H.G. 'Young Children's understanding of Society', in McGurk, H. (Ed.) *Issues in Childhood Social Development*, Methuen, 1978 p. 236.
45. FURTH, H.G., 1979 (*op. cit*) pp. 17–18.
46. FURTH, H.G., 1979 (*op. cit*) p. 27.
47. FURTH, H.G., 1979 (*op. cit*) pp. 29, 49–51.
48. FURTH, H.G., 1978 (*op. cit*) p. 255.
49. For a general treatment of differences in children's strategies and styles of learning and interaction, see the whole series of publications from the ORACLE project, and especially GALTON, M. and WILLCOCKS, J. *Moving from the primary classroom*, Routledge & Kegan Paul, 1983.
50. GRAY, J. *Case Study No 16, A whole school approach, St. Peters C.E. School, Chorley,* IY 86 (*op. cit*).
51. GUNNING, S. and D. and WILSON, J. *Topic Teaching in the Primary School*, Croom Helm, 1981 pp. 10–11, 19–20.
52. HALES, S.P., Chapter 7.
53. HARLEN, W. in the two Match and Mismatch Project publications: *Raising questions* and *Finding answers*, OLIVER and BOYD, for Schools Council, 1977. See also the same author's *Guides to assessment in education: science*. Macmillan Education, 1983.
54. HIGGINSON, P. 'Profit on Paper, Milltown pupils see the writing on the wall', *Times Educational Supplement* 12.4.85, p. 21.
55. HIMMELWEIT, H.T., HALSEY, A.H. and OPPENHEIM, A.N. 'The

views of adolescents on some aspects of the social class structure', *British Journal of Sociology*, 3, 1952.

56. HOLMES S. and JAMIESON I. 'Further uses of "Adults Other than Teachers" ' in Watts A. (Ed.), *Work Experience and Schools*, Heinemann, 1983.

57. INDUSTRY YEAR 1986 *Education and Industry* (i) *Initial Training of Teachers* Sept. 13–14, 1985 Conference Report.

58. *Industry Matters Primary and Middle Schools*, RSA, September 1985.

59. INNER LONDON EDUCATION AUTHORITY, *The Study of Places in the Primary School*, ILEA 1981 p. 4.

60. These processes are outlined in ILEA *Social Studies in the Primary School*, London, 1980. The encounter with the Netsilik group was as part of a theatre-in-education programme mounted by the Cockpit Theatre, *How we live*, 1980.

61. INNER LONDON EDUCATION AUTHORITY, *Social Studies in the Primary School*, ILEA, 1981.

62. JAHODA, G. 'Development in the perceptions of social differences in children from 6 to 10', *British Journal of Psychology*, 50, 2, 1959.

63. JAMIESON, I.M. (Ed.) *We Make Kettles: studying industry in the primary school*, Longman, 1984.

64. JAMIESON, I.M. (Ed.) 'Industry and the primary school', in Jamieson, (Ed.) *We Make Kettles: studying industry in the primary school*, Longman, 1984.

65. JAMISON, I.M. and LIGHTFOOT, M. *Schools and Industry,* Schools Council Working Paper 73, Methuen Educational, 1982.

66. JAMIESON, I.M. and LIGHTFOOT M. *Schools and Industry*, Schools Council Working Paper 73, Methuen Educational, 1982.

67. KOELLER, S. *A Review of the Research in Economics in Early Childhood/ Elementary Education*, ED 171 412, 1979, pp. 78.

68. KOURILSKY, M. 'The Kinder Economy: A Case Study of Kindergarten Pupils' Acquisition of Economic Concepts', *The Elementary School Journal*, 77 1976–77 p. 183.

69. LAWTON, D. *Social Change, Educational Theory and Curriculum Planning*, University of London Press, 1973.

70. LAWTON D., CAMPBELL J. and BURKITT, V. *Social Studies 8–13* (Schools Council Working Paper 39), Evans/Methuen, 1971.

71. LAWTON, D., CAMPBELL, J. and BURKITT, V. *Social Studies 8–13* (Schools Council Working Paper 39), Evans/Methuen, 1971.

72. LOCKWOOD, H. 'Curriculum development in the junior school', *Social Science Teacher* 9, 4/5, 1980.

73. MCGOWAN, D.B. and GALLIMORE, M.J., Case Study No 20 *Awareness and Importance of Industry*, Mossley CE Primary School, Congle-

ton, Industry Year (1986) North West Primay Regional Conference, April 1986.

74. McNaughton, J.H. 'Piaget's theory and Primary School Social Science', *Educational Review*, November 1966.

75. Margerison, C.J. 'Island: a social studies experiment', *Ideas,* 8/9 Goldsmiths College Curriculum Laboratory, 1968.

76. Page, R. and Nash, M. *Teenage Attitudes to Technology and Industry*, SCSST 1980.

77. Piaget, J. *Judgement and Reasoning in the Child*, Routledge & Kegan Paul, 1928.

78. Piaget, J. and Weill, A.M. 'The development in children of the idea of the homeland and of relations with other countries', *International Social Science Bulletin*, 3, 1951.

79. Piaget, J. and Inhelder, B. *The child's conception of space*, Routledge & Kegan Paul, 1965.

80. Pollard, A. *The social world of the primary school*, Holt Education, 1985.

81. Purkis, S. *Oral History in Schools*, Oral History Society, University of Essex, 1979.

82. Rogers, V. *The Social Studies in English Education*, Heinemann, 1968.

83. Ross, A. *School Curriculum Industry Project: Primary and Middle Schools-Industry Conference Proceedings*, SCDC 1985.

84. Ross, A. 'The Bottle Stopper factory: talking all together', *The English Magazine* (ILEA) 11, 1983.

85. Ross, A. 'In-service and Curriculum Development: An approach to curriculum development dissemination based on in-service education within a single authority: the case-study of social studies in ILEA primary schools', *British Journal of In-Service Education*, 9, 2, 1982.

86. Ross, A. 'Children becoming historians . . .', *Language Matters*, Issue 1/2, 1984.

87. The activities in this school project have been described by the author in several articles: most fully in *Social Science Teacher*, 13, 2, 1984; *Employment Gazette* (Department of Employment), 1985; and 'Modelling the world of work: active learning about industry in the primary school', *Primary Teaching Studies*, 1, 1, 1985.

88. See the treatment of discussion by Alistair Ross in Chapter 2.

89. Alistair Ross, the author of Chapter 2, has experimented with a picture-sorting technique to assess children's understanding of hierarchy in an enterprise. Initial unpublished results were promising.

90. Ross, A., Chapter 2.

91. Ross, A. and Smith, D. *Schools and Industry 5–13: Looking at the World of Work: Questions Teachers Ask*, School Curriculum Industry Project, SCDC, 1985.

92. Ross, A. and Smith D. *Schools and Industry 5–13, Looking at the World of Work: Questions Teachers Ask*, School Curriculum Industry Project, SCDC, 1985.

93. Ross, A. and Smith, D. *Schools and Industry 5–13: Looking at the World of Work: Questions Teachers Ask*, School Curriculum Industry Project, SCDC, 1985.

94. Russell, D. *Children's Thinking*, Ginn, 1965.

95. Rowland, S. *The Enquiring Classroom: an approach to understanding children's learning.* Falmer Press, 1984. See also Raven, J. *Opening the primary classroom*, Edinburgh/Scottish Council for Research in Education, 1985, for a different perspective on similar approaches to teaching.

96. School Curriculum Development Committee Planning Conference Report on Economic Awareness July 1986.

97. School Curriculum Development Committee (1986) Conference, Report on Economic Awareness (*op. cit*) p. 21.

98. Schools Council *The Practical Curriculum*, Working Paper 70, Methuen Educational, 1981.

99. Schools Council *Primary Practice*, Working Paper 75, Methuen Educational, 1983.

100. Schools Council *Curriculum Planning in History, Geography and Social Science*, Blyth, W.A.L. (Ed.), Collins/ESL, 1976.

101. Schools Council *The middle years of schools* (Schools Council Working Paper 22), HMSO, 1969.

102. Schools Council/Merton Education Authority *The New Approach of the Social Studies*, Schools Council, 1981.

103. Schug, M.C. 'What Educational Research Says About the Development of Economic Thinking', *Theory and Research in Social Education*, Fall 1981, Vol 9, No 3 p. 27.

104. Schug, M.C. and Birkley, C.J. *The Development of Children's Economic Reasoning*, San Francisco California, November 22 1983, Paper to National Council for the Social Studies.
See also Schug, M.C. 'Children's Understanding of Economics', *Elementary School Journal*, Spring 1987.

105. Shipman, M.D. *Assessment in primary and middle schools.* Croom Helm, 1983.

106. Smith, D. (Ed.) *Industry Education in the Primary School: Case Studies from the National Primary Schools Industry Competition 1986*, SCDC, 1987.

107. Smith, D. 'Industry in the Primary School', *Dialogue in Education*, Vol. 1, No 2, p. 9.

108. SMITH, D. 'Britannia High School, Industrial Relations Case Study' in Jamieson,I. and Lightfoot, M. *Schools and Industry,* Schools Council Working Paper No 73, Methuen Educational, 1982.

109. SPENDER, D. *Invisible women: the schooling scandal,* Writers and Readers Publishing Cooperative, London, 1982.

110. SUTTON, R.S. 'Behaviour in the attainment of Economic Concepts', *The Journal of Psychology,* 1962, Vol 53 pp. 37–46.

111. STRAUSS, A.L. 'The development and transformation of monetary meanings of a child', *American Sociological Review,* 1952, Vol 17 pp. 275–286.

112. TABA, H., DURKIN, M.C., FRAENKEL, J.M. and McNAUGHTON, A. *Teachers' Handbook of Elementary Social Studies: An inductive approach,* Addison Wesley, 1971.

113. 'Early look at economics' *Times Educational Supplement* 25.7.86.

114. TIZZARD, B. and HUGHES, M. *Young Children Learning,* Fontana, 1984.

115. TOUGH, J. *Talk for teaching and learning.* Ward Lock Educational, for Schools Council Communication Skills Projects, 1979 (especially chapter 6).

116. The example of Forsbrook Infants' School is instructive here: in successive years children have made kettles, ovens and mugs. VINCENT, G. 'We Make Kettles', in Jamieson, I.M. (Ed.) *We Make Kettles: studying industry in the primary school,* Longman, 1984.

117. WAGSTAFF, S. *People Around Us: Unit 1 — Families,* (1978) *Unit 2 — Friends,* (1979); *Unit 3 — Work,* (1970); all published by the ILEA, the first two also by A. & C. Black.

118. WAITE, P.E. 'Industry and the Primary Classroom' *Education 3–13,* Vol 12 No. 1 pp. 37–40.

119. WAITE, P.E. in association with PENNINGTON, M. 'Industry Year 1986 and beyond', *Primary Science Review* 1987 (forthcoming).

120. See also Chapter 4, Waite, P.E.

121. WAITE, P.E., Chapter 4.

122. Some developments of this kind have been introduced by teachers working with two members of the Schools/Industry (5–13) Research Group, Patrick Waite and John Garwell.

123. WARD, D. and BENFIELD, E. Department of Trade and Industry/ Industry/Education Unit, 'Industry in primary classrooms', *View* 28 Summer 1986 pp. 8–9.

124. WATTS, A.G. *Work Shadowing,* Longman for the School Curriculum Development Committee, 1986.

125. Adapted from WILDSMITH, B.D. 'Primary Education and Industry',

Bulletin, *LRDG* (Learning Resource Development Group of Colleges and Institutes of Higher Education) 12, January 1985, pp. 23–24.

126. WOODS, P. (Ed.), *Pupil strategies: explorations in the sociology of the school*, Croom Helm, 1980.

List of Contributors

Janice Anderson   taught for a number of years in secondary schools before moving into primary work. Currently she has responsibility for mathematics within the school.

Elizabeth Benfield   is a primary teacher in an inner city school in Salford. During 1985–86 she was a teacher fellow working on industry linked projects with a range of schools and age groups.

Alan Blyth   is Emeritus Professor of Education at the University of Liverpool. He taught in schools and colleges and in the Universities of Keele and Manchester and has written extensively about curriculum and social organization in primary schools. He was the first Director of the Schools Council Project, *Place, Time and Society 8–13*, and is now investigating the assessment of primary humanities.

Shelia Burleton   is a primary school teacher in Sefton with responsibility for language development throughout the school. She has taught in a number of schools on Merseyside.

Roger Carter   taught in London and Shropshire before moving to Madeley College of Education. He is now county inspector for Geography.

Ciaran Clerkin   has spent most of his teaching career working in East London. He is now head teacher at Manor School in the London Borough of Newham.

Sandra Cross   spent seven years in the Personnel Department of a large electronics company before going into primary teaching. She is responsible for environmental studies within her present school.

Shirley Fitzpatrick   teaches at Forsbrook Infants School in Staffordshire where she began school–industry links and project work. She has contributed to a number of primary workshops throughout the country on the subject of school and industry links.

John Garwell   worked in industry and commerce before becoming a secondary school teacher in Birmingham. He lectured for 17 years at Gwent College of Higher Education, focusing particularly on industry studies in the primary school.

Steven Hales   has worked in primary schools in Hereford and Worcester and Dudley. He is now headteacher at Higham on the Hill Primary School and Community Centre in Leicestershire.

Peter Holdsworth   has taught English and careers education in the ILEA. After working for a year as an advisory teacher for careers education and guidance, he was appointed as the DISCO/SCIP coordinator for Greenwich.

John Murphy   has taught PE and general subjects in two London comprehensive schools. He was head of department before becoming deputy head of St Mary's School in Eltham where he is currently acting head.

Robert Richards   is currently headteacher of Catbrook Primary School, Gwent. He has wide experience and knowledge of environmental studies which he is using to develop links with local industry.

Alistair Ross   taught for eight years in primary schools in the ILEA before joining the Department of Teaching Studies at the Polytechnic of North London as Principal Lecturer. He directs the Primary Schools and Industry Centre based there and chairs the SCIP 5–13 Research group.

Duncan Smith   taught in secondary schools in Wiltshire and was Senior Lecturer in Education and Teaching Studies at Worcester College of Higher Education before being seconded to the Schools Council Industry Project in 1980. He is currently Research Director for the School Curriculum Industry Partnership at its Midland base in the University of Warwick.

Patrick Waite   is Principal Lecturer at Edge Hill College of Higher Education. He was one of the founder members of the SCIP 5–13 Research group. He is editor of the RSA's *Industry Year Primary Report* and consultant to a number of colleges and LEAs in the area of economic awareness for the 5–16 age range.

Index

absurdities tests, 48, 56
active learning, 132–3, 137, 155
  see also experiential learning
'adults other than teachers' (AOTs), 9, 10, 31,
  14–15, 58, 74–88, 107, 111–12, 115,
  117–18, 133–5, 137, 159, 160–61, 167–9,
  171, 193
  and planning of projects, 76–8, 83–4, 88,
  93–4, 113–16, 124–30
  preparation and briefing of, 14, 18, 79, 83,
  86, 126, 129–30, 133, 137,
  see also parents
Alexander, R. J., 45, 205
Anderson, Janice, 213
  see also Garwell and Anderson
AOTs: *see* 'adults other than teachers'
appraisal/assessment of industry education,
  37–56
  AOTs and, 82, 88, 111–12, 136–7
  case studies, 54–5, 101, 110–12, 117, 136–8,
  181, 189–90, 194
  defined, 42–6
  formative assessment, 52
  norm-, criterion- and self-referenced
  assessment, 46–7
  recall assessment and transfer assessment,
  46–51, 52, 54
  summative assessment, 47, 52–3
  see also attitudes; concepts
Arael Primary School, Abertillery: *see* Garwell
  and Anderson
Armento, B. J., 69–70, 205
Armstrong, M., 42, 43, 205
art and craft, 11, 98, 108, 117, 119–20, 142,
  153, 174, 176–8, 186–8, 194–5
Ascension Primary School, Salford: *see*
  Benfield, Elizabeth
assessment: *see* appraisal
attitudes/values:
  and appraisal/assessment, 39–41, 47, 48–9,
  54
  bias and imbalance, children's reactions to,
  19–20, 186
  to industry and commerce, ix, x–xi, 9–10,
  12, 94, 111–12, 172, 180

to trade unions, 12, 14, 108, 118
autonomous learning, 22–3, 170, 201–2

Barnes, D., 27, 205
Benfield, Elizabeth (Ascension and St Phillip's
  Primary Schools, Salford), 10, 11, 13,
  172–81, 213
Birkley, C. J.: *see* Schug and Birkley
blind people: *see* handicapped workers
Blyth, W. A. L. (Alan), 6, 8, 10, 11–12, 16, 24,
  25, 37–56, 61, 73, 82, 170, 205, 213
  Place, Time and Society 8–13, 25–6, 32, 38,
  205
board games, 150–51
Broadfoot, P. M., 45, 205
Bruner, J. S., 25, 206
Burkitt, V.: *see* Lawton, Campbell and Burkitt
Burleton, Sheila (Freshfield Primary School,
  Formby), 8, 11, 13, 54, 78, 91–101, 213
Burris, V. I., 63–6, 206
business games, 17

Campbell, R. J., and Lawton, D., 27, 206
  see also Lawton, Campbell and Burkitt
Carter, Roger, 192–200, 213
Catbrook Primary School, Chepstow: *see*
  Richards, Robert
Central Advisory Committee for Education,
  Plowden Report, 23–5, 206
Clerkin, Ciaran (Manor Primary School,
  Newham), 11, 54, 78, 87, 182–91, 213
Coal Clough Primary School, Burnley, 56
commerce: *see* industry and commerce
communication: *see* language and
  communication skills
computers, 5, 10, 100
  see also micro-computers
concepts:
  and appraisal/assessment, 38–41, 47, 52, 53,
  62
  categorical, 38–41
  formation/development of, 22–3, 31–3,
  60–62
  key concepts in industry education, 7–8, 26,
  32; conflict, 11, 32, 156–70, 186; division

217